THOMAS WASOW

Departments of Linguistics and Philosophy
Stanford University

ANAPHORA IN GENERATIVE GRAMMAR

1979

E. STORY-SCIENTIA P.V.B.A.

SCIENTIFIC PUBLISHERS

GHENT - ANTWERP - BRUSSELS

D/1979/0009/27

ISBN 90 6439 162 9 (Sigla 2)

ISBN 90 6439 160 2 (the series)

© 1979 by E. STORY-SCIENTIA GENT

ACKNOWLEDGEMENTS

A number of people have provided me with valuable advice and support in the preparation of this monograph. Foremost among them is Noam Chomsky, without whose assistance and encouragement I would never have begun (much less finished) this project. Others who (knowingly or unknowingly) have made valuable contributions include Adrian Akmajian, Avery Andrews, Emmon Bach, Joan Bresnan, Peter Culicover, Bob Fiengo, Ken Hale, Morris Halle, Michael Helke, Larry Horn, Ray Jackendoff, Jerry Katz, Paul Kiparsky, Howard Lasnik, William Leben, Julius Moravcsik, Tom Roeper, Haj Ross, and Henk van Riemsdijk. Financial support for much of the research was provided by National Institutes of Health Grant # 5TOIHDOOIII during my years in graduate school. A grant for typing and duplicating costs was provided by the office of the Dean of the College of Hampshire College, for which I have Myron Lunine to thank. Finally, I owe a special debt of gratitude to my wife, Judith, who has consistently supported me in every imaginable way. I wish to thank all of these people for their help, while taking sole responsibility for any defects in what follows.

PREFACE

Although linguistics is commonly defined as "the scientific study of language," a more honest characterization might be "anything anyone has to say about language that someone else is willing to listen to." "Linguistics" is an umbrella term used to cover a wide variety of only loosely connected disciplines.

One of these disciplines is generative grammar. Generative grammar aims to characterize formally what it means to "know a language." In principle, a generative grammarian seeks to write a set of rules (known as a "grammar") which will enumerate all (and only) the well-formed sentences of a language. Most generative grammarian agree that this enumeration should include information about the meaning and the pronunciation of these sentences. Further, it is widely held that a grammar of a language should explicate certain intuitions which speakers have regarding relatedness among sentences and regarding relationships among elements within a single sentence.

In fact, however, work on generative grammar has consisted less of actual attempts to write grammars than of discussions regarding what kinds of rules such grammars should employ. This is not surprising, in light of the newness of the field and the broader implications of these more theoretical questions. There is a good deal of disagreement among generative grammarians regarding basic theoretical questions. The present monograph continues in this theoretical vein. Discussions of specific rules will be oriented towards trying to discover what categories of rules grammars must include. This orientation is especially evident in Part II, which is less concerned with reviewing existing arguments than is Part I.

I will not attempt to provide definitions for all of the technical terms employed ; nor will I attempt to outline the full history of every issue discussed. I assume that the issues considered here are of interest primarily to people already well versed in the literature of generative grammar. Hence, I take the reader to be familiar with the "standard theory" of transformational grammar (as outlined by Katz and Postal (1964) and Chomsky (1965)), with the inadequacies of that theory discovered in the late 1960's, and with the "interpretive" and "generative semantic" theories which have been developed to try to remedy these inadequacies. Specifically, I assume familiarity with the basic ideas outlined in such work as Chomsky (1971, 1972), Jackendoff (1972), Lakoff (1965, 1970c), McCawley (1970), Postal (1970b, 1971), and Ross (1967a). I will feel free to use such terms as "transformation," "base," "deep structure," "derivational constraint," "lexical insertion," and "cycle" without detailed explanation. The reader who is unfamiliar with these works and terms should expect to encounter difficulties.

This monograph is a revised and expanded version of my 1972 MIT dissertation, *Anaphoric Relations in English*. Much has been written in the last six years that bears on the issues raised here. For the most part, however, I have not made major revisions to accomodate these later works ; rather, I have tried to work out more thoroughly and carefully the ideas in my thesis. I believe that many of these ideas are relevant to much current work, and I hope readers will forgive the sketchiness of my references to the most recent literature.

One inadequately referenced item which deserves special mention is Gilles Fauconnier's 1971 University of California at San Diego dissertation, *Theoretical Implications of Some Global Phenomena in Syntax*. There are a number of points of striking overlap between Fauconnier's ideas and mine, most notably in § 3.1.1 and Appendix I. In other places, Fauconnier's work disagrees with mine and poses serious problems for an approach like mine. I did not have an opportunity to read Fauconnier's work until this monograph was nearly completed. Rather than delay publication further, so that I could take his work into account, I have chosen simply to cite its existence and relevance here, and to recommend it to the reader.

CONTENTS

Chapter One

BACKGROUND

0. *Introduction*

The native speaker of any natural language knows that special relationships, called *anaphoric relationships*, exist between certain pairs of elements in the language. When two items A and B in a given discourse are anaphorically related, the full specification of the meaning of B involves (i) referring to the fact that A and B are anaphorically related, and (ii) repeating some part of the meaning of A. The items playing the role of B in this characterization will be referred to as *anaphoric elements* or *anaphors*. The items upon which anaphors depend for the specification of their meanings are called their *antecedents*. The collective term for anaphoric relations in general is *anaphora*.

In some cases, items which may serve as anaphors may also appear in contexts in which they are not associated with an antecedent. In such a case, other (possibly non-linguistic) factors must provide sufficient information for the determination of the meaning of the item in question.

The classic example of an anaphoric relation is that between definite pronouns and their NP antecedents.

(1) (a) *The President* has promised that *he* will end the war.
    (b) *Nixon* can't expect black people to vote for *him*.
    (c) *A man* does what *he* thinks best.[1]

Numerous other anaphoric relations have been discussed by generative grammarians. Examples of several of these are given in (2).

(2) (a) When Billy saw Mary's *tricycle*, he wanted *one*, too.
    (b) *John* shaved *himself*.
    (c) After Pete *tried LSD*, Karen did $\begin{cases} \textit{it, too} \\ \textit{so, too} \\ \textit{the same thing} \\ \textit{likewise} \end{cases}$
    (d) The book says to *add the water to the beans*, but I did just *the opposite*.

(f) Fred *got reclassified I-A*, and *it* happened to George too.

(g) The police claim that *Mike* and *Dan* robbed a bank, and *the former* has confessed, although *the latter* claims to have an alibi.

In addition to cases like these, if we allow anaphors to be phonetically null, it is possible to treat instances of ellipsis (or what has been called "deletion under identity") as anaphoric relations. Examples of null anaphors are given in (3).

(3) (a) *Mary* enjoys _____ singing to herself.

(b) John *left*, but Bill didn't _____

(c) *John left*, but he didn't say why _____ .

1. *Goals*

Intuitively, it is clear why languages have anaphoric relations: anaphora reduces redundancy, thereby shortening (and hence simplifying) sentences. In order for this simplification to be possible, however, it is necessary that the speaker of a language be able to identify correctly the elements participating in an anaphoric relation and to determine correctly the meaning of the anaphor on the basis of meaning of the antecedent. If a grammar is to reflect the linguistic competence of a native speaker of a language, it must include mechanisms of associating anaphor and antecedent and for specifying correctly the reading of the anaphor as a function of the reading of the antecedent.

In the past decade, a voluminous yet depressingly inconclusive literature has grown up around the problem of representing anaphora in the grammar of English. This monograph is an attempt to clarify the issues involved and to indicate in a general way how the grammar of English might reflect the speakers' intuitions regarding anaphora.

More specifically, I will consider the following questions:

(A) What sorts of mechanisms are best suited for representing anaphora in a grammar?

(B) What are the conditions on the rule(s) associating anaphors with antecedents?[2]

(C) Do the various cases of anaphora form a linguistically significant class of phenomena, and, if so, how can the grammar capture this fact? That is, is it proper to speak of "anaphoric relations" in general, or should, e.g., definite pronouns be treated quite differently from elliptical constructions?

(D) What do the answers to (A) - (C) entail for linguistic theory?

In Part I, I will be concerned primarily with questions (A) and (B) and
I will concentrate on reviewing and evaluating much of the existing literature
on definite pronominal anaphora. Part II continues to explore (A) and (B)
but places greater emphasis on (C) and (D).

2. *Extrinsic Factors*

It should be noted here at the beginning that some instances of anaphora
involve factors which are clearly non-linguistic, and hence, presumably not
represented in linguistic theory. For example, facial expressions or hand
gestures (pointing) may indicate the intended referent of a definite pronoun,
even when no antecedent is included in the linguistic context. To try to
incorporate gestures into grammar would be tantamount to requiring grammar
to describe not just language, but all means of communication. Such an
extension of the goals of linguistic theory (even assuming it to be possible
and desirable) is well beyond the scope of this monograph and will hence
not be considered.

A related point which ought not to require repeating is that people do use
anaphoric elements in ways which violate the various anaphora rules which
have been and will be proposed. Thus, for example, Robert Rardin claims
that his grandmother uses sentences like (4), where *she* refers to Mrs. Smith.

(4) I saw Mr. Smith the other day; you know she died last year.

No theory of anaphora ever proposed (or likely to be proposed) can assign
she the proper meaning. Facts like these in no way invalidate the attempt
to formulate such rules. Rather, they re-emphasize the need to distinguish
between linguistic competence and performance (see Chomsky (1965)).
Here, as in all linguistic research, the intelligibility and even the use of
examples violating the proposed rules is of little consequence, so long as
the native speaker knows the examples to be deviant. Of course, the acceptability of such examples must ultimately be explained, presumably in terms
of extra-grammatical mechanisms.

It is similarly an unreliable test of a sentence's grammaticality to embed
it in a context and submit it to the perusal of numerous graduate students.
The context can easily force an abnormal interpretation on a sentence in such
a way that its deviance is overlooked. An especially clear example of this is
Hammerton (1970). Hammerton questions Chomsky's assertion (Chomsky
(1968)) that (5) does not permit the indicated anaphoric relation.

(5) *Learning that *John* had won the race surprised *him*.

In support of this position, Hammerton submitted the passage in (6) to
twenty speakers of English, with the result that all of them interpreted the

penultimate occurrence of *him* as referring to John.

> (6) John is a very happy man this morning; though he was thoroughly
> miserable last night. He got home convinced that he had come in
> second in the race and that Bill had won it. In fact, he was so
> sour about it that he could hardly bring himself to listen to the
> report on the radio. Learning that John had won the race sur-
> prised him. It delighted him, too.

Hammerton's result is hardly surprising and quite irrelevant. The deviance
of (5) is not a matter requiring statistical confirmation. The fact that a
discourse like (6), in which John is the subject under discussion, allows any
occurrence of *him* to be interpreted as referring to John has no bearing on
the question of what anaphoric relations are possible within a sentence. All
that can be legitimately be concluded from (6) is that, in linguistics, as in
any empirical science, extraneous factors may obscure the data.

One reason why anaphoric relations appear to be especially susceptible
to this technique of suggesting alternative intrepretations by providing a
context is that anaphora is in part a discourse phenomenon. That is, anaphoric
relations may hold between elements in different sentences, as was illustrated
in (6) above. Examples with other anaphoric relations are given in (7).

> (7) (a) John *tried to seduce Mary.* Bill did *so*, to.
> (b) Nobody believes *that John will win.* Even he doesn't believe
> *it.*
> (c) John plans to *come.* He claims that Mary will _____ , to.
> (d) *Mayor White is running for re-election.* I can't imagine why

------

Notice that intersentential anaphora is possible only if the antecedent occurs
earlier in the discourse than the anaphor, and only if the anaphor and
antecedent are in fairly close proximity.

> (8) (a) **He* went to the store. *John* bought some bread there.
> (b) ??John *went to the store.* It was a small market near the
> corner of Elm and Maple, and free samples of a new brand
> of peanut butter were being given away there. Mary, how-
> ever, decided not to _____

It seems, then, that inter-sentential anaphora can be described reasonably
straightforwardly. The only readily apparent problems are making precise
the notion of "close proximity," and accounting for the similarities between
intersentential and intrasentential anaphora. These problems will not be
considered, and the remainder of this monograph will be concerned only
with antecedents and anaphors which are contained in a single sentence.

In all that follows, therefore, an element will be termed "anaphoric" only if it has an antecedent in the same sentence.

One final comment along these lines: when different informants differ in their judgments regarding the grammaticality of a sentence, it is not necessarily an indication of dialect or "idiolect" differences. This is especially true when the speakers in question are linguists with competing theories to defend. In general, such situations arise because of the marginal character of the data. The fact that supposed dialect differences among linguists so often correlate with differences in theoretical orientation is a good indication that it is frequently not simply a matter of dialects. This is not, of course, to deny that genuine dialects exist. However, there is a tendency among generative grammarians to attribute confusion regarding marginal and unreliable data to dialect differences. Instead of worrying so much about dialects, linguists would be better off trying to find clearer examples on which to base their analyses. This policy will be adopted in the present work.

3. *Assumptions*

Before going on to consider (A) - (E) in detail, it seems advisable to make explicit the theoretical framework and background assumptions upon which the remainder of this monograph is to be based. This is necessary because of the current theoretical split among generative grammarians which has cast into question almost every substantive or methodological proposal ever put forward under the name of generative grammar. Because this controversy is so far reaching and deep, it would go beyond the scope of this monograph to attempt to justify these background assumptions in any detail. Rather, references will be given to work supporting the assumptions, and, in some cases, the arguments will be summarized. Of course, any productive results that may come out of the present work provide indirect evidence for the assumptions underlying that work.

The fundamental problems of linguistics, as has been stated many times elsewhere (see e.g., Chomsky (1971)), is to account for the fact that a child learning a language is able, in the space of a few short years and on the basis of very limited and largely degenerate data, to master a system so fantastically complex. The only plausible explanation of this remarkable feat appears to be that human beings are innately equipped with a highly structured language-learning mechanism, and that much of the complexity of language is not learned, but is rather a reflection of the structure of this innate mechanism. This hypothesis entails that many of the structural properties of any language are in fact manifestations of the structure of the innate language-learning mechanism, and are hence necessarily common to all languages. Thus, the discovery of linguistic universals serves to corroborate the hypothesis of innate structure, and the primary goal of linguistic research is the discovery of linguistic universals. (For more on the innateness hypothesis, see Wasow (1973b)).

From these very general considerations emerge certain conclusions about desirable properties for a theory of language. Most importantly, a theory should be maximally restrictive, in the sense that it should minimize the number of possible descriptions of a given phenomenon (subject, of course, to limitations imposed by the data, i.e., by the diversity of languages). This restrictiveness serves to explain the ease with which languages are acquired. In striving for restrictiveness, it is to be expected that linguistic theory will be highly structured. That is, the theory will postulate a variety of different kinds of mechanisms, each with highly specialized functions. In terms of methodology for research, this means that the linguist should not be afraid to postulate new sorts of rules, if he can simultaneously constain their operations and the operations of the already established kinds of rules.

In particular, these considerations refute the methodological arguments of Postal (1972c) in favor of what he calls a "homogeneous theory." This argument (and similar ones by Postal (1970a) and Lakoff (1970a, 1970c)) is based on the false assumption that the theory which most serverely limits the categories of rules necessary is to be preferred over all others. In fact, however, it is the theory with the most limited generative capacity which is to be preferred. Further, this preference is dictated by facts, not methodology. The goal of linguistic theory must be explanation, not homogeneity.

The conclusion that the primary aim of the linguist must be to constrain linguistic theory is reinforced by the theorems of Peters and Ritchie (1969) and Kravif (1971), demonstrating that various versions of linguistic theory are too powerful for their stated purpose. That is, they show in effect that any algorithm at all can be formulated as a transformational grammar.[3] If linguistic theory is to explain language acquisition by restricting the notion of "possible human language," then this result constitutes a significant setback for the theoretical linguist.[4] Consequently, generative grammarians must orient their research towards limiting the generative capacity of their theories.

Paradoxically, the work of recent years has for the most part tended to do just the opposite. Thus, the past decade has seen the introduction into linguistic theory of syntactic rule features (Lakoff (1965)), language-particular constraints on deep structure and surface structure (Perlmutter (1968)), derived structure interpretive rules (Jackendoff (1969) and others), derivational constraints of various kinds (Lakoff (1969) and others), transderivational constraints (Lakoff (1973)), and numerous (deservedly) more obscure innovations. In contrast, the number of proposals for constraining linguistic theory is quite small. The most notable examples are Ross (1967a), Emonds (1970), Postal (1971), and Chomsky (1970b, 1971).

One possible escape from this unhappy state of affairs, which has been suggested by Bach (1971), is that there might be a relatively small number of specific rule types available for the description of languages. Rather stringent constraints would be placed on each type of rule, so that the rule types could almost be thought of as universal rules. In other words, the notion, "rule of grammar" would be constrained by enumerating a set of narrowly defined categories of rules from which all grammars must be constructed. A theory of this sort will be designated "heterogeneous."

Such a proposal receives initial support from the fact that a number of rules which have been studied in English have close analogues in a variety of other languages (see, e.g., Ross (1970) for a discussion of one such rule).

Bach's proposal that we should aim to construct a heterogeneous theory is extremely attractive for a number of reasons. First of all, it offers hope of solving the problem raised by the Peters and Ritchie theorem; if all grammatical rules are of certain very specific types, then it is likely that all languages will be of rather specific types as well. Secondly, it offers hope of providing a resolution of many of the issues dividing generative semantics from interpretivism. For example, while some of these rule types might be global (in the sense of Lakoff (1970a)), the objections of interpretivists to such rules would be met by a sufficiently narrow specification of the kinds of global rules possible.[5] In addition, the question of whether there is a distinction between syntactic and semantic rules becomes purely academic, once the appropriate categories of rules have been established; the question of whether these labels are attached to categories loses all empirical content once the categories themselves are agreed upon.

One of the main points of this monograph is to argue for the appropriateness of a heterogeneous conception of linguistic theory in dealing with anaphoric relations. I will argue in Part II below that it is futile to argue over the question of whether anaphora should be handled in the semantic component or the syntactic component. Rather, I will attempt to show that anaphora rules dealing with a variety of phenomena have much in common with one another and little in common with grammatical rules of other sorts. Thus, I will argue that anaphora rules constitute a separate, narrowly constrained category of rules.

I should add that opting for heterogeneity does not resolve all of the issues dividing generative semantics from interpretivism. For example, a heterogeneous theory is neutral with respect to the question of whether it is possible to order all lexical insertion transformations in a block. On such issues I generally take the more conservative position, i.e., the position of the standard theory of Chomsky (1965). Thus, for example, I will assume that lexical insertion can be done in a block, and that the level preceding lexical insertion is defined by a context-free phrase structure grammar. In other

words, I will assume that it is possible to define a level of deep structure
distinct from semantic representation (this level being the level immediately
following lexical insertion).

It must be emphasized here that in striving for a heterogeneous theory,
I am not arguing for arbitrary multiplication of the available rule types.
Rather, I am saying that it is desirable to distinguish different rule types
where this makes it possible to constrain these types in ways which help to
restrict the generative capacity of linguistic theory. For example, Emonds'
(1970) division of grammatical transformations into root, structure-pre-
serving, and minor movement rules is to be adopted, if possible, because
it allows us to impose on grammars his Structure Preserving Constraint, which
says that root transformations apply only to root sentences (i.e., main clauses).
In contrast, some proposed mechanisms, such as syntactic rule features and
derivational constraints involving arbitrary levels of structure, have not led
to any constraints on linguistic theory. Hence, in the absence of overwhelming
empirical evidence showing such rule types to be necessary (see Kayne
(1969a), Baker and Brame (1971), and Appendix II to this monograph),
I will assume that they are not needed.

In general, then, I will be operating within the standard theory, augmented
by those innovations which have served to constrain that theory. Innovations
which do not serve this function will generally be avoided. The one notable
exception to the above generalization is that I accept the need for what are
variously referred to as derived structure interpretive rules or two-point
derivational constraints involving semantic representation. Since the need for
these is virtually universally accepted (see, e.g., Jackendoff (1972) and
Lakoff (1970c)), there should be no objection to my decision to accept them.

NOTES

[1] Throughout this monograph italics or underlining will be used to indicate an anaphoric
relation. This notation is adopted rather than the more common device of indexing (cf. Chomsky (1965) pp. 145-146 and Chapter 2, § 1 below) because of the widespread confusion
resulting from the use of the term "referential" in association with indices (see, e.g., Karttunen
(1969) or Lakoff (1968)). Both notations fail to distinguish anaphor from antecedent. This may
well require the introduction of a new notation altogether. No such move is made in this
monograph, however.

[2] (A) and (B) are distinct questions. This can be seen from the fact that (B) needs to be
answered regardless of the answer to (A). At least four distinct proposals have been made
in regard to (A): (i) grammatical transformations (Lees and Klima (1963)); (ii) lexical
insertion transformations (McCawley (1970)); (iii) global derivation constraints (Postal
(1970)); and (iv) rules of semantic interpretation (Jackendoff (1969)). Each of these
proposals (with the possible exception of (iii)) is compatible with various formulations of
specific conditions on the rule(s) and rule ordering.

[3] This assumes the validity of "Church's Thesis", i.e., that the notion "recursively anumerable" is an adequate formalization of the concept "describable by an algorithm" (cf. Rogers (1967)).

[4] It is not, however, as serious a setback as is widely believed. Although they did demonstrate the excess power of their formalization of linguistic theory, they also proposed some rather natural constraints — which are consistent with almost all existing proposals within transformational grammar — which would limit the class of transformational languages to a subclass of the recursive sets.

[5] Note that interpretive rules constitute one (or more) type of global rules.

PART I

Pronominal Anaphora

Chapter 2

THE PRONOMINALIZATION AND REFLEXIVIZATION TRANSFORMATIONS

1. *History*

The first generative treatment of anaphora was Lees and Klima's (1963) paper, "Rules for English Pronominalization." They were concerned primarily with distinguishing the privileges of occurrence of ordinary pronouns, reflexives, and reciprocals. Since in the theory current at the time, transformations were the only available mechanism for formalizing their insights, Lees and Klima proposed that these elements be derived transformationally from full NP's under identity with some other NP in the sentence. No attempt was made to differentiate between anaphoric and non-anaphoric pronouns. This should occasion no surprise, since, at the time, generative grammarians dealt with questions of meaning only peripherally. It seems doubtful, however, that they could have intended their Pronominalization transformation to account for non-anaphoric pronouns. Under these circumstances, one wonders why they proposed the transformation at all, for they could have accounted for anaphoric pronouns with whatever mechanism they meant to use in deriving non-anaphoric pronouns.

Lees and Klima contributed two ideas which have had a lasting effect on subsequent studies of pronominal anaphora. The first is the proposal for a Pronominalization transformation; such a rule was an accepted part of all work in generative grammar for several years. The other was the idea that reflexives constitute a special class of anaphoric pronouns, namely those which are in the same clause as their antecedent.

The purpose of this chapter is to present arguments against both of these ideas. This is necessary because the ideas in question have had such a powerful influence on the study of anaphora.

In order to discuss the merits of Lees and Klima's proposals, it will be useful first to recapitulate briefly some of the subsequent work elaborating on their ideas. This work contains some fundamental insights which have been incorporated into alternative approaches to anaphora, and which will be discussed at greater length in later chapters.

The first important modification of Lees and Klima's proposals was suggested by Chomsky (1965), and was necessitated by the work of Katz and Postal (1964), which argued (roughly) that deep structure determines meaning. Since the Katz-Postal hypothesis entails that the operation of the Pronominalization and Reflexivization transformations cannot affect meaning, these transformations needed to be modified, for, as originally formulated, they would relate such examples as the (a) and (b) sentences of (1) and (2).

(1) (a) The President says that the President should be treated with respect.

(b) *The President* says that *he* should be treated with respect.

(2) (a) John hurt John.

(b) John hurt himself.

These pairs are not synonymous because different occurrences of the same NP need not refer[1] to the same thing. For example, in sentence (1a) it is possible for the first occurrence of "the President" to refer to a particular individual and for the second occurrence to refer to the office of the Presidency. Thus (1a) may mean (roughly) that Nixon says we should treat all Presidents with respect, but (1b) may not be so paraphrased. More strikingly, in (2a) the two occurrences of "John" must refer to different individuals, whereas in (2b), "John" and "himself" designate the same person. Hence, the Katz-Postal hypothesis requires that the identity condition in the Pronominalization and Reflexivization transformations include identity of reference. Chomsky (1965) proposed to accomplish this by assigning an index to every NP in deep structure. Two NP's will then be interpreted as coreferential if and only if they have the same index, and two NP's with different indices cannot fulfill the identity condition included in the Pronominalization and Reflexivization transformations. This makes it possible to determine identity of reference in deep structure, in keeping with the demands of the Katz-Postal hypothesis.

The next major advance in the study of pronominal anaphora came with the investigation of the criteria for "backwards pronominalization," i.e., pronominalization in which the anaphor precedes the antecedent in the sentence. Lees and Klima only considered instances of forward pronominalization.[2] Later researchers noticed that backwards pronominalization was also possible, although only in certain environments. The structural description of the Pronominalization transformation required a specification of these environments, and a number of linguists set to work to discover what they are. Several investigators (including Postal, Matthews, Gross, G. Lakoff, and Ross) arrived independently at the following solution:

(3) Backwards pronominalization is possible only if the anaphor is

dominated by a subordinate clause which does not dominate the antecedent.

Langacker (1966) formulated the same condition somewhat differently.[3]

(4) Backwards pronominalization is possible unless
  (a) the anaphor and the antecedent are in different conjuncts of a coordinate conjunction, or
  (b) the anaphor commands the antecedent.

"Command" can be defined as follows:

(5) Node A commands node B if every S node dominating A dominates B.

The constraint given in (3) and (4) (which I will refer to as the "precede-command condition") will be discussed in detail in Chapter 4. For the present, it suffices to note that it remains an accepted part of almost all analyses of pronominal anaphora. (6) exemplifies its operation (see Chapter 4 for a multitude of further examples and counterexamples).

(6) (a) *John* stays when you ask *him* to leave.
  (b) **He* stays when you ask *John* to leave.
  (c) When you ask *John* to leave, *he* stays.
  (d) When you ask *him* to leave, *John* stays.

The basic ideas of Lees and Klima were elaborated in a number of other papers (e.g., Postal (1966)), but the modifications outlined above (viz., indices plus the precede-command condition) are the only ones that became generally accepted as part of "the Standard Theory."

Before discussing the shortcomings of this theory, I would like to review one other proposed modification of the Lees and Klima account, namely Ross' (1967b) suggestion that Pronominalization should be a cyclic rule. According to the analysis developed by Langacker and others, forward pronominalization should always be possible; the condition given in (3) and (4) constrains only backwards pronominalization. Ross (1967b) noticed that (7a) constituted an apparent counterexample to this prediction.

(7) (a) *Realizing that *Oscar* was unpopular disturbed *him*.
  (b) Realizing that *he* was unpopular disturbed *Oscar*.

Ross argued that this example can be handled by the standard Pronominalization rule if we make the following three assumptions: (i) Pronominalization is an obligatory transformation; (ii) Pronominalization is a cyclic transformation; and (iii) there is a transformation of Equi NP Deletion (henceforth Equi) which deletes the subject of certain embedded sentences under identity with an NP in the matrix sentence, and the derivation of examples like (7) involves Equi.

Given these assumptions, (7a) cannot be generated. (iii) guarantees that the deep structure of (7a) will be something like (8).

(8)

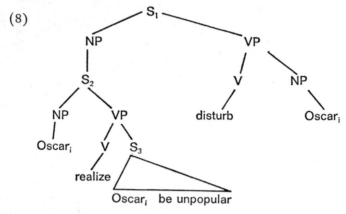

Applying pronominalization cyclically and obligatorily, as (i) and (ii) require, we are forced to pronominalize the bottommost occurrence of *Oscar*$_i$ on the S$_2$ cycle: if we did not pronominalize at all, we would violate (i); if we pronominalized backwards, we would violate (3) and (4). Now it is clear that (7a) can never be derived, since (i) and (ii) force its deep structure, (8), to be realized as (7b). Thus, given (i)-(iii), (7a) is out for the same reason that (9) is out.

(9)   *He* realized that *Oscar* was unpopular.

This argument has great appeal, and much has been written about these examples. It is for this reason that it is mentioned here. An alternative analysis of example (7a) is presented in Chapter 4, § 3.1.1.

These, then, are the landmarks in the development of the transformational analysis of Pronominalization: Lees and Klima's original paper, Chomsky's introduction of indices, Langacker, et. al.'s discovery of the precede-command condition, and Ross' argument for cyclicity.

In the last five to ten years, a number of arguments have been put forward showing the untenability of this entire approach to pronominal anaphora. The next section consists of a summary of some of these.

2. Arguments Against Pronominalization

2.1 Perhaps the strongest argument against deriving pronouns transformationally is due to Bresnan (1970).

She points out that, in sentences like (10a), either Pronominalization or

There-insertion, but not both, may apply, as (10b-d) demonstrate.

(10) (a) Some students said that some students had been in the office.
      (b) *Some students* said that *they* had been in the office.
      (c) Some students said that there had been some students in the office.
      (d) **Some students* said that there had been *they* in the office.

The reason that (10d) is ill-formed is, of course, that There-insertion applies only to sentences with indefinite subjects, so that it cannot apply to sentences like the complement clause of (10b). In a theory with a transformation of Pronominalization, however, this explanation cannot be formalized, since the pronominalization (and hence the definitization) of *some students* would have to follow the insertion of *there*. This can be seen from the fact that, whereas There-insertion is known to be a cyclic transformation (see Wasow (1975) for an argument showing the cyclicity of *There* insertion) and hence applies on the cycle of the complement clause, Pronominalization cannot apply until the matrix cycle, owing to the identity condition involved in its operation. Thus, the only means of excluding (10d) in a theory incorporating Pronominalization would be with some ad hoc constraint blocking Pronominalization if the NP to be pronominalized had been involved in the insertion of *there*. But such an analysis fails to capture the obvious fact that what excludes (10d) is the definiteness of the pronoun.[4]

Similar arguments can be given on the basis of special conditions on the transformations of Particle movement and Dative movement. Both of these rules are blocked in sentences whose direct objects are pronominal (assuming that the formulations of the rules in question given by Emonds (1972) are correct). This is illustrated in (11) and (12).

(11) (a) John turned the girl away.
      (b) John turned away the girl.
      (c) John turned her away.
      (d) *John turned away her.

(12) (a) John gave a book to Mary.
      (b) John gave Mary a book.
      (c) John gave it to Mary.
      (d) *John gave Mary it.

Consider now sentences like (25).

(13) (a) The girl claims that John turned the girl away.
      (b) Bill bought the book after John gave the book to Mary.

If Particle movement and Dative movement apply cyclically (and there are good arguments that they should — See Emonds (1972)), then in a theory incorporating a Pronominalization transformation, they could apply in sentences like (13) before Pronominalization applied, and sentences like (14) would be produced.

(14) (a) *The girl claims that John turned away her.
   (b) *Bill bought the book after John gave Mary it.

Examples (14), like example (10d) above, seem to require that an ad hoc constraint be added to Pronominalization, blocking its application just in case certain other transformations have applied earlier. Such constraints are clearly undesirable, and any analysis requiring them must be regarded with the utmost suspicion.[5]

Still another argument can be constructed along the same lines on the basis of Bresnan's (1971a) insightful reanalysis of English sentential stress. Bresnan showed that certain apparent counterexamples to the Nuclear Stress Rule (NSR) can be accounted for if the NSR applies at the end of each transformational cycle. She also argued that pronouns did not have any word stress, and hence did not participate in the operation of the NSR.[6] Given this analysis, suppose we try to assign sentence stress to an example like (15) in a theory including Pronominalization.

(15) *John* believes Mary loves *him*.

The derivation is summarized in (16).

(16) John$_i$ believes Mary loves John$_i$

I	I	I	I	I	Word Stress
		2	2	I	NSR
				him$_i$	
				[-stress]	Pronominalization
2	I	3	3		NSR

On the first cycle, the NSR assigns main stress to *John* (thereby reducing the stress on the other words in that clause), just as it does in (17).

(17) Mary loves Jóhn.

On the second cycle, Pronominalization applies, thus destressing *him* and leaving *believes* as the rightmost primary stress in the sentence. Hence, the NSR assigns the main stress in the sentence to *believes*, giving the incorrect (18a) instead of (18b).

(18) (a) *Jóhn belíeves Mary loves *him*.

   (b) *John* believes Mary lóves *him*.

The problem with (16) is, of course, the Pronominalization transformation. The derivation of anaphoric pronouns from full NP's forces the NSR to reduce stress where it should not be reduced. The well-motivated cyclic ordering of the NSR makes it impossible to pronominalize before this incorrect stress reduction would take place.[7]

2.2 Dougherty (1969) advances a number of arguments against the existence of a Pronominalization transformation. These arguments consist basically of two sorts of examples: sentences which can have no source if Pronominalization exists, and sentences whose alleged sources would also underlie ungrammatical sentences. Examples of the first sort are given in (19).

(19) (a) *Each of the men* thought that *he* was the tallest.
(b) *Neither of the siamese twins* was bold enough to ask the other to scratch *his* back in those places that *he* couldn't reach himself.
(c) You can have an *ice cream, a soda,* or *both.*[8]

A transformation of Pronominalization would have to derive (19a-c) from the deviant sources (20a-c).

(20) (a) *Each of the men thought that each of the men was the tallest.
(b) *Neither of the siamese twins was bold enough to ask the other to scratch neither of the siamese twins' back in those places that neither of the siamese twins could reach himself.
(c) *You can have an ice cream, a soda, or (both) an ice cream, a soda.

Examples which a transformational theory of Pronominalization could not derive without similarly deriving deviant sentences are given in (21).

(21) (a) *Each of Mary's sons* hated *his* brothers.
(b) *Each of Mary's sons* was hated by *his* brothers.

The sources for (21) would be essentially the sentences in (22).

(22) (a) Each of Mary's sons hated each of Mary's sons' brothers.
(b) Each of Mary's sons' brothers hated each of Mary's sons.

But such a theory could also generate the ill-formed example of (23) from (22).

(23) (a) *Each of Mary's sons' brothers was hated by *him.*
(b) *Each of Mary's sons' brothers hated *him.*

Notice, furthermore, that the examples in (21) are not synonymous with their supposed sources in (22), since the latter, but not the former, implies

that each of Mary's sons hates himself.[9] Sentences of this sort, in which the
application of the Pronominalization transformation would affect meaning,
constitute a further argument against the existence of Pronominalization.
Additional examples are provided in (24).

(24) (a) *Most politicians* believe that everyone loves *them.* ≠
     (b) Most politicians believe that everyone loves most politicians.
     (c) *Some adolescents* claim that *they* are bored with life ≠
     (d) Some adolescents claim that some adolescents are bored with
         life.
     (e) *Every bride* hopes that *she* will have a happy marriage. ≠
     (f) Every bride hopes that every bride will have a happy
         marriage.

The non-synonymy of such examples with their purported sources requires
the postulation of some interpretive mechanism ordered after Pronominalization which will assign the appropriate readings to the pronouns. But if such
a mechanism is needed anyway, then it is possible to generate all pronouns
in the base and subject them all to the interpretive mechanism, thereby
rendering the transformation superfluous.[10]

Observe that the postulation of referential indices in deep structure reduces
the force of this argument; it might be possible to argue that the transformation only appears to have changed meaning because of the failure to mark
coreference in (24b, d, & f). It seems to me, however, that indices do not
suffice to account for these facts. Even if both occurrences of "some adolescents" in (24d) are understood as referring to the same specific group of
adolescents, (24c) still allows an interpretation absent from (24d), viz., one
in which each adolescent makes claims only about him or herself.

It is interesting to note that all of the examples in (24) involve quantifiers.
Hence, it might be objected that an appropriate analysis of quantifiers could
nullify the above argument (the analysis outlined by Lakoff (1970c) is a
natural candidate). Since evaluation of such an objection would take us too
far afield, I will simply remark that there appear to be significant problems
with all such analyses of quantifiers (see Jackendoff (1971c). I am therefore
unconvinced by this way of avoiding the difficulty presented by (24).

2.3 The mode of reasoning utilized above — that independent evidence for
an interpretive mechanism to account for anaphora makes a Pronominalization
transformation unnecessary — is employed by Jackendoff (1969, 1972) and
Dougherty (1969) in connection with anaphoric relations not involving
pronouns. They point out that it is highly implausible to derive the anaphors
in (25) from underlying NP's identical to their antecedents.

(25) (a) *John* told Mary that he loved her, but *the bastard* didn't mean it.

(b) *Each* of the workers hated *the rest* of the workers.

This being so, it is possible to purchase a certain degree of economy in the grammar of English by dispensing with the transformation of Pronominalization and employing whatever mechanism accounts for the anaphoric relations in (25) to assign antecedents to definite pronouns.

Postal (1972d) attempts to rebut this argument by deriving "anaphoric epithets" such as (25a) from appositive clauses, as illustrated below.

(26) (a) *John* told Mary that he loved her, but *he*, who is a bastard, didn't mean it. $\Longrightarrow$

(b) *John* told Mary thay he loved her, but *the bastard* didn't mean it.

While such an analysis might make it possible to account for anaphoric epithets in a manner consistent with the transformational derivation of pronouns, the lack of independent evidence (together with the failure of this solution to generalize to cases like (25b)) render this approach dubious. Nevertheless, Postal's suggestion weakens the force of the anaphoric epithets argument against a Pronominalization transformation.

2.4 The best known argument against Pronominalization consists of what is known as the Bach-Peters paradox (Bach (1970)). This argument shows that the standard assumptions about the identity condition associated with the transformation of Pronominalization are incompatible with the rather fundamental tenet of transformational grammar that phrase markers are finite (i.e., have only finitely many branches). Consider sentence (27).

(27) *The pilot who shot at it* hit the mig that chased *him*.

If every anaphoric definite pronoun is derived from a structure identical to the full NP which serves as its antecedent, then *it* and *him* in (27) must be derived from (28a) and (28b), respectively.

(28) (a) the mig that chased him
(b) the pilot who shot at it

But (28a) and (28b) themselves contain the definite anaphoric pronouns *him* and *it*, so they must in turn be derived from (28b) and (28a). Clearly, this procedure can be continued indefinitely. Since the antecedent of each of the pronouns contains the other, there can be no hope of eliminating the anaphors by replacing them with their antecedents.

Although the Bach-Peters paradox certainly shows that some assumptions that had been made about the operation of pronominalization are untenable,

Karttunen (1971) shows that most linguists who have considered the paradox have suggested much more radical alterations in the theory of pronouns than the argument itself necessitates.

Karttunen observes that (29) can serve as the input to the Pronominalization transformation, if it is assumed that relative clauses have the structure

NP
NP   S   at this stage, and further, that the bottom of these two NP's may

serve as the antecedent for Pronominalization.

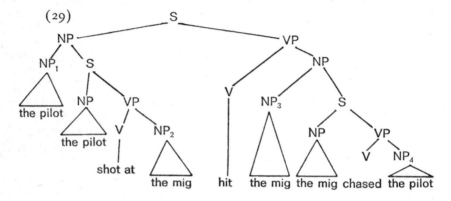

Applying Pronominalization to NP_2 and NP_4 under identity to NP_3 and NP_1, respectively, (29) yields (27). Thus, the force of the Bach-Peters paradox is considerably weakened.

In Wasow (1973a), repeated here as Appendix I, I have argued that Karttunen's analysis predicts that examples like (27) ought to be infinitely ambiguous, and that such examples do, after all, provide an argument against a Pronominalization transformation.

2.5 Another argument against deriving anaphoric pronouns transformationally from full NP's is presented by Wasow (1973c). Consider an underlying structure like (30) (irrelevant details have been ommitted).

(30) The woman John$_i$ loved told John$_i$ that John$_i$ was a dope.

The transformation theory of pronominal anaphora would be unable to block the derivation of (31) from (30).

(31) *The woman *he* loved told *him* that *John* was a dope.

This derivation is accomplished in two stages: First of all, the middle occurrence of *John*$_i$ is pronominalized under identity with the first occurrence. This stage of the derivation cannot be blocked without similarly blocking the derivation of (32b) from (32a).

(32) (a) The woman John$_i$ loved told John$_i$ that you were a dope.
      (b) The woman *John* loved told *him* that you were a dope.

Thus, the intermediate form (33) is derived.

(33) The woman *John*$_i$ loved told *him* that John$_i$ was a dope.

Pronominalization can now apply to (33) yielding (31). This stage of the derivation cannot be blocked without likewise blocking the derivation of (34b) from (34a).

(34) (a) The woman John$_i$ loved told me that John$_i$ was a dope.
      (b) The woman *he* loved told me that *John* was a dope.

Thus the transformational theory of pronominal anaphora cannot be prevented from deriving the ungrammatical string (31).

2.6 There are no doubt further reasons for abandoning the idea of a transformation converting NP's into pronouns under conditions of identity[11] (e.g., Kayne (1971) presents an ordering paradox that arises if the grammar of French is assumed to contain such a transformation). However, the arguments in this section suffice to justify the abandonment of the transformational theory of pronominal anaphora.

The fact that the transformational approach encounters so many difficulties is not terribly surprising in light of the lack of syntactic motivation for such a transformation. As Dougherty (1969) observed, the syntactic properties of anaphoric pronouns are essentially the same as those of non-anaphoric pronouns; but, as we have seen, pronouns do behave differently from full NP's in many respects. Dougherty's formulation of this fact has been severely criticized in the literature (Postal (1972b) and MacColl (1972)), but I think it is fundamentally correct (see § 4 below for a modification and defense of his position). Hence, any analysis which uses a grammatical transformation for distinguishing anaphoric from non-anaphoric pronouns can be expected to encounter difficulties.

3. *Reflexivization*

Whereas Lees and Klima's analysis of ordinary pronouns has been generally abandoned for the reasons given above, their approach to reflexives remains widely accepted. In essence, this analysis (which will be referred to as "the Reflexivization analysis") involves transforming the second of two identical NP's into a reflexive form if they command one another (i.e., if they are in the same clause). In a theory with indices, the identity condition includes identity of reference, and the Reflexivization transformation can be

made obligatory. This makes it possible to account for the following paradigms.

(35)   *I hurt me.   You hurt me.   He hurt me.
       I hurt you.   *You hurt you.   He hurt you.
       I hurt him.   You hurt him.   *He hurt *him*.

       I hurt myself.   *You hurt myself.   *He hurt myself.
       *I hurt yourself.   You hurt yourself.   *He hurt yourself.
       *I hurt himself.   *You hurt himself.   He hurt himself.

(36)   (a) I want you to love $\left\{ \begin{array}{c} \text{me} \\ \text{*myself} \end{array} \right\}$.

       (b) You saw the man who mugged $\left\{ \begin{array}{c} \text{you} \\ \text{*yourself} \end{array} \right\}$.

       (c) *John* denies the claim that you upset $\left\{ \begin{array}{c} \text{*him* } \\ \text{*himself} \end{array} \right\}$.

       (d) We believe that they hate $\left\{ \begin{array}{c} \text{us} \\ \text{*ourselves} \end{array} \right\}$.

       (e) *Our opponents* realize that we hate $\left\{ \begin{array}{c} \text{*them* } \\ \text{*themselves} \end{array} \right\}$.

The Reflexivization analysis predicts that anaphoric pronouns and reflexives
are in complementary distribution. These examples seem to bear that prediction out, and they serve as the principle justification for this approach.

Helke (1970) demonstrates a number of defects of the Reflexivization
analysis, and develops a preferable alternative analysis. This section summa-
rizes Helke's insights.

Helke's most direct argument against the Reflexivization analysis is the
observation that reflexives and anaphoric pronouns are not, after all, in
complementary distribution, as the following examples show.[12]

(37)   (a) *The young woman* took it upon $\left\{ \begin{array}{c} \text{*her* } \\ \text{herself} \end{array} \right\}$ to lead the
            revolution.

       (b) *Mrs. Cabot* wrapped the stole around $\left\{ \begin{array}{c} \text{*her* } \\ \text{herself} \end{array} \right\}$.

       (c) It annoys *John* that a picture of $\left\{ \begin{array}{c} \text{*him* } \\ \text{himself} \end{array} \right\}$ is hanging
            in the post office.

       (d) *John* remarked that, as for $\left\{ \begin{array}{c} \text{*him* } \\ \text{himself} \end{array} \right\}$, he didn't care
            who we voted for.

In addition to the fact that reflexives and anaphoric pronouns are not in complementary distribution, Helke observed a difference between them that suggests that they should be handled by separate rules. Reflexives differ from anaphoric pronouns in that the latter, but not the former, may have what are known as "split antecedents." This is illustrated in (38).

(38) (a) *John* told *Mary* about the man *they* were meeting.
      (b) *John told Mary about themselves.[13]

On the basis of these observations, Helke proposed an alternative to the Reflexivization analysis. The central feature of Helke's analysis is that reflexives consist of a head noun *self* with a possessive pronominal determiner. The necessary agreement between this determiner and some other NP in the same clause is accounted for by a transformation which inserts pronominal copies of NP's into empty determiner nodes. This transformation is independently necessary for examples like (39).

(39) (a) The man lost $\left\{ \begin{array}{l} \text{his} \\ \text{*her} \end{array} \right\}$ way.

      (b) The dog Wagged $\left\{ \begin{array}{l} \text{its} \\ \text{*the cat's} \end{array} \right\}$ tail.

      (c) The police lost $\left\{ \begin{array}{l} \text{their} \\ \text{*our} \end{array} \right\}$ heads.

The constraint that reflexives and their antecedents must be in the same clause (or, in Helke's terminology, "have the same sentential ancestry") is accounted for by Chomsky's "insertion prohibition" (Chomsky (1965), p. 146):

(40) "no morphological material... can be introduced into a configuration dominated by S once the cycle of transformational rules has already completed its application to this configuration."[14]

Given (40), Helke's analysis accounts automatically for the facts in (36). No special conditions are required on the copying transformation; whereas the Reflexivization analysis provides a description of (36), Helke's provides an explanation, and is hence preferable.

Notice that Helke's analysis also accounts for most of (35): in his system, reflexives can arise only through copying, and in many of the examples in (35), the reflexive differs in person from the other NP in the sentence. The remaining examples in (1) are accounted for by the following universal constraint:

(41) Given the configuration NP_1-V-NP_2, NP_1 and NP_2 have non-intersecting reference.[15]

(41) is needed on independent grounds in order to rule out examples like (42).

(42) ??I hurt us.   *You (plural) hurt you (singular).
       *We hurt me.   *You (singular) hurt you (plural).

(41) also serves to explain why, in an example like (43), *the soldiers* and *the officers* are understood as denoting disjoint sets.

(43) The soldiers dislike the officers.

The main advantage of Helke's analysis over the Reflexivization analysis is that each of the three devices Helke employs (viz., the copying transformation, the insertion prohibition, and constraint (41)) has independent motivation. Thus, Helke simplifies the grammar of English by eliminating the Reflexivization transformation and performing its function with independently necessary mechanisms. In addition to these rather basic considerations, there are a few minor advantages to Helke's analysis. For example, its bifurcation of of reflexives correctly predicts that they will receive final stress, and that expressions like *my own self* and *your little self* are possible alternates for the normal reflexives.[16]

For the purposes of the present monograph, what is important about Helke's work on reflexives is that it demonstrates that anaphoric pronouns and reflexives should be handled rather differently.[17] The copying transformation which produces reflexives cannot be used to account for ordinary anaphoric pronouns without violating the insertion prohibition, since ordinary pronouns may be in lower clauses than their antecedents. Thus, ordinary anaphoric pronouns require a fundamentally different sort of analysis. This conclusion contrasts markedly with the views of Lees and Klima (1963) and most subsequent investigators.

4. *Anapornia*

4.0 Probably the most fundamental difference between reflexives and ordinary pronouns is that the former must always be understood anaphorically, whereas the latter can be understood non-anaphorically. As mentioned above, Dougherty (1969) argued against deriving anaphoric pronouns transformationally on the basis of his claim that any anaphoric pronoun also allowed a non-anaphoric interpretation. This purported relationship between anaphoric and non-anaphoric pronouns (which Dougherty dubbed "the Anaporn Relation") must be considered accidental within a transformational theory of Pronominalization, but it is very naturally captured within a theory which distinguishes between the problems of generating pronouns and assigning antecedents to them. In a theory of the latter sort, one need only specify which pronouns can receive an anaphoric interpretation, and all pronouns can be assumed to allow non-anaphoric interpretations.

Unfortunately, the anaporn relation as Dougherty stated it simply does not hold. This can readily be seen from a consideration of examples like (39) above. The inaccuracy of Dougherty's claim has been used as a basis for criticizing his work (e.g., Postal (1972b)). However, I believe that to abandon the anaporn relation altogether would be to miss an important insight. Helke's work discussed above suggests a way of salvaging the spirit, if not the letter, of Dougherty's proposal. Further, this bears on some important theoretical issues raised by Jackendoff (1969) and Postal (1970b).

4.1 Consider some typical counterexamples to the Anaporn relation.

(44) (a) *Mary* washed *herself*.
    (b) *The President* lost *his* head.
    (c) *The chairman* gnashed *his* teeth.
    (d) *The losers* had to buy beer for the winners, didn't *they?*
    (e) *She* is a happy girl, is *Sue*.
    (f) *The man who shot Liberty Valance, he* was the bravest of them all.
    (g) *He* is a very wise man, *the Maharishi*.[18]

Examples like (44a-c) have already been discussed in connection with Helke's analysis of reflexives. It was concluded that the pronouns in such exemples all result from application of a transformation which makes pronominal copies of certain NP's. Examples like (44d) have been frequently discussed in the literature (see, e.g., Katz and Postal (1964) and Culicover (1970)), and it is widely believed that such pronouns are also a result of copying transformations. Culicover (1970) analyzes the pronoun in (44e) similarly as the output of a copying transformation. Ross (1967a) mentions transformations of Left and Right dislocation, which are allegedly involved in the derivations of (44f) and (44g) (but cf. van Riemsdijk and Zwarts (1974)). These transformations would move NP's, leaving pronominal copies behind.[19]

These facts are highly suggestive. If all counterexamples to the anaporn relation involve pronouns resulting from the application of copying transformations, then it might be possible to salvage the anaporn relation in spirit by stipulating that copying transformations which involve an NP always produce a pronoun whose antecedent is that NP.

One immediate advantage of such a stipulation is that it accounts for the fact that some of the pronoun-antecedent pairs in (44) seem to be in relative positions in which pronominal anaphora relations are usually prohibited. In (44e) and (44g), for instance, the pronoun is to the left of its antecedent, and might plausibly be argued to command the antecedent,[20] in which case no anaphoric relation should be possible. In addition, (44f) exhibits an abnormal pronoun-antecedent relation, as can be seen from the ungrammaticality of (45), in which the relevant phrases presumably bear exactly the same structural relationship as in (44f). (See Chapter 4 for discussion of the constraint involved).

(45)   *Behind *the man who shot Liberty Valance, he* saw a light.

If copying transformations necessarily stipulate an anaphoric relation between the copy and the NP copied, then these anomalies are accounted for. Another similar case is that of Extraposition, if the pronoun *it* in sentences like (46) is said to be in an anaphoric relation with the complement clause. The existence of such an anaphoric relation requires an explanation, since the pronoun is to the left of its antecedent and commands it.

(46)   (a) *It* is possible *that John will come.*
       (b) *It* is impossible *for John to come.*

By supposing Extraposition to be formulated so as to move the complement, leaving *it* as a copy, it is possible to account for this unusual anaphoric relation. Further, such an analysis accounts for the impossibility of associating *it* with any other antecedent in such sentences — given, of course, the above proposal about copying transformations.

Another class of counterexamples to the anaporn relation as Dougherty presents it consists of relative pronouns. These must always be anaphorically related to their heads. For example, in (47), *which* must necessarily be anaphorically related to *the book.*

(47)   *The book which* was lying on the table belongs to me.

Chomsky (personal communication) has pointed out that such cases, although they may be inconsistent with the details of the formulation of the anaporn relation, are perfectly consistent with the point Dougherty makes, viz., that for elements which are sometimes interpreted anaphorically, those environments where they may be so interpreted are a proper subset of those where they may be interpreted non-anaphorically. Since relative pronouns must always be interpreted anaphorically, they are not really relevant to Dougherty's conclusion. The fact that relative pronouns must be anaphorically related to their heads can be incorporated into the grammar by including in the rule (or rules) involved in forming relative clauses a stipulation that the head must be the antecedent of the relative pronoun. This would replace a condition in almost all existing analyses of relatives that stipulates identity between the head and an NP internal to the relative.

Notice now that the traditional method of formulating copying transformations would also involve stipulation of identity between NP's (viz., between the NP copied and the copy). This suggests that it might be possible to dispense with the notion of identical NP's altogether, in favor of the notion of anaphorically related NP's. This could be accomplished by replacing the term "identical to" with "under the influence of" in all grammatical rules, where "under the influence of" is defined in (48).

(48) (a) NP_1 is under the influence of NP_2 if and only if NP_1 is a pronoun and NP_2 is its antecedent.

(b) If A and B are constituents other than NP, A is under the influence of B if and only if A and B are identical.[21]

With this definition, it is possible to avoid mention of anaphora in the formulation of the transformations involved in (44). Instead, operations which copy NP's can simply be formulated as inserting an NP under the influence of another NP. This bears on an important theoretical issue raised by Jackendoff (1969), which will be discussed below.

Another beneficial consequence of adopting (48) is that it accounts automatically for the requirement that relative pronouns be anaphorically related to their heads. This is accomplished without significant alteration of the rules involved in the formation of relative clauses.

In addition, replacing the notion of identity by that of under the influence of makes other predictions which seem to be borne out. For example, it predicts that no transformation needs to refer to true identity between NP's. In fact, the linguistic literature seems to support this prediction. I know of no cases of grammatical rules or constraints which involve identical NP's (as opposed to anaphorically related NP's).

Another prediction of (48) is that all transformations which delete NP's "under identity" actually delete pronouns under anaphora. It is rather striking that Postal (1970b) makes precisely this claim on quite different grounds. Postal proposes (48), under the title, "Universal Deletion Constraint."

(49) If a transformation T deletes an NP_a subject to the existence of a coreferent NP, NP_b, in the same structure, then at the point where T applies, NP_a must be pronominal.

Although most of Postal's reasons for proposing (49) are inapplicable in the present framework, there do not appear to be any counterexamples to the proposal at hand among deletion rules. All in all, the substitution of "under the influence of" for "identical to" seems to be quite well supported.

4.2 Recall at this point that the discussion leading up to (48) was introduced in order to attempt to salvage Dougherty's anaporn relation. The reader might, at this point, ask in what sense the proposal above accomplishes this end. In answer to this question, consider what conclusion Dougherty draws from the anaporn relation: If, as Dougherty claims, every pronoun which could be interpreted anaphorically could also be interpreted non-anaphorically then it would be most unnatural to propose that anaphoric pronouns have an entirely different source from non-anaphoric pronouns, for implicit in such an analysis would be the claim that the anaporn relation is entirely accidental. Such a theory would derive anaphoric pronouns from NP's fully identical to their antecedents, whereas non-anaphoric pronouns would have to be generated in the base (unless the definition of transformation were so altered as to allow transformations to refer to information — including non-linguistic information — outside of the sentence being operated on). Thus, the anaporn relation, if it held, would strongly support a theory of anaphora which would require all pronouns to be generated in the base and would postulate a filtering mechanism to determine which pronouns may have an anaphoric interpretation. (Every pronoun would be allowed a non-anaphoric interpretation).

Notice now that a minor modification of such a theory, viz., the replacement of "identical to" by "under the influence of," would serve to account for the fact that the only counterexamples to the anaporn relation are pronouns involved in a transformation which stipulates anaphora between the pronoun and its antecedent. All pronouns not produced by copying transformations would be generated in the base, and, of these, the only ones which are obligatorily anaphoric are those whose non-anaphoric interpretations are filtered out by transformations which mention that they are under the influence of another NP. Thus, (48) makes it possible to account for the fact that most pronouns are ambiguous between anaphoric and non-anaphoric interpretations, and to utilize this fact as an argument in favor of generating most pronouns in the base and against a transformation of Pronominalization. In this way, the arguments for incorporating (48) into linguistic theory and those against a Pronominalization transformation reenforce one another.

4.3 Jackendoff (1969) asserts that "coreferentiality, a purely semantic concept, cannot be referred to in transformations, and conversely, semantic rules cannot depend on what transformation have taken place, but only on the resulting structural configurations." Moreover, it is clear from the context in which this quote appears that a still stronger claim is intended, for it is on the above grounds that Jackendoff rejects Postal's "Cross over Constraint" (Postal (1971)). The Cross over Constraint, contrary to what Jackendoff seems to be suggesting, is neither a transformation nor a semantic rule. Rather, it was proposed as a universal constraint on the operation of a class of transformations in environments where certain anaphoric relations obtain. Thus, it seems that Jackendoff is claiming that the independence of syntax

and semantics is such that no constraint affecting the operation of transformations may refer to semantic information.

On general methodological grounds Jackendoff is correct in wishing to
maintain the distinctness of the components of a generative grammar. This
is in keeping with the goal outlined in Chapter 1 of maximizing heterogeneity
in the interests of making linguistic theory more restrictive. Thus, if possible,
semantic features should not be made available to individual syntactic transformations.

Notice, however, that these considerations do not apply to the Cross over
Constraint. Postal proposed this constraint as a linguistic universal, i.e., as
part of linguistic theory. As such, it restricts the operation of transformational
rules on the basis of semantic information, without requiring the transformations to make mention of the semantic features involved.[22] The Crossover
Constraint, if factually correct, would provide a universal statement of one
of the ways in which syntax and semantics are linked, and, as such, it would
restrict the class of grammars formulable within linguistic theory. Hence, the
Crossover Constraint is the sort of mechanism which is *a priori* desirable,
and the burden of proof, contrary to Jackendoff's implication is on its
opponent.[23]

Returning now to Jackendoff's claim that transformations may not refer
to coreferentiality, consider what this implies, in conjunction with Helke's
analysis of reflexives. Since Helke proposes that the pronominal determiner
portion of a reflexive is the product of a copying transformation, and
Jackendoff would insist that the necessary coreferentiality between this determiner and the NP of which it is a copy be assigned by a semantic rule, it
follows that reflexives would have to be associated with antecedents by a
rule other than the copying transformation which produces them. This
semantic rule, however, cannot be the same as the rule utilized to account
for the anaphoric relations of ordinary pronouns, as (50) shows.

(50) (a) Mary asked *Sue* to wash *her* car.
     (b) *Mary* asked Sue to wash *her* car.
     (c) Mary asked *Sue* to wash *her*self.
     (d) *Mary asked Sue to wash *her*self.

In fact, it is evident that the antecedent of the pronominal determiner of a
reflexive must always be the NP of which that determiner is a copy. In other
words, the conditions on the semantic rule must be identical to those on the
syntactic transformation. This is clearly an unsatisfactory situation.

It would seem, then, that Jackendoff's wish to keep syntactic rules from
mentioning anaphora is incompatible with Helke's analysis of reflexives. This
conflict is resolved, however, by substituting the notion of "under the
influence of" for "identical to." Making this substitution, it is possible for

transformations to mark anaphoric relations, but it is not necessary for transformations to mention anaphora (or "coreferentiality"). Rather, linguistic theory determines which transformations will mark anaphoric relations (viz., transformations traditionally formulated as involving identical NP's). In this manner, the notion of "under the influence of" permits us to accept Helke's analysis of reflexives (and various other analyses mentioned in § 4.1) without giving up Jackendoff's goal of restricting the power of the syntactic component.

5. *Conclusion*

In addition to summarizing some of the early history of generative studies of anaphora, this chapter has attempted to refute two ideas which played an important role in that earlier research. I have argued against deriving anaphoric pronouns transformationally from full NP's. Further, I have argued that the best existing analysis of reflexives cannot be generalized to cover ordinary anaphoric pronouns, thereby denying the traditional claim that reflexives and anaphoric pronouns should be accounted for in the same manner. Finally, I have claimed that particular grammars need never refer to identity between NP's (but only to anaphora), and I have proposed a definition which formalizes this idea.

Although I have outlined an analysis of reflexives to replace the standard one, I have said little about what sort of mechanism can do the work of the Pronominalization transformation without running into the difficulties described in § 2 above. The next chapter will be devoted to exploring the merits of two existing proposals for solving this problem.

NOTES

[1] I realize that I am using the word "refer" rather sloppily here. It would be much more prudent to use the phrase "used in referring." I will discuss this to some extent in Chapter 4. My sloppy usage here is in keeping with the general practice of linguists.

[2] In fact, Lees and Klima's rule is restricted to cases in which the antecedent is "in a matrix sentence" and the anaphor is "in a constituent sentence embedded within that matrix sentence" (p. 152). I have no idea why they limited themselves to such cases.

[3] Ross (1967b) claimed that these formulations make different predictions, but it seems to me that he was wrong unless he intended to define "subordinate clause" in a manner other than the obvious one.

[4] Notice that this same argument applies to any analysis (such as Kuroda (1969) or Postal (1966)) which includes a transformation of Definitization in the generation of pronouns.

[5] John R. Ross (personal communication) has suggested that facts like those in (11) and (12) should not be accounted for by conditions on the rules themselves, but rather by a

surface structure constraint ruling out sentences with pronominal direct objects which are not adjacent to the verb. Such an alternative would invalidate my argument, since the relevant ungrammatical examples would be ruled out at surface structure, rather than cyclically. (Incidentally, such a constraint would have to be global, since the notion of "direct object" is not definable in terms of surface structure).

Another alternative has been proposed by Howard Lasnik (personal communication). Lasnik suggested that pronominal direct objects should be encliticized cyclically. This alternative would not invalidate my argument, since the encliticization rule would apply on the complement cycle, but Pronominalization would not apply until the matrix. Observe, by the way, that this alternative requires that Particle Movement be done "backwards", i.e., leftwards, as proposed by Emonds (1972).

The contrast in (i) shows that either Ross' or Lasnik's alternative is to be preferred over an analysis which accounts for (11) and (12) by means of conditions on the rules themselves.

    (i) (a) Stanford owns — or so I was led to believe — the Dumbarton Bridge.

        (b) *Stanford owns — or so I was led to believe — it.

Crucial evidence in choosing between Ross' and Lasnik's proposals would consist of examples like (ii).

    (ii) ?John was given it.

Lasnik's analysis would rule (ii) out (since encliticization would have to precede Dative Movement, which in turn precedes Passive), whereas Ross' would allow it. Unfortunately, I find it marginal, and I am consequently unable to choose decisively between these alternatives.

Notice, however, that in all of the examples in (iii)-(vi), the (b)-sentences are significantly worse than the (a)-sentences.

    (iii) (a) John was given this house by his father.

        (b) ?John was given it by his father.

    (iv) (a) ?John is hard to give birthday presents.

        (b) *John is hard to give them.

    (v) (a) ?It was John that we gave the camera.

        (b) *It was John that we gave it.

    (vi) (a) John, we gave a camera.

        (b) *John, we gave it.

Lasnik's proposal predicts that the (b) sentences should be worse, whereas Ross' does not. It seems, then, that a surface structure constraint is probably not the best mechanism for accounting for the kinds of facts in question. Hence, the argument in this section does not appear to be weakened by Ross' observations.

  6 This does not, of course, prevent pronouns from receiving contrastive stress.

  7 Notice that this argument shows that the analysis of Siegel (1973) cannot be correct. Siegel argues that there should be a Pronominalization transformation only for what she calls "pronouns of laziness" (see Geach (1969)). The pronoun in (15) is such a pronoun. For a fuller discussion of this point, see Wasow (1975).

  8 Example (19c) is relevant only if it is assumed that *both* is related to its antecedents in the same way as ordinary definite pronouns are related to their antecedents. Notice, however, that exactly the same difficulty arises with examples of what have been called "split antecedents." Thus, if Pronominalization is a transformation which converts an NP into a pronoun under identity with another NP, then (i) can have no source.

    (i) *John* told *Mary* that *they* were lost.

Given an analysis incorporating a Pronominalization transformation, the most plausible underlying structure for (i) is (ii).

    (ii) John told Mary that John and Mary were lost.

If (ii) is the source of (i), however, the identity condition involved in Pronominalization cannot be one of syntactic identity, since the NP *John and Mary* occurs only once in (ii). What kind of condition could replace a strict syntactic identity condition in this case is not clear. Certainly, no adequate answer has been given to the question.

[9] This is so because each of Mary's sons is one of Mary's sons' brothers, so long as Mary has at least two sons. Mary is presupposed to have at least two sons by the use of the definite NP, *Mary's sons' brothers.*

[10] Lakoff (1968) proposes a theory of anaphora which includes both a Pronominalization transformation and surface structure rules of interpretation (Lakoff calls them "output conditions"). A careful reading, however, will reveal that he offers no motivation whatever for the postulation of the transformation.

[11] One more argument against the transformational approach to pronouns should be mentioned. Bach (1969) attempts to prove that there can be no Pronominalization transformation on the grounds that it is impossible to order such a transformation. His arguments is divided into three parts : (i) evidence that Pronominalization is not a precyclic transformation ; (ii) evidence that Pronominalization is not a cyclic transformation ; and (iii) evidence that Pronominalization is not a post-cyclic or last-cyclic transformation. Although much of the evidence Bach presents is of interest (and generalizes to the other approaches to anaphora), the conclusion that he attempts to establish does not follow from his evidence, because the arguments for (ii) are faulty. Bach presents two arguments for (ii). One depends on the claim that WH-fronting (Bach calls it "Question movement") must either be last cyclic or apply on the cycle following the one determined by the clause in which the WH-word appears. Both Chomsky (1971) and Jackendoff (1969) argue against this assumption, and it does not appear to be adequately justified. The other argument offered by Bach against cyclic Pronominalization depends crucially on the supposition that an optional cyclic rule which has failed to apply to a particular structure on one cycle may subsequently apply to the same structure on a later cycle in the same derivation. Chomsky (1971) has argued that the transformational cycle should be defined in such a way as to preclude such derivations. Thus, Bach's arguments against cyclic Pronominalization are inadequate. Postal (1970) and Lakoff (1968b) have also argued against a cyclic transformation of Pronominalization, but their arguments are subject to much the same criticism as Bach's. See Chapter 4 and Appendix II for further discussion of ordering problems.

[12] Helke notes that speakers differ in their reactions to examples like those in (37), but he observes that almost all speakers do allow free variation between anaphoric pronouns and reflexives in some environments.

[13] It is possible to get split antecedents for "picture noun reflexives," as (i) illustrates.
    (i) *John* showed *Mary* a picture of *themselves.*
This is not inconsistent with Helke's analysis, for his use of the (universal) Insertion Prohibition (see below) in place of the usual "simplex sentence" condition forces him to find another source for picture noun reflexives anyway. Helke's solution is to derive picture noun reflexives from emphatic reflexives (e.g., *them themselves,* in the case above) by deletion. Under such an analysis, the reflexive in (i) does not really have a split antecedent ; it is the deleted pronoun which has a split antecedent.

[14] Chomsky (1971) replaces (40) with another, more general, formulation. The distinction is irrelevant for the present purposes. A number of arguments have been given in support of the insertion prohibition (see, e.g., Chomsky (1971), Helke (1970), and Kayne (1969b)). Unfortunately, all of these depend on highly controversial analyses. Perhaps the best support for it to date is the nonexistence of a convincing counterexample. Note that the following paradigm lends some support to it (if it is assumed that phrases such as "I believe" may be generated as some sort of sentential modifiers, as first suggested by Bresnan (1968)) :
    (i) I believe John has claimed that Nixon is telling the truth.
    (ii) John, I believe, has claimed that Nixon is tell ng the truth.
    (i i) John has, I believe, claimed that Nixon is telling the truth.
    (iv) John has claimed, I believe, that Nixon is telling the truth.
    (v) *John has claimed that Nixon, I believe, is telling the truth.
    (vi) *John has claimed that Nixon is, I believe, telling the truth.
    (vii) *John has claimed that Nixon is telling, I believe, the truth.
    (viii) John has claimed that Nixon is telling the truth, I believe.

The ungrammatical sentences are precisely those in which the parenthetical "I believe" has been inserted into a lower sentence, thus violating (40).

15 This is the formulation of Chomsky (1971), not of Helke (1970). However, it is perfectly consistent with everything Helke says. Notice, by the way, that (41) involves the assumption that the referent of a reflexive is not the same as that of its antecedent. This seems plausible, especially if a reflexive consists of an NP with the head noun *self*.

16 This is not to claim that Helke's analysis solves all of the problems confronting the Reflexivization analysis. For example, sentences like (37) provide difficulties for both theories. See Helke (1970) for possible solutions to these difficulties. Notice, however, that the variability of judgements regarding (37a&b) supports Helke's analysis weakly : under it, the occurrence of reflexives in prepositional phrases is lexically marked and hence likely to be variable ; under the Reflexivization analysis, whether the object of a preposition is a reflexive or an anaphoric pronoun is a function of whether the prepositional phrase is derived from an underlying clause (see Chomsky (1965), pp. 146-7), and one would not expect this to vary much among speakers.

17 Jackendoff (1969, 1972) presents a different alternative to the Reflexivization analysis. For our purposes, the crucial difference between Jackendoff's and Helke's analyses is that Jackendoff tries to handle reflexives and anaphoric pronouns with a single rule. Since I am arguing against such a uniform treatment, it is incumbent on me at this point to give reasons for rejecting Jackendoff's analysis. First of all, I will simply note that almost none of the arguments for Helke's approach work for Jackendoff ; that is, the reasons for rejecting Reflexivization in favor of Helke's theory are also reasons for rejecting Jackendoff's theory. Further, Jackendoff's rule makes some wrong predictions. For example, Jackendoff's rule permits reflexives to be marked anaphorically related to only one other NP (see Jackendoff (1972), p. 176). This makes it impossible to derive (i), in which the reflexive must be the controller of the gerund (as can be seen by considering the meaning of (ii)).

    (i) John reprimanded himself for picking flowers.
    (ii) John reprimanded Bill for picking flowers.

Finally, by collapsing the rules for reflexives and anaphoric pronouns, Jackendoff (1972) is led to make the obviously false claim that backwards pronominal anaphora is impossible if the antecedent is inanimate. The falsity of this claim is demonstrated by (iii).

    (iii) If you want to read *it, my book* will soon be out.

Jackendoff is led into this error by his wish to combine the two rules, for in those special cases in which a reflexive may precede its antecedent, it does obey this constraint, as (iv) and (v) show.

    (iv) A picture of himself appears in Pete's scrapbook.
    (v) *A story about itself appears on the newspaper's front page.

This difference is further evidence for treating reflexives and anaphoric pronouns differently.

18 Postal (1972b) gives a number of other supposed counterexamples to the anaporn relation in which the anaphoric interpretation of the pronoun is necessitated by the stress contour. The linguistic literature is full of ambiguous sentences which can be disambiguated by considering intonational factors. This has not led anyone to deny that those sentences are ambiguous. Rather, it has led to work on how the intonational features are linked to the meaning difference. Thus, for example, Lasnik (1972) notes that Lakoff's familiar example (i) can be disambiguated on the basis of intonation, but that does not lead him to deny that it is ambiguous.

    (i) George doesn't beat his wife because he loves her.

Hence, it seems rather discriminatory for Postal to single out Dougherty and to chastise him for claiming ambiguities where stress serves to disambiguate.

19 Postal (1971) suggests instead that examples like (44f) be derived from sentences like (i).

    (i) As for the man who shot Liberty Valance, he was the bravest of them all.

Notice, however, that (i) allows an interpretation in which the antecedent of *he* is *Liberty Valance*, whereas (44f) does not, so that Postal's analysis leaves the non-ambiguity of (44f) with respect to anaphora unaccounted for. Further, the contrast between the (a) and the (b) sentences in (ii) - (iv) casts additional doubt on Postal's analysis.

(ii) (a) As for George, I'd rather Bill got the job.
    (b) ??George, I'd rather Bill got the job.
(iii) (a) As for *John,* I've never met *him.*
    (b) ?*John,* I've never met *him.*
(iv) (a) As for what Pete said about Bill, don't believe a word he said.
    (b) *What Pete said about Bill, don't believe a word he said.

[20] This depends on the appropriate structure for such examples. If (44e) and (44g) have structures like (i) and (ii), respectively, then this argument clearly fails.

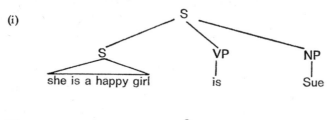

(i)

On the other hand, if (iii) and (iv) are the appropriate trees, then the argument holds.

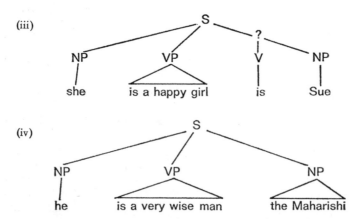

It is not clear to me which (if any) of these structures are correct. If (i) and (ii) are right, then (v) and (vi) should be grammatical.

(v) ?She was afraid of *him,* was the woman who jilted *your brother.*
(vi) ?He loved *her,* the man who shot *your sister.*

Unfortunately, the data are too marginal to be of much help. Since the point is rather minor, it will not be pursued.

[21] Evidence might be found to suggest that (48a) generalizes to constituents other than NP. I do not insist on the precise formulation of (48). I am merely asserting that the evidence suggests that the symmetric relation of identity between NP's is not relevant to the formula-

tion of grammatical rules, whereas the asymmetrical anaphora relation is. Gilles Fauconnier has done some very interesting work relevant to this issue.

22 The fact that Postal viewed referential indices as syntactic features and hence made no effort to avoid referring to them in transformations is irrelevant. The fact remains that Postal's Cross over Constraint can be formulated as a universal without requiring transformations to refer to anaphora.

23 Nevertheless, I believe the Cross over Constraint to be incorrect on empirical grounds. Some of the arguments against it are to be found in Jackendoff (1969, 1972) and others below in Appendix II. Further, it should be noted that Helke's analysis of reflexives, which was defended above, eliminates many of Postal's arguments in favor of the Cross over Constraint.

Chapter 3

ALTERNATIVES TO PRONOMINALIZATION

o. *Introduction*

The inadequacy on the transformational approach to pronominal anaphora has been widely recognized for some time now. There are basically two alternative approaches which have been suggested in its place.[1] The purpose of this chapter is to describe and compare these alternatives.

In order to facilitate their evaluation, it will be useful to recapitulate briefly the arguments against the transformational approach. The following is a list of the arguments presented in § 2 of Chapter 2:

(A) Bresnan's argument and several arguments modeled after it, showing that the sensitivity of certain rules (There insertion, Dative movement, Particle movement, and the Nuclear Stress Rule) to properties that differentiate full NP's from pronouns is incompatible with a Pronominalization analysis;

(B) Dougherty's observation that a Pronominalization analysis encounters both syntactic and semantic difficulties in the derivation of pronouns whose antecedents contain quantifiers;

(C) The problem of accounting for anaphoric epithets;

(D) The Bach-Peters paradox;

(E) My observation that Pronominalization derives certain ungrammatical sentences (e.g., sentence (31) of Chapter 2);

(F) The Anaporn relation.

Because of the many complications and controversies that have arisen in connection with the analysis of quantifiers, (B) will not be used as criterial in evaluating the analyses to be presented below. Further, it should be noted that the force of arguments (C), (D), and (F) has been questioned; although I maintain that these are valid arguments against Pronominalization (see Chapter 2 and Appendix I), I acknowledge their controversial status. Hence, I will rely most heavily on arguments (A) and (E) in the discussion below.

Opinions of the analyses of pronominal anaphora outlined below reflect accurately the current split among generative grammarians: generative seman-

ticists generally propound the lexical substitution approach to anaphoric pronouns, interpretivists naturally support the interpretive approach, and pro-
fessed neutrals try to concentrate on issues which do not require that they
choose between these approaches (e.g., Partee (1973)). Thus, in presenting
and evaluating these alternative approaches to anaphora, I will be considering
one of the central issues dividing the two camps, and the conclusions I reach
will be relevant to the choice between their competing theories.

1. *The Lexical Substitution Approach*

1.0 While generative semanticists, most notably Postal, have written extensive
criticisms of various proposals for dealing with pronominal anaphora, they
have provided surprisingly few positive proposals for remedying the defects
of these other analyses. Of the leading proponents of generative semantics,
so far as I know only McCawley (1970) has actually outlined an analysis.[2]
Under these circumstances, I will deal with McCawley's analysis as the prime
alternative to the interpretive approach. A variant of McCawley's analysis is
presented by Harman (1972) and will be considered as well.

1.1 McCawley's Analysis

McCawley (1970) suggests that the underlying structure of a sentence
consists of two parts: a "proposition" and a set of noun phrases. Such a
proposition is essentially what philosophers sometimes call an "open sentence," i.e., a representation of a sentence with free variables in place of the
NP's. The set of NP's includes a specification of which variable stands for
which NP.[3] As an illustration, McCawley uses sentence (1a), to which he
assigns the underlying representation (1b).

(1) (a) The man killed the woman.

(b)[4]

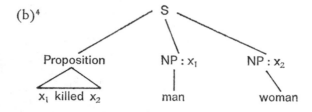

Such underlying structures are converted into more familiar looking phrase
markers by a transformation which substitutes NP's for the appropriate
variables. It is this transformation which takes the place of Pronominalization
in McCawley's theory. If a variable occurs several times in one structure, then
the corresponding NP is substituted for only one of its occurrences, and

"[t]hose occurrence... for which the substitution is not made are then filled by pronouns" (p. 176). The precede-command condition can be built in "by saying that a noun phrase may be substituted for any occurrence of the corresponding index which either precedes or is in a 'higher' sentence than all other occurrences of that index"[5] (p. 176).

This analysis can be illustrated with the underlying structure in (2).

(2)

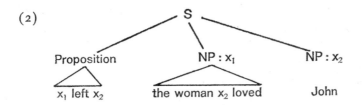

Substituting first for x_1, we get an intermediate structure in which there are two occurrences of x_2, the rightmost of which is the "higher" one. This allows us two choices in substituting for x_2, and we can derive either of the sentences in (3).

(3) (a) The woman *he* loved left *John*.
    (b) The woman *John* loved left *him*.

McCawley (1970) argues in favor of adopting such a derivation of NP's. Consideration of his arguments would take us too far afield. My objective in discussing McCawley's proposal is simply to consider its tenability as a theory of pronominal anaphora, in light of the arguments against Pronominalization presented above.

1.2 The arguments grouped together under (A) above all apply to McCawley's analysis. I will illustrate this with Bresnan's original argument, on which the others are based. A detailed account of the applicability of (A) to analyses like McCawley's is provided by Wasow (1975).

Notice first of all that McCawley's lexical substitution transformation cannot apply until rather late in a derivation. In particular, it cannot apply until after passivization takes place, if it is to avoid deriving (4).

(4) *He* was shot by the woman who hated *John*.

Now consider (5).

(5) There was known to be an agent in the crowd.

The derivation of this sentence involves the transformation of There insertion operating on the embedded clause (*an agent be in the crowd*) and passivization of the main clause. In order for passivization to move *there* into the position of subject of the main clause, There insertion must apply before passivization takes place.[6] It follows that There insertion applies to the embedded clause before lexical substitution can occur in the main clause.

Now consider the underlying structure in (6).

(6)

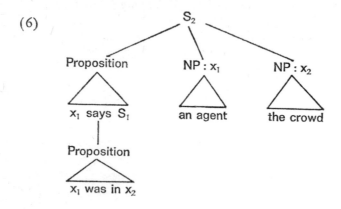

There insertion may apply to S_1, and will do so before *an agent* is substituted for x_1 (for the reasons just given). Now, when lexical substitution occurs, *an agent* will replace the first (leftmost) occurrence of x_1, and the other occurrence will become a pronoun, resulting in the ungrammatical string (7).

(7) *An agent* says there was $\left\{ \begin{array}{c} he \\ him \end{array} \right\}$ in the crowd.

McCawley's variables may stand for either definite or indefinite NP's, and There insertion operates only on sentences with indefinite subjects. Since There insertion must apply before lexical substitution, it will sometimes apply where it shouldn't, as in (7).

Parallel arguments can be constructed using Dative movement, Particle movement, or Number Agreement (see Wasow (1975)). In fact, the arguments against Pronominalization cited in (A) above carry over to McCawley's analysis largely without modification. Thus, McCawley's theory of pronominal anaphora fails its first test.

1.3 Anaphoric epithets appear to provide the same argument against Mc-Cawley's proposal as against Pronominalization. Of course, Postal's (1972a) rebuttal of this argument against Pronominalization carries over to McCawley's analysis, too, but it has no more independent motivation in this context that it did in the other. The point is that neither of these analyses can be generalized in a natural and motivated way to account for the fact that phrases like *the bastard, the fool*, etc. can be interpreted anaphorically.

1.4 McCawley (1970) discusses how his analysis avoids the Bach-Peters paradox. A sentence like (8) will have a finite underlying structure like (9).

(8) *The pilot who shot at it hit the mig that chased him.*

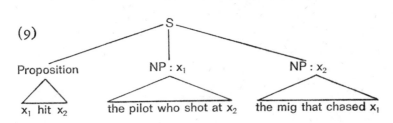

(9)

Thus, the Bach-Peters paradox does not arise in McCawley's analysis of anaphoric pronouns.[7]

1.5 McCawley's analysis also has no trouble excluding sentences like (10).

(10) *The woman *he* loved told *him* that *John* was a dope.

The underlying structure for (10) would be (11).

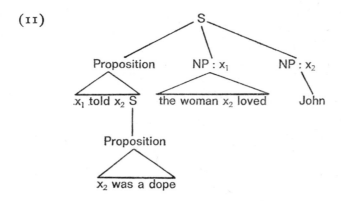

(11)

After substituting for x_1, McCawley would be left with (12).

Now, of the three occurrences of x_2, the first is the leftmost and the second is the highest; the final occurrence of x_2 is both to the right of and below (i.e., commanded by) the second occurrence. Hence, according to McCawley's rule, *John* may be substituted for either of the first two occurrences of x_2, but not for the last one. (10) is the result of making this forbidden substitution. Thus, McCawley's analysis correctly predicts the ungrammaticality of (10), as well as the grammaticality of (13a & b).

(12)

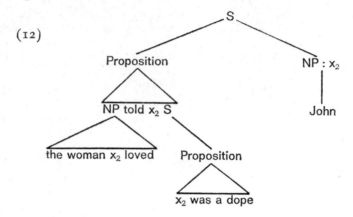

(13) (a) The woman *John* loved told *him* that *he* was a dope.
     (b) The woman *he* loved told *John* that *he* was a dope.

1.6 Does the Anaporn relation (as modified in the previous chapter) constitute evidence for or against McCawley's analysis? It is difficult to answer this question because McCawley says nothing about the source of non-anaphoric pronouns. One plausible guess might be that non-anaphoric pronouns are the surface realization of underlying free variables, i.e., of indices with no corresponding NP's. Given such an analysis, it is fairly clear that the modified Anaporn relation would be a natural consequence. Consider, for example, a sentence like (14).

(14) John realizes that Mary hates him.

Him in (14) can be understood either anaphorically or non-anaphorically, and McCawley's theory could plausibly assign to it the underlying structures in (15) for the two readings.

(15) (a)

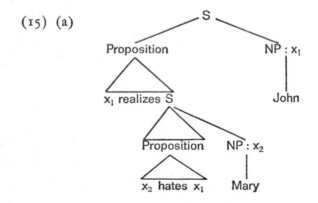

(b)

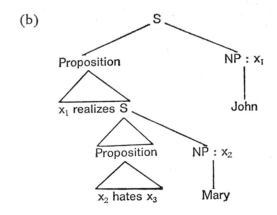

In similar fashion, any pronoun which allows an anaphoric interpretation can be derived from either a bound or a free variable, thus allowing a non-anaphoric interpretation as well. Hence, a plausible extension of McCawley's analysis accounts naturally for the Anaporn relation.

1.7 It seems, then, that McCawley's lexical substitution approach to pronominal anaphora fares somewhat better than Pronominalization. It does, however, encounter some of the same difficulties. In particular, it is subject to Bresnan's argument and the variants of it presented in Chapter 2, § 2.1. Further, if anaphoric epithets constitute an argument against Pronominalization then they argue against McCawley's analysis as well. In sum, McCawley's proposal for pronominal anaphora is an improvement, but not enough of one.

1.8 Harman (1972) proposes a variation of McCawley's analysis, which he attributes to R. Grandy. Harman's analysis differs from McCawley's in that Harman allows an NP to be substituted only for the leftmost occurrence of the corresponding variable. In order to account for cases of backwards anaphora (i.e., cases where the anaphor precedes the antecedent), Harman postulates a rule which moves subordinate clauses to the left. This rule and the NP substitution rule may apply in either order.

Harman asserts that the usual precede-command condition is ad hoc. He argues that his analysis is to be preferred because it eliminates this condition.

Harman's proposal can be faulted on a number of grounds. For example, it might be asked why adding an otherwise unnecessary transformation and dropping the requirement that transformations be strictly ordered is less ad hoc than the precede-command condition. Further, it should be noted that there are special conditions on backwards anaphora (see Chapter 4) which are not naturally statable in Harman's analysis. At this point, however, I will limit myself to the observation that Harman's analysis is subject to the same criticisms as McCawley's.

The differences between Harman's and McCawley's analyses are quite irrelevant to Bresnan's argument and its variants. The attempt to eliminate the backwards condition on the NP substitution rule is completely unconnected to the problem of determining the definiteness of variables. Hence, Harman's theory is no better than McCawley's on this account.[8] Harman's analysis also shares with McCawley's the inability to account for anaphoric epithets in a natural way.

In sum, then, neither version of the lexical substitution analysis appears to be satisfactory.

2. *The Interpretive Approach*

The other alternative to Pronominalization has been outlined by, among others, Dougherty (1969) and Jackendoff (1969, 1972). The fundamental feature of this approach is the idea that all pronouns are generated in deep structure, and that the association of pronouns with appropriate antecedents is accomplished by a special class of interpretive rules which operate on derived structure. This has the effect of separating the problem of associating pronouns with antecedents from the problem of generating them. Proponents of the interpretive approach claim that the confusion of these two problems is the fundamental flaw in the Pronominalization analysis.

The interpretive approach postulates a rule (or perhaps a set of rules) which marks certain pairs of NP's as anaphorically related.[9] This marking may take the form of a "table" of anaphorically related pairs (as Jackendoff suggests) or it might be accomplished by some other device, such as indexing. The point is inessential; the important facet of the interpretive approach is the idea that deep structure pronouns are somehow marked for anaphora by rules operating on derived structure. I will now consider the applicability of the arguments against Pronominalization to this approach.

2.1 The arguments listed in (A) all depend on syntactic properties of pronouns which are common to anaphoric and non-anaphoric pronouns. The conclusion these arguments point to is that definite pronouns must be inserted into phrase markers prior to the operation of certain rules; further, they show that in some cases, the determination of anaphoric relations cannot be made until after these rules have operated. Hence, these arguments suggest a theory in which the insertion of pronouns into phrase markers is a process separate from and preceding the determination of anaphoric relations. That is, the arguments in (A) support the fundamental idea of the interpretive approach to anaphora. Thus, (A) provides very strong grounds for adopting the interpretive approach.

2.2 Anaphoric epithets provide further motivation for adopting the interpretive approach. There is nothing inherent in this approach that would restrict the operation of the interpretive anaphora rules to pronouns. The extension of the domain of interpretive rules to certain full NP's seems much more natural than Postal's (1972d) proposal to derive anaphoric epithets from non-restrictive relative clauses with pronominal heads.

2.3 The interpretive approach encounters no difficulties with the Bach-Peters paradox. In fact, Wasow (1973a) (Appendix I in the present monograph) argues that the Bach-Peters examples provide evidence in support of the interpretive approach.

2.4 My argument against Pronominalization based on examples like (10) (repeated here for convenience) carries over to the interpretive approach.

(10) *The woman *he* loved told *him* that *John* was a dope.

Since any interpretive analysis must somehow incorporate the precede-command condition (or something close to it — see Chapter 4), it must allow anaphoric relations to hold between *he* and *him* and between *he* and *John*. Hence, the interpretive approach incorrectly predicts that (10) should be grammatical.

2.5 The anaporn relation is an immediate consequence of adopting an interpretive approach in which the anaphora rule is optional. This was Dougherty's (1969) reason for citing the Anaporn relation.

2.6 The interpretive approach appears to avoid all but one of the arguments against pronominalization. Thus, like the lexical substitution approach, it seems to be an improvement, but not enough of one.

3. *Choosing an Alternative*

Since neither of the alternatives discussed above seems to be entirely adequate (at least as presented), we must now look either for ways to remedy their defects or for still another alternative approach to pronominal anaphora. I will take the former tack. Initially, it might seem difficult to decide which approach to try to modify. Disregarding the controversial anaphoric epithets argument, we are left with one argument against each theory and no obvious clues as to which approach might be most easily and naturally patched up.

However, a close examination of the problems with the two approaches does reveal a basis for choosing. The applicability of arguments (A) to the lexical substitution approach is an unavoidable consequence of the derivation of pronouns and full NP's from the same source; such a derivation makes it impossible to differentiate pronouns from full NP's early in the derivation, and the arguments in (A) show that it is necessary to do so (see Wasow (1975)). Deriving pronouns and full NP's from the same source is a fundamental feature of the lexical substitution approach. Hence, this approach would require a rather substantial modification if the arguments in (A) are to be avoided. By comparison, the problem with the interpretive approach is rather minor. In a theory (like the interpretive one) which treats anaphora as a binary relation, it is not logically required that it be a transitive relation. Examples like (10) show that pronominal anaphora is transitive. (This will be explained more fully and more formally in the next section). There is no fundamental conflict between this conclusion and the basic premises of the interpretive approach. Hence, this approach seems to be the more plausible candidate for modification.

There is another reason for choosing to try to salvage the interpretive approach. One of my primary purposes in this monograph, it will be recalled, is to argue for what I called a heterogeneous theory. That is, I intend to show that the rules governing anaphora share a number of properties which differentiate them from other categories of rules needed for the description of languages. If anaphora rules are to be treated as a specifiable class, then it is natural that they should be formally alike. That is, one of my goals in this monograph would be undermined if different anaphoric relations were not treated uniformly. Hence, it is desirable to choose an approach to pronominal anaphora which generalizes naturally to other anaphoric relations (e.g., VP anaphora). The interpretive approach lends itself naturally to such generalization, as I will show in Chapter 6.

In contrast, I know of no proposals for generalizing the lexical substitution approach, and my own speculations regarding how such a generalization might be accomplished have left me skeptical as to its feasibility.

One final remark must be made concerning my decision to adopt the interpretive approach. One of my goals is to show the advantages of treating anaphora rules as a distinct category, obeying different constraints from other types of rules. Hence, in saying that I support the interpretive approach, I do not mean to lump anaphora rules together with other types of interpretive rules which have been proposed. On the contrary, I will argue in Chapter 5 that the properties of anaphora rules distinguish them both from syntactic transformations and form other types of interpretive rules. Further, the question of whether anaphora rules are syntactic or semantic seems to me to be without empirical content. Again, among my aims will be to demonstrate the properties shared by the various rules for associating anaphors with antecedents. In saying that I adopt an interpretive approach, all I mean is that I believe that the anaphors are present in deep structure, with their antecedents determined by rules operating on derived structure.

4.0 The Transitivity Condition

Having opted for the interpretive approach, I must now devise a means of avoiding the argument against it presented in § 2.4. To this end, I propose that (16) be incorporated into linguistic theory.

> (16) The Transitivity Condition
>   If A, B, and C are elements in a sentence such that A and B are anaphorically related, and B and C are anaphorically related, then the sentence is ungrammatical unless A and C are anaphorically related.[10]

(16) serves to rule out (10) (repeated here for convenience) as follows: let *him* = A, *he* = B, and *John* = C.

> (10) *The woman *he* loved told *him* that *John* was a dope.

(17a) shows that A and B may be anaphorically related, and (17b) shows that B and C may be anaphorically related; therefore, by the Transitivity Condition, (10) is ungrammatical, since A and C cannot be anaphorically related, as (17c) demonstrates.

> (17) (a) The woman *he* loved told *him* that I was a dope.
>   (b) The woman *he* loved told me that *John* was a dope.
>   (c) *The woman I loved told *him* that *John* was a dope.

In effect, the Transitivity Condition says that in sentences containing more than two anaphorically related elements, the anaphora rules must mark every pair of elements. Put another way, (16) says that the symmetric relation "is anaphorically related to" is also a transitive relation.

4.1 Since transitivity is a property of many relations in common use, this seems like a natural constraint to impose upon anaphora. (In fact, it seems so natural that it has sometimes been erroneously suggested that it is unnecessary to state such a constraint — that it is true by definition). Furthermore, there is some independent empirical evidence in favor of the Transitivity Condition.

Consider example (18).

> (18) *The man who he* said Mary kissed was lying.

It is clear that an anaphoric relation holds between relative pronouns and their heads. Furthermore, every existing theory of anaphora would permit an anaphoric relation to be established between the head of a relative clause and a pronoun in the clause, since the head both precedes and commands the clause. In (18), then, *the man* and *who* may be anaphorically related, and *the man* and *he* may be anaphorically related. (19) shows that *who* and *he* cannot be anaphorically related (for reasons discussed in Appendix II).

(19) *Who did *he* say Mary kissed?

In order that the same explanation suffice to account for (18) and (19), it is necessary to adopt the Transitivity Condition. Otherwise, it would be necessary to rule out anaphora between *the man* and *he* in (18), in addition to ruling out anaphora between *who* and *he*.

4.2 Further independent evidence for the Transitivity Condition can be found in Chapter 4, § 3.1 and Chapter 5, § 1.2. The Transitivity Condition also figures prominently in my solution to an ordering paradox discovered by Postal. This is discussed in Appendix II.

The variety of independent support for the Transitivity Condition shows that it is not merely an ad hoc device for ruling out (10). Further, notice that although the lexical substitution approach rules (10) out automatically, it cannot handle some of the other facts used to motivate the Transitivity Condition, especially those cited in Chapter 5 (see Wasow (1973c)). The Transitivity Condition, then, is a rather natural and well-motivated constraint; and, as such, it serves to nullify the one argument for preferring the lexical substitution theory of pronominal anaphora over the interpretive approach.

With the motivation for adopting the interpretive approach established, we are now in a position to investigate some of the conditions on the pronominal anaphora rule. This will be the subject of the next chapter.

NOTES

[1] This statement is slightly misleading for a couple of reasons. First of all, there have been other proposals, e.g., hybrids (such as Witten (1970) or Siegel (1973)). Further, there is no unanimity among the proponents of either approach, as the discussion below will show.

[2] Lakoff (1968b) suggested an analysis which cannot properly be labeled generative semantics, since it assumes the framework of the Standard Theory. In fact, as noted in Chapter 2, footnote 10, Lakoff's proposals constitute an interpretive analysis in everything but terminology.

[3] McCawley (1970) uses the term "index", rather than "variable", suggesting that these indices are essentially the same as those suggested by Chomsky (1965, p. 145) (cf. Chapter 2, § 1). That McCawley's conception of indices differs from Chomsky's is evident from the fact that the former claims that "each index... corresponds to the 'intended referent' of that noun phrase occurrence" (p. 172). Chomsky prudently avoids making any similar claim.

[4] McCawley glosses over the question of why the NP's in (1b) lack articles. This is of no consequence for the present discussion, however.

[5] McCawley's formulation is a bit sloppy here. Note, for example, that it would not allow the derivation of (i), unless "higher" were taken in a rather peculiar sense.

(i) The fact that *he* lost upset the woman who had predicted that *John* would win. Further, notice that in (ii) the antecedent neither precedes all anaphors, nor is it in a higher sentence than all of them.

(ii) That the woman who loved *him* left *John* upset *him*.

These defects of McCawley's analysis are rather trivial, however. A more careful formulation of the condition on the substitution transformation would correct them. Hence, they need not concern us.

6 Note that it is also possible to derive (i).

(i) There was an agent known to be in the crowd.

In (i), There insertion applies to the main clause (not the embedded clause) after passivization.

7 Karttunen (1971) claims that examples like (8) provide an argument for Pronominalization and against McCawley's analysis. That the first of these claims is incorrect is demonstrated by Wasow (1973a) (reprinted here as Appendix I). Further, Dik (1973) asserts that a natural elaboration of McCawley's analysis makes it possible to avoid Karttunen's argument against it.

8 It might be thought that Harman's explicit rejection of the transformational cycle and strict ordering among rules might allow him to avoid Bresnan's argument, but, in fact, he cannot. Harman admits that passivization must always be accomplished prior to NP substitution. Given this, there is no way he can avoid deriving (i).

(i) *According to *a witness,* there was believed to be $\left\{ \begin{array}{c} he \\ him \end{array} \right\}$ testifying.

In this example, There insertion had to apply before passivization, which in turn had to take place before NP substitution. The same is true in (ii).

(ii) There was believed to be a witness testifying.

Therefore, in both (i) and (ii), There insertion operates at a point in the derivation at which the subject of the embedded clause is still a variable. Since variables are not marked for definiteness, there is no way to rule out (i) while still deriving (ii).

9 It might alternatively be possible to formulate the rule so as to mark the impossibility of anaphora between certain pronouns and NP's (see Lasnik (1976)).

10 Various other similar proposals have appeared in the literature. For example, Jackendoff (1969) says :

(i) Three or more NP's can be understood as mutually coreferential
only if they have been marked pairwise coreferential.   (p. 44)

He attempts to formalize this idea by adopting the following convention :

(ii) (Noncoreferentiality Convention)
If a pair of NP's... does not appear in the table of coreference,
they are noncoreferential.   (p. 56)

(The elements appearing in the table of coreference are precisely those which have been marked coreferential by an interpretive rule.) Since coreferentiality is by definition a transitive relation, (i) follows from (ii). Unfortunately, (ii) is untenable, for reasons discussed by Postal (1972b). The problem has to do with the fact that terms like *the morning star* and *the evening star* may have the same referent without being anaphorically related. (16) is my attempt to formulate (i) in such a way as to avoid Postal's criticism. However, the basic insight is Jackendoff's, and I gratefully acknowledge my debt to him.

Williams (1971) proposes a constraint equivalent to the Transitivity condition. Although I arrived at (16) independently, I do make use of some of Williams' examples in what follows.

Chapter 4

THE PRONOMINAL ANAPHORA RULE

In this chapter I will consider the problem of determining the conditions governing the establishment of an anaphoric relation between a definite pronoun and an NP. In other words, I will be trying to formulate the rule for definite pronominal anaphora. Since the literature on this subject is quite extensive, this problem is best approached by considering some past proposals.[1]

1. *Past Proposals*

1.1 One essentially trivial condition on pronominal anaphora is that the pronoun must agree with its antecedent in person, gender, and number.[2] The sentences in (1) - (3) are examples of this.

(1) (a) *The Jones'* said that *they* were leaving.
    (b) *We said that *they* were leaving.
    (c) *John* denied that *he* was a communist.
    (d) *You denied that *he* was a communist.[3]
(2) (a) *The young lady* claimed that *she* didn't drink.
    (b) *The young lady claimed that *he* didn't drink.
    (c) *The young lady claimed that *it* didn't drink.
(3) (a) *The policemen* drew *their* guns.
    (b) *The policemen drew *his* gun.
    (c) *The policeman* drew *his* gun.
    (d) *The policeman drew *their* guns.

1.2 Another condition on almost all formulations of the pronominal anaphora rule is some version of the precede-command condition discussed in Chapter 2, § 1, repeated here as (4).

(4) An NP may not serve as the antecedent of a pronoun which both precedes and command it.

In other words, an anaphoric relation may be established only if the pronoun is in a subordinate clause not containing the NP. (4) is illustrated in (5) with a number of different types of subordinate clauses.

(5) (a) The fact that *he* was a moron didn't bother *John*.
  (b) *It didn't bother *him* that *John* was a moron.
  (c) The man who shot *him* didn't know *John*.
  (d) *He* was unknown to the man who shot *John*.
  (e) The man who shot *him* claimed that *John* had attacked first.
  (f) The man who shot *him* didn't know the woman *John* loved.
  (g) Because *he* was famous, *John* always wore dark glasses.
  (h) *He* always wore dark glasses because *John* was famous.
  (i) After meeting *his* wife, Mary wouldn't see *John* anymore.
  (j) *Mary wouldn't see *him* anymore after meeting *John's* wife.
  (k) The evidence that *he* was innocent cleared *John*.
  (l) *He* was cleared by the evidence that *John* was innocent.

1.3 Another frequently mentioned condition on rules for pronominal anaphora is (6) (see, e.g., Postal (1970b)).

(6) If a definite pronoun is to the left of an NP, the NP may serve as the antecedent for the pronoun only if it is definite.

The examples in (7) are given by Postal (1970b) in support of (6).

(7) (a) ?*The fact that *he* lost amused *somebody in the crowd*.
  (b) *Somebody in the crowd* was amused by the fact that *he* lost.
  (c) *The man who lost *it* needs to find *something*.
  (d) The man who lost *something* needs to find *it*.
  (e) ?*His* realization that the world was exploding worried *someone*.
  (f) *Someone* was worried by *his* realization that the world was exploding.

1.4 A further condition on the assignment of pronoun-antecedent pairs is proposed by Lakoff (1968b). Lakoff's condition is essentially equivalent to (8).

(8) An NP may not serve as antecedent for a pronoun if
  (a) the NP is to the left of and commands the pronoun,
  (b) the pronoun is not a relative pronoun,
  (c) the pronoun is the surface structure subject of its clause, and
  (d) the NP is prominent with respect to the clause containing the pronoun.[4]

While (8) is certainly inadequate as given (see footnote 4), the basic idea behind it — that subjects may behave differently from nonsubjects with respect to left-to-right anaphora — is not implausible.

(9) (a) In *Mary's* apartment, a thief assaulted *her*.
(b) *In *Mary's* apartment, *she* was assaulted by a thief.
(c) *Bill's* apartment, Mary always talks to *him* about it.
(d) **Bill's* apartment, *he* always talks to Mary about it.
(e) It was *John's* dog that bit *him*.
(f) *It was *John's* dog that *he* hit.

2. *Revisions of Past Proposals*

Each of the last three conditions on pronominal anaphora mentioned has certain shortcomings. In the cases of (6) and (8), there exist outright counterexamples; in the case of (4), the condition is merely insufficiently general.

2.1 Consider first of all examples like (10).

(10) (a) The portrait of *his* mother always depresses *John*.
(b) The story about *him* that was making the rounds cost *John* many friends.

In such examples, the pronoun is to the left of and in the same clause as its antecedent, so according to (4), no anaphoric relation should be possible.

The lexicalist hypothesis (Chomsky (1970b)) provides a rather straightforward solution to the difficulty presented by (10). Chomsky has pointed out that the internal structure of certain NP's (such as the subjects of (10a & b)) bears many striking similarities to the structure of sentences, and he has further argued rather persuasively that there are a number of special properties which are common to such NP's and sentences. Among these properties is that of being the domain of a transformational cycle ("cyclic" for short). Much recent work has indicated that the notion of cyclic node may be relevant for the formulation of certain constraints. (10) suggests that the term "subordinate clause" should perhaps be replaced by the term "cyclic node" in the statement of the precede-command condition given in Chapter 2, (3), or, alternatively, that the phrase "cyclic node" should replace the phrase "S node" in the definition of "command" (Chapter 2, (5)).[5]

Notice now that there are still other instances of anaphora violating (4), in which the pronoun is not embedded in an NP with the internal structure of a sentence. Consider the examples in (11).

(11) (a) Near *him*, *John* saw a snake.
(b) In *her* apartment, *Mary* was assaulted by a thief.

Lakoff (1968b) has shown that it is impossible to account for the inconsistency between these examples and (4) by means of rule ordering. Thus, (11) constitutes genuine counter-evidence to (4). Similarly, examples like (12), though not fully grammatical, are nowhere near as bad as those in (13), contrary to what (4) predicts.

(12) (a) ?*His* mother loves *John*.
    (b) ?*Their* maid speaks well of *the Smiths*.
    (c) ?*Her* friends gave *Mary* a going-away present.

(13) (a) **He* loves *John's* mother.
    (b) **They* speak well of *the Smith's* maid.
    (c) **She* gave *Mary's* friends a going-away present.

In cases like (12), speakers of English exhibit a wide range of reactions, from full acceptance to almost total rejection. This indicates that the criterion involved in right-to left anaphora may vary somewhat among speakers. Suppose, then, that (4) is reformulated as (14).

(14) If an NP serves as the antecedent of a definite pronoun to its left, the pronoun must be at least as deeply embedded as the NP.

Linguistic theory must place certain limitations on the notion of "depth of embedding," but within these limits, there can be room for individual variation. Thus, if a pronoun is dominated by a cyclic node not dominating the NP, then the pronoun will be considered, by convention, to be at least as deeply embedded. Similarly, if the pronoun is part of a prepositional phrase, the NP is not, and the NP commands the pronoun, then the pronoun is at least as deeply embedded. On the other hand, if the pronoun is the subject or object of a sentence containing the NP, then the pronoun is less deeply embedded. Finally, if the pronoun is a possessive determiner, linguistic theory will not specify whether the pronoun is as deeply embedded as the NP, so that individual speakers are free to make their own determination.[6]

2.2 Counterexamples to (6) are quite numerous. In fact, Postal (1970b) gives several in the course of defending (6). Some of these are presented in (15).

(15) (a) If *he* has an ugly wife, *a man* should find a mistress.
    (b) When *they* are angry, *gorillas* can be awfully mean.
    (c) Men who hunt *them* will tell you that *gnus* are smelly beasts.
    (d) The fact that *he* is being sued should worry *any businessman*.
    (e) The girl who *he* is going to marry can upset *any bridegroom to be*.

Postal correctly observes that the indefinites in (15a-c) are interpreted as generics and concludes that generics do not obey (6). He fails to note that (15d & e) also have generic force, so he makes a separate and unnecessary exception to (6) for them. There are, in addition, other exceptions to (6) which Postal does not mention.

(16) (a) After Bill kissed *her*, *a certain young lady* blushed repeatedly.
(b) That *he* was not elected upset *a certain leading politician*.
(c) The woman *he* loved betrayed *a man I know*.

The examples in (16) suggest that (6) should be extended to allow specific indefinites to serve as antecedents of pronouns to their left.[7]

Notice that the two classes of exceptions to (6) mentioned above are characterized in semantic terms. The notions of genericness and specificity refer to the manner of interpretation, not to any syntactically definable properties. There are no diagnostic environments for genericness or specificity, and, in fact, attempts to characterize these properties in syntactic terms have not been very successful (see Baker (1966), Bowers (1969), Fodor (1970), Jackendoff (1971)). Definiteness, on the other hand, is a syntactic property. There exist a number of diagnostic environments for definiteness (see Postal (1966)), and definiteness is best characterized in terms of these. It seems somewhat unnatural that a rule of grammar like (6) which defines a criterion for anaphora in purely syntactic terms should have classes of exceptions which can be characterized only in semantic terms. It would be much more natural if the criterion of definiteness in (6) were replaced by some semantic property. This property would have to be a property common to specific and generic indefinites, if these are not to remain exceptional. No such property has been discussed in the literature, so a new term will have to be introduced, its semantic content indicated, and the consequences of reformulating (6) in terms of it explored.

What do specific and generic indefinites have in common that distinguishes them from nonspecific nongeneric indefinites? The answer is that specifics and generics are used in referring. Specific NP's are used in referring to individuals, and generic NP's are used in referring to sets. An NP is more likely to be interpreted specifically (i.e., to be used in referring to an individual) if the context provides information narrowing down the class of possible referents. The class of possible referents of a generic NP is the singleton consisting of the set to which the NP is being used to refer. Thus, the possibility of backwards pronominalization is a function of the amount of information provided regarding the identity of possible referents. In what follows, generic and specific indefinites will be designated as "determinate" because of the extra information they supply regarding the identity of possible referents.[8] (6) can now be reformulated as (17).

> (17) If a definite pronoun is to the left of an NP, the NP may serve
> as the antecedent for the pronoun only if it is determinate.[9]

So far, all that has been accomplished is a terminological change, plus an attempt to provide an intuitive basis for it. It now remains to be shown that the intuitive characterization of "determinate," together with (17) lead to correct predictions.

One prediction that (17) makes is the following: an anaphoric relation rendered impossible by (17) should be improved by the addition of information narrowing the class of possible referents. Although intuitions vary a good deal on this point, most speakers agree that the addition of tags like *guess who*, or *but I don't know which one* improve such examples. More clearly, the addition of relative clauses to indefinite antecedents improves backwards anaphora.

> (18) (a) *The fact that *he* lost upset *somebody*.
> (b) ?The fact that *he* lost upset *somebody*, and I'll bet you can't guess who.
> (c) *Since *it* didn't bother him, John ignored *something*.
> (d) Since *it* didn't bother him, John ignored *something that might have alarmed other people*.

The marginal character of examples like (18b), together with the variability among speakers on this point, suggests that determinateness is a property of which various degrees are possible (see footnote 8).

Another consequence of replacing (6) by (17) is that (17) allows for the possibility that definite NP's may be subject to the same constraint. It is well-known that genericness is independent of definiteness, i.e., that both definite and indefinite NP's may be either generic or nongeneric. Partee (1970) suggests that the same may be true of specificity. She argues that the distinction between referential and attributive NP's among definites (see Donellan (1966)) may actually be the same as the specific-nonspecific distinction among indefinites. A discussion of specificity and referentiality would be too involved to be undertaken here, being inevitably linked with the problem of opacity (see Fodor (1970)). However, if Partee's suggestion is accepted, it would be reasonable to expect that some definites might be indeterminate and that (17) might therefore have applications to definite NP's.

Clear examples for testing the applicability of (17) to definites are hard to find. This is in part due to the fact that virtually all definite NP's may be interpreted referentially, so that (17) must be tested by considering whether certain sentences involving left-to-right anaphora allow ambiguities absent from the corresponding sentences in which the pronoun is to the left of the antecedent. Intuitions regarding this question tend to be delicate.

Consider sentence (19).

(19) If you are looking for *the fountain of youth*, you'll never find *it*.

The NP *the fountain of youth* can be understood either referentially, i.e., as the name of an object assumed by the speaker to exist, or attributively, i.e., as a description to which it may or may not be possible to assign a referent. These two interpretations can be distinguished by adding to one of the two clauses in (20).

(20) (a) because it is so well hidden.
(b) because it doesn't exist.

If (17) generalizes to definite NP's, then an NP serving as the antecedent of a pronoun to its left should not permit this kind of ambiguity, allowing instead only the referential interpretation. This does indeed appear to be the case, as (21) shows.

(21) If you are looking for *it*, you'll never find *the fountain of*

youth $\left\{\begin{array}{l} \text{because it is so well hidden.} \\ \text{*because it doesn't exist.} \end{array}\right.$

Further examples of the same sort are given in (22) - (24).

(22) (a) If *the Winner of the election* ends the War, *he* will be very popular.
(b) If *he* ends the war, *the winner of the election* will be very popular.

(23) (a) Whenever I read *the newspaper*, I am disgusted by *it*.
(b) Whenever I read *it*, I am disgusted by *the newspaper*.

(24) (a) Although very few Romans ever met *the Emperor*, they all hated *him*.
(b) Although very few Romans ever met *him*, they all hated *the Emperor*.

In each of these examples, the (a) sentence readily permits an interpretation which is unnatural for the (b) sentence. For example, (22a) but not (22b) could naturally be uttered if the election had not yet taken place and the phrase *the winner of the elecion* could not yet be associated with a specific person. The contrast is clearer if *the winner of the election* is replaced by *whoever wins the election*, which tends to allow only the attributive interpretation. Thus, (25b) is substantially less natural than (25a).

(25) (a) If *whoever wins the election* ends the war, *he* will be very popular.
     (b) ??If *he* ends the war, *whoever wins the election* will be very popular.

Similarly (23a) but not (23b) allows an interpretation in which no particular newspaper is under discussion, and (24a) but not (24b) may be interpreted to mean that all Romans hated whoever happened to be emperor.

Additional evidence is provided by examples (26) and (27).

(26) (a) ??A guy who didn't believe *it* interrupted *someone's story.*
     (b) *Someone's story* was interrupted by a guy who didn't believe *it.*

(27) (a) *Very few countries' presidents* really care about the people *they* govern.
     (b) ??The people *they* govern really concern *very few countries' presidents.*

In these sentences, the antecedent NP's are definite, so (6) does not apply. Since the determiners tend to be interpreted nonspecifically, however, the NP's are most naturally interpreted as indeterminate. Thus, (17) accounts for the contrasts in these examples.

All of this follows from (17) if referential NP's are said to be determinate and attributive NP's are indeterminate. These data therefore provide strong support for the decisions to replace the criterion of definiteness in (6) and to extend the notion of determinateness to definite NP's.[10]

2.3 The third condition on definite pronoun anaphora, given above as (8), cannot be correct as stated. Chomsky (personal communication) and Akamajian and Jackendoff (1970) have pointed out that examples like (9b & d) are considerably improved if extra morphological material is inserted between the antecedent and the pronoun. This is illustrated in (28).

(28) (a) In *Mary's* newly furnished apartment, *she* was assaulted by a thief.
     (b) ?*Bill's* recently redecorated apartment, *he* always talks to Mary about it.

These examples suggest that the subject-nonsubject distinction Lakoff uses in accounting for (9) is in fact irrelevant, and that the difference in the behavior of subjects and objects in (9) is a result of the fact that the object is always further to the right, and hence further from the proposed NP. This suggestion would receive support from examples in which the object is excluded from an anaphoric relations with a preposed NP by virtue of their

proximity. It is possible that such examples could be constructed using impera-
tives, in which the lack of an overt subject brings the object nearer to the
front of the sentence. Unfortunately, such examples are not as bad as might
be hoped, as can be seen from (29).

(29) (a) ?With all due respect to *my worthy opponent,* don't believe
           him.
      (b) ?In a conversation with *the sergeant,* call *him* "sir."
      (c) ?On a camping trip with *John,* trust *him.*

However, the fact that these examples are not fully grammatical does support
Chomsky's proposal over Lakoff's.

   If Chomsky is correct about (9), then the constraint involved is of a
rather different type than the other conditions on anaphora discussed above,
for properties like length are generally assumed to be irrelevant to the problem of writing grammars. Rather, they tend to be linked with such aspects
of linguistic performance as memory limitations (see Chomsky and Miller
(1963)).[12] Since the constraint involved does not appear to interact in any
interesting way with processes in the grammar of English, there is no reason
to assume that the distance criterion suggested by Chomsky to account for
(9) needs to be stated in the grammar. Instead, such examples as (9b & d)
and (29) can be considered grammatical but unacceptable because of the
following performance constraint.

(30) If a preposed NP serves as the antecedent for a pronoun in the
      same clause which is too close to it, the sentence is unacceptable.

The problem of specifying what "too close" means will not be considered
here, since the problem at hand is to discover what *grammatical* devices are
involved in English anaphoric relations.[13]
2.4 A rough initial statement of the grammatical criteria determining possible pronoun-antecedent pairs in English can now be made. It is given in (31).

(31) Given an NP and a definite pronoun in the same sentence, the
      NP may serve as the antecedent for the pronoun unless
      (a) the pronoun and the NP disagree in gender, person, or
           number;
      (b) the pronoun is to left of the NP and the pronoun is less
           deeply embedded than the NP; or
      (c) the pronoun is to the left of the NP, and the NP is
           indeterminate.

3. *Ordering*

One aspect of pronominal anaphora which has received a great deal of attention in the literature is the ordering of the rule. This section will be devoted to a consideration of the ordering of (31).

Although a tremendous number of arguments have been advanced concerning the ordering of one version or another of the rule for definite pronominal anaphora, the majority of these depend crucially on particular and often unjustified details of the formulation of the rule (or of other rules). For this reason, it might be wise to consider some of the better known arguments, and to see in what respects they fail to apply to (31).

3.1.1 Consider the most famous ordering argument for Pronominalization, viz., that advanced in John R. Ross' elegant paper, "On the Cyclic Nature of English Pronominalization." Ross' argument, reproduced in detail in Chapter 2, § 1, holds that the ungrammaticality of examples like (32) can be accounted for on the basis of the usual precede-command condition, if this condition is applied cyclically.

(32)   *Realizing that *John* was a failure upset *him*.

Assuming (as was commonly done at the time the article was written) that definite pronominal anaphora results from the application of a transformation of Pronominalization and that the "understood" subjects of subjectless infinitives and gerunds are present in deep structure, but get deleted by a transformation of Equi NP deletion (Equi for short — see Chapter 7), Ross claims that (32) would have an underlying structure essentially like (33).

(33) $[S_1 [S_2$ John's realizing $[S_3$ that John was a failure $S_3] S_2]$ upset John $S_1]$.

If Pronominalization is cyclic, he argues, it will apply first of the S_2 cycle, converting the middle occurrence of *John* to the pronoun *he*. It is then impossible to derive the surface structure (32) from (33).

Lakoff (1968b) and Postal (1970b) argue against Ross' conclusion and present alternative means of accounting for (32). Jackendoff (1969, 1972) refutes Lakoff's and Postal's arguments, and attempts to resurrect Ross' argument for his own interpretive theory of pronouns. He concludes his discussion of the matter with the words, "This redeems Ross' argument, at least for the interpretive theory" (1969, p. 127). This claim is in fact not fully justified: while Jackendoff succeeds in refuting the arguments against cyclic Pronominalization, in his system, sentences like (32) are handled by independently necessary mechanisms and hence have no bearing on the question of the cyclicity of Pronominalization. Thus, Jackendoff does not redeem Ross' argument, but only (perhaps) his conclusion. Since the framework adopted here can account for (32) in almost the same manner as Jackendoff's could, the reason for the ungrammaticality of (32) will be explained in detail. The question of the relevance of (32) to the problem of determining whether the pronominal anaphora rule is cyclic will have been laid to rest, at least for the remainder of this monograph.

In the framework adopted here, the underlying structure of (32) would be something like (34), where the curly brackets indicate that the subject of S_2 might be either a dummy element or a definite pronoun, depending on whether Equi should be formulated as a deletion rule of as some kind of anaphora rule (see Chapter 7 for arguments regarding the choice between these two possibilities).

(34) $[S_1 [S_2 \begin{Bmatrix} his \\ \triangle \end{Bmatrix}$ realizing $[S_3$ that John was a failure $S_3] S_2]$ upset him $S_1]$.

That the subject of S_2 cannot be the full NP *John* follows from the discussion in Chapter 2, § 4. Recall that the subject of S_2 can only be deleted if it is under the influence of (i.e., anaphorically related to) another NP (because of the universal constraint that deletions must be recoverable). Hence, the subject of S_2 must be anaphorically related to *him* if Equi is a deletion rule. If Equi is not a deletion rule, then the subject of S_2 must be a dummy element, say $\triangle$, and it must be anaphorically related to *him* in order to receive an interpretation. In either case, there is an anaphoric relationship between the subject of S_2 and *him*. Therefore, if an anaphoric relationship held between *John* and *him* (i.e., if (32) were grammatical), the Transitivity Condition would require that an anaphoric relation hold between *John* and the subject of S_2. But this is excluded by (31b).[14] Hence (32) is ungrammatical. Notice that neither (31) nor Jackendoff's alternative to (31) need apply cyclically for this argument to hold. Thus, Ross' argument is not valid, given either the present framework or Jackendoff's, and there can be no way to redeem that argument (even though its conclusion may hold).

3.1.2 Jackendoff (1969) does present an argument of his own for the cyclic ordering of his pronominal anaphora rule. He claims that the rules of Reflexivization and Equi (both of which are interpretive rules in his system) share certain conditions with the pronominal anaphora rule, so that it is necessary to collapse these rules. Further, he argues, both Reflexivization and Equi are generally agreed to be cyclic rules, and he gives the arguments supporting this position. It follows that the pronominal anaphora rule must apply cyclically.

In the framework adopted here, this argument will not work. Helke's arguments, repeated in part in Chapter 2, § 3, show that Reflexivization is less closely connected to the pronominal anaphora rule than is generally believed. The arguments in Chapter 2, § 3 eliminate the motivation for collapsing the pronominal anaphora rule with the Reflexivization rule. In fact, as was argued in Chapter 2, there is good reason to believe that they are very different kinds of rules and hence incapable of being collapsed. Those properties which anaphoric pronouns do, in fact, share with reflexives can, for the most part, be accounted for by independently motivated universals, such as the definition of "under the influence of" given in Chapter 2, § 4.1.

What of the properties common to the pronominal anaphora rule and Equi; do these constitute a convincing argument for a cyclic ordering of the former? Within a heterogeneous theory, the answer would have to be "no." If Equi is a deletion rule, then it can only delete elements "under the influence of" other elements (see Chapter 2, § 4.1); that is, it will delete only anaphoric pronouns, so it is freed from having to be collapsed with the pronominal anaphora rule. If Equi is an anaphora rule (as Jackendoff claims it is — cf. Jackendoff (1972), Chapter 5), then it must share certain properties with other anaphora rules, including the pronominal anaphora rule. It is not necessarily possible, however, to collapse all anaphora rules, so arguments for ordering Equi cyclically would not automatically carry over to the pronominal anaphora rule. On the other hand, notice that a theory in which all anaphora rules can be ordered in a block is more restrictive than and hence (on methodological grounds — see Chapter 1, § 3) preferable to a theory in which they cannot. For these reasons, although arguments for ordering Equi cyclically would not constitute arguments for ordering the pronominal anaphora rule cyclically, they would provide motivation for seeking such arguments. Given this tenuous connection between the problem at hand and the ordering of Equi, I will not consider the merits of the existing arguments bearing on the latter.[15]

3.1.3 While there are no convincing arguments for the cyclicity of the pronominal anaphora rule, it is also true that the existing arguments against cyclicity are invalid, if certain independently motivated assumptions are made. Two of the arguments in question are due to Bach and were briefly discussed and dismissed in Chapter 2, footnote 11. A third argument, due to Postal (1970b), depends crucially on the claim that WH-fronting is either last-cyclic or post-cyclic. In conjunction with the fact that the pronominal anaphora rule must follow WH-fronting (see § 3.2.1 below), this claim leads Postal to the conclusion that the pronominal anaphora rule cannot be cyclic. To consider in detail the issues bearing on the validity of this argument would take us quite far afield, so I will limit myself to a few comments on some of them. First of all, I must point out that the question of whether WH-fronting is a cyclic rule is extremely controversial and far from settled (cf. Bresnan (1972a)), a fact which casts doubt on one premise of Postal's argument. Secondly, I will observe that Jackendoff (1972), pp. 126-128, suggests that Postal's argument goes through only if pronominal anaphora is accounted for by an obligatory Pronominalization transformation; since such a theory has been shown to be untenable, Jackendoff's suggestion, if correct, renders Postal's argument irrelevant. The question of ordering (31) with respect to WH-fronting and with respect to several clearly last-cyclic or post-cyclic transformations is discussed in § 3.2.1 below; for the moment, however, it is sufficient to note that Postal's (1970b) argument against cyclicity depends upon assumptions which we do not need to make here. Hence, this argument is not compelling in the present framework.

The remaining arguments against the cyclicity of the pronominal anaphora rule depend on the existence of a transformation for deriving what have been referred to as "action nominalizations" (Fraser (1970)). Since there are rather strong arguments against the existence of such a transformation (see Wasow and Roeper (1972)), it follows that none of the existing arguments regarding the cyclicity of the pronominal anaphora rule holds in the present framework.

3.2.1 There are, nevertheless, a number of examples which do bear on the ordering of (31). For instance, (35) - (39) show that several well-known transformations, viz., Passive, Tough movement, It replacement, Extraposition, and Extraposition from NP, affect the possible anaphoric relationships in the sentences to which they apply, thus indicating that (31) should follow them all.

(35) (a) The woman *John* loved rejected *him*.
      (b) **He* was rejected by the woman *John* loved.
      (c) **He* loved the woman who rejected *John*.
      (d) The woman who rejected *John* was loved by *him*.

(36) (a) It was easy for the woman who loved *John* to please *him*.
      (b) **He* was easy for the woman who loved *John* to please.
      (c) **It* was easy for *him* to please the woman who loved *John*.
      (d) The woman who loved *John* was easy for *him* to please.

(37) (a) It seemed to *John* that *he* was unpopular.
      (b) **He* seemed to *John* to be unpopular.

(38) (a) That *John* was not chosen mystifies *him*.
      (b) **It* mystifies *him* that *John* was not chosen.

(39) (a) A man who *John* trusted turned *him* in.
      (b) **A man turned *him* in who *John* trusted.

Similar evidence shows that (31) must apply after WH-fronting, regardless of whether it is the formation of questions or relatives which is involved.

(40) (a) *The members of the team* all hoped that the pros would
         draft some of *them*.
     (b) ?*Which of *them* did *the members of the team* all hope
         that the pros would draft.
     (c) **He* married one of the girls that *Bill* had been dating.
     (d) Which of the girls that *Bill* had been dating did *he* marry?

(41) (a) The woman who lived next door to *the Morgans* didn't
         share the old man's faith in *them*.
     (b) ??We all laughed at the old man whose faith in *them* the
         woman who lived next door to *the Morgans* didn't share.
     (c) **She* denied vigorously that *Mary* was guilty.
     (d) The man whose claim that *Mary* was guilty *she* had denied
         so vigorously finally produced some proof.

Notice that the judgements in (41) are independent of whether the relatives
are read as restrictive or non-restrictive. As noted above, the fact that the
pronominal anaphora rule must follow WH-fronting has been the basis of
a number of (largely erroneous) claims about the ordering of the anaphora
rule. It also proves to be the basis for an apparent ordering paradox which
is discussed in Appendix II.

Jackendoff (1969), pp. 54-55, mentions several other transformations
which appear to increase the number of possible pronoun-antecedent pairs in
a sentence. Sentences (42) - (45), due to Jackendoff, show this.

(42) (a) **He* is fond of the girl *John* kicked yesterday.
     (b) How fond of the girl *John* kicked yesterday *he* is!

(43) (a) **He* secretly loves the girl who kicked *John*.
     (b) The girl who kicked *John*, *he* secretly loves.

(44) (a) **Though *he* is fond of the girl *John* kicked yesterday, I like
         her even more.
     (b) Fond of the girl *John* kicked yesterday though *he* is, I like
         her even more.

(45) (a) **We all bet that Mrs. Provolone would kick someone, and
         his mother did kick the girl *John* hates.
     (b) We all bet that Mrs. Provolone would kick someone, and
         kick the girl *John* hates *his* mother did. (Where John is
         understood to be Mrs. Provolone's son).

In each of (42) - (45), the (b) sentence is alleged to differ from the (a)
sentence by the operation of a transformation. An important fact about these

rules is that none of them is cyclic, as evidenced by the fact that none of them applies in embedded clauses (cf. Emonds (1970)).

(46) (a) *Mary thinks how brave Bill is!
      (b) *Bill realizes (that) beans you'll never eat.
      (c) ??Mary forgot that handsome though Bill was, John was handsomer still.
      (d) *Mary believed that John would pay up, and Jane believed (that) pay up he did.

In order for the operation of these transformations to affect anaphoric relations, as (42) - (45) show that they do, they must apply before all anaphoric relations have been marked. Since (46) shows the rules in question to be either last-cyclic or post-cyclic, it follows that the pronominal anaphora rule is either cyclic, last-cyclic, or post-cyclic. That is, if the transformations in question are post-cyclic, then the pronominal anaphora rule must also be post-cyclic, in order for it to follow them in the derivations of (42b) - (45b); if the transformations are last-cyclic, then they can precede the pronominal anaphora rule on the last cycle, even if the latter is cyclic or last-cyclic.[16]

Suppose now that an example could be constructed with the following properties: (i) it contains a pronoun and an NP, such that both are in the domain of some transformational cycle other than the last; (ii) if none of the rules operating in (42)-(45) applies, then the pronoun and the NP may enter into an anaphoric relation; and (iii) if one of the rules from (42)-(45) applies, then the pronoun and the NP may not be anaphorically related. From such an example, it would follow that (31) must apply after or near the end of the last transformational cycle, for, otherwise, the anaphoric relation excluded by (iii) could be marked on some cycle before the last one. Unfortunately, the attempt to construct examples of this sort results in sentences which are so awkward that it becomes difficult to judge whether the relevant anaphoric relations are possible.[17]

(47) (a) I think the man who seduced *John's* wife is like *him*.
      (b) ??How like *him* I think the man who seduced *John's* wife is.

(48) (a) Though the man who seduced *John's* wife is like *him*, I still disapprove.
      (b) ?Like *him* though the man who seduced *John's* wife is, I still disapprove.

(49) (a) We all bet that Jane would kick someone, and Mary thinks the girl *John* loves did kick *his* mother.
      (b) ??We all bet that Jane would kick someone, and kick *his* mother Mary thinks the girl *John* loves did. (where Jane is the girl John loves).

These data are too marginal to be taken as evidence on any serious empirical issue. Thus, evidence for or against the cyclicity of (31) must be sought elsewhere. Nevertheless, notice that the data in this section have established that (31) must apply either at surface structure, last-cyclically, or late in the transformational cycle. The fact that (47)-(49) are not worse than they are suggests that the last of these possibilities is the most plausible.

3.2.2 It is natural, therefore, to ask whether there are any transformations which must apply after (31). Bach (1969) mentions two rules which he claims must follow the assignment of pronominal anaphora. One of these is Equi, which Bach orders after Pronominalization in order to account for data like (32). It was seen above, however, that (32) is excluded by mechanisms other than ordering, which are independently necessary parts of linguistic theory. Thus, the first of Bach's cases does not apply in the present framework. His second case has to do with the formation of pseudocleft sentences and involves some rather intricate reasoning.

Bach points out that sentence (50) is ambiguous.

(50) What *Descartes* discovered was a proof of *his* existence.

As Bach explains it, (50) "can mean either that Descartes discovered a proof of his existence, or that Descartes discovered something and that someone concluded from the nature, quality, extent or whatnot of this discovery that Descartes existed." I will refer to the former interpretation as the "equative reading" and to the latter as the "predicative reading." Bach assumes without argument that these two meanings are associated with different underlying structures. He also claims that there is no reason to postulate any surface structure difference between the two readings. Thus, he concludes that the two interpretations of (50) cannot be distinguished on structural grounds after the transformation of Pseudocleft formation has applied. He notes, however, that (51), in which the pronoun and antecedent have been reversed, is unambiguous, allowing only the predicative reading.

(51) What *he* discovered was a proof of *Descartes'* existence.

Bach proposes to account for these puzzling facts by using Pseudocleft sentence formation in the derivation of (50) under its equative reading but not under its predicative reading. That is, according to Bach, Pseudocleft sentence formation can have applied in the derivation of a sentence only if that sentence has an equative interpretation. Now the differential behavior of the two readings of (50) with respect to anaphora would follow from Bach's suggestion that Pseudocleft sentence formation follows the pronominal anaphora rule. Given this ordering, the equative reading of (51) would be excluded, since at the point at which the anaphora rule applied, the structure underlying this reading would be something like (52), which does not allow *Descartes* and *he* to be anaphorically related.

(52) He discovered a proof of Descartes' existence.

Notice that the above argument involved three plausible but completely unsubstantiated assumptions: (i) that the two readings of (50) are associated with different deep structures; (ii) that (50) has only one surface structure; and (iii) that the difference between (50) and (51) with respect to anaphora reflects a structural difference at some level. Akamjian (1970) argues at length against assumption (i). Akmajian asserts that pseudoclefts do indeed have two possible deep structures, but that the ambiguity of sentences like (50) is a function of surface structure, not of deep structure. Assumption (iii) is cast into doubt by the fact, discussed in § 2.2 above, that non-structural, purely semantic factors do affect the possibilities of anaphora. Thus, Bach's observations do not constitute very compelling evidence that Pseudocleft formation must apply later than (31).

Consider, further, the constrasts in (53) and (54).

(53) (a) What aggravated *him* was what *John* wouldn't tell us.
    (b) *What aggravated *him* was that *John* was unpopular.

(54) (a) What irritated *him* was the least of *John*'s problems.
    (b) *What irritated *him* was the photograph of *John*'s mother.

In these examples, the (a) sentences have predicative readings, while the (b) sentences (ignoring for the moment their anomaly with respect to anaphora) have equative readings. Thus, according to Bach's analysis, only the (b) sentences are derived via Pseudocleft sentence formation. Given Bach's claims about ordering, this means that the pronominal anaphora rule applies to these examples at a point where they have essentially the form of the examples in (55).

(55) (a) That *John* was unpopular aggravated *him*.[18]
    (b) The photograph of *John*'s mother irritated *him*.

Hence, the indicated anaphoric relations in (53b) and (54b) should be just as good as those in (55). This prediction is false. Thus, the interaction between anaphora and the formation of pseudocleft sentences appears to be rather more complex than Bach suggests.[19]

Another transformation which might need to apply after (31) is the rule involved in the derivation of the sentences in (56) from sources like (57).

(56) (a) After the thief they ran.
    (b) Into the air the balloon flew.
    (c) Above the rooftops it soared.
    (d) Over the fence he scrambled.

(57) (a) They ran after the thief.
     (b) The balloon flew into the air.
     (c) It soared above the rooftops.
     (d) He scrambled over the fence.

If this rule applied before (31), it could be expected to produce configurations which would allow anaphoric relations not possible in the source sentences. In other words, paradigms like those in (35)-(41) could be expected.
That they do not appear is shown by (58).

(58) (a) ?*After the man who assaulted *Mary she* ran.
     (b) ?*Into the house where *Bill* had seen an orgy in progress
         he dashed.
     (c) ?*Above the city *Bill* loved so well *he* soared.
     (d) ?*Over the fence that separated *Bill's* yard from the neigh-
         bors' *he* scrambled.

This suggests that the rule in question applies after (31). It has been pointed
out by some informants, however, that the complexity of the proposed
phrases in (58) renders these examples marginal at best, quite apart from
questions of anaphora. That this seems to be so is demonstrated by (59).

(59) (a) ??After the man who assaulted Mary I ran.
     (b) ??Into the house where Bill has seen an orgy in progress
         we dashed.
     (c) ?Above the city Bill loved so well John soared.
     (d) ?Over the fence that separated your yard from the neigh-
         bors' Bill scrambled.

The complexity of the preposed phrases is necessary in order to avoid violating the constraint stated in (30). Thus, the evidence regarding the relative
ordering of (31) and the rule relating (56) and (57) is somewhat questionable, and, hence, so far, no clear example has been produced of a rule which
must follow (31).

3.3 The evidence presented so far regarding the ordering of (31) seems to
be consistent with three possibilities: That (31) applies after all transformations have applied, that (31) applies last-cyclically, but before some transformations, or that (31) applies cyclically, but after most (or perhaps all)
of the cyclic transformations. The evidence in (58), though inconclusive,
tends to favor, the second or third of these conclusions. The fact that (47b)-
(49b) are not worse than they are suggests that (31) ought to apply cyclically. However, the very marginal character of these data makes any conclusion based on them extremely speculative.

One possibility which has not been discussed so far is that different portions of (31) apply at different levels. While this would be a highly plausible means of escaping from any legitimate ordering paradox which might arise, there is at this point no motivation whatever for adopting such an analysis. Moreover, it will now be shown that the existing proposals to this effect are incompatible with the facts considered so far.

Williams (1969) suggests that there should be two rules for associating definite pronouns with their antecedents: one based on left-to-right order, and one based on the relation of command. The latter would apply at the level of deep structure, the former at surface structure. This proposal was defended by Wasow (1970) as a means of escaping the apparent ordering paradox of Postal (1970b). It has already been noted that the ordering arguments of Postal (1970b) do not hold in the present framework, so Williams' proposal is not well motivated. In addition, his proposal would incorrectly predict that anaphoric relationships cannot be altered by transformationally induced changes in the command relationships. That is, Williams' analysis would allow anaphoric relations based on command relations to be established in deep structure, and subsequent transformational alterations of the command relations would not affect these anaphoric relations. Examples (37a & b), repeated here for convenience, show that this analysis does not work.

(37) (a) It seemed to *John* that *he* was unpopular.
     (b) **He* seemed to *John* to be unpopular.

Williams' analysis would mark the anaphoric relation in (37a) at the level of deep structure; the subsequent application of the transformation of It replacement would result in (37b), and there would be no way to rule out the anaphoric relation at this point.

Witten (1970) makes a similar proposal, but he divides the pronominal anaphora rule on the basis of the definiteness of the antecedent, rather than according to the structural relationship of pronoun and antecedent. That is, he argues that indefinite NP's are marked for anaphora in deep structures,[20] while pronouns with definite antecedents are transformationally derived from full NP's. Aside from the objections to the latter half of this proposal, some of which are summarized in Chapter 2, § 2. Witten's analysis cannot be correct, for transformations can alter possible anaphoric relations involving indefinite antecedents. For example, Witten's proposal could not account for the constrasts in (60) and (61).

(60) (a) The dog which *a friend of mine* bought bit *him*.
     (b) **He* was bitten by the dog which *a friend of mine* bought.

(61) (a) **He* beat the mistress of *a famous actor*.
     (b) The mistress of *a famous actor* was beaten by *him*.

The argument here is parallel to the argument against Williams' proposal. If anaphoric relations involving indefinites are marked in deep structure, then the operation of transformations should not affect anaphoric relations involving indefinites. Examples (60) and (61) show that they do.

3.4 One further factor ought to be considered with respect to the ordering of (31), viz., stress. It has often been noted (Lakoff (1968b), Akmajian and Jackendoff (1970), Jackendoff (1969)) that stress and anaphora interact. Perhaps if the nature of this interaction is made explicit, it might reveal something about the ordering of (31) in relation to the stress marking rules.

Akmajian and Jackendoff (1970) suggests that at least part of the connection between anaphora and stress is simply "that reduced relative stress level on both the NP and the pronoun is essential for a coreferential interpretation." Although they are certainly on the right track, their use of the term "essential" here is too strong, as their own example, given here as (62), shows.

(62) *John* hit Bill and then George hit *HIM*.[21]

(62) suggests that, while stress may be reduced on elements participating in an anaphoric relation, this does not prevent contrastive stress from being assigned to these elements. In fact, (63) suggests that contrastive stress may apply to elements participating in anaphoric relations just as freely as to any other elements.

(63) (a) *John* hit Bill and then George hit *HIM*.
     (b) John hit Bill and then George hit JOHN.
     (c) *John hit *Bill* and then George hit *HIM*.
     (d) *John hit Bill and then George hit BILL.
     (e) John hit *Bill* and then George hit *him*.
     (f) John hit Bill and then George hit Bill.
     (g) **John* hit Bill and then George hit *him*. (normal stress)
     (h) *John hit Bill and then George hit John. (normal stress)

However, Akmajian and Jackendoff deny this conclusion, claiming instead that there are interactions between anaphora and contrastive stress.
They support this claim with examples like (64).

(64) (a) After *he* woke up, *John* went to town.
     (b) *After *HE* woke up, *John* went to town.
     (c) *After *he* woke up, *JOHN* went to town.

A little reflection, however, will reveal that (64b & c) are perfectly acceptable, given the proper contexts. For example, the discourse in (65a) is quite acceptable, and (64c) may be used as an answer to (65b).

(65) (a) Was it after YOU woke up that John went to town? No. After *HE* woke up, *John* went to town.

(b) After *he* woke up, *one of my roommates* went to town. Do you know which one?

Notice, by the way, that the above seems to be violating the methodological suggestion (Chapter 1, § 2) that wider contexts should not be used in judging possible anaphoric relations. The difference in this case is that contrastive stress always requires a wide enough environment to provide a contrast. The reason the anaphoric relations in these examples are impossible in isolation is that the lack of a wider context allows only one possible contrast, viz., a contrast between *John* and *he*. Since anaphors are in some sense replacements for their antecedents, it is rare or impossible for anaphor and antecedent to be in contrast. But this need not be built into the anaphora assignment mechanism, nor into the stress rules. Rather, (64b & c) are assigned inconsistent readings, in which items are at once necessarily co-referential and contrasted, and this accounts for their deviance.

Akmajian & Jackendoff's further examples along these lines are similar, although it is more difficult to construct the appropriate contexts for them. Thus, (66a), which they judge as anomalous, is acceptable as an answer to (66b).

(66) (a) That George would be *TOM*'s thesis advisor never occurred to *him*.

(b) That George would be *a certain student*'s thesis advisor never occurred to *him*. Do you know who I mean?

Notice that (66b) is itself awkward, since there seems to be a tendency to choose a definite antecedent for a definite pronoun, if one is available. Replacing *George* by *Mary* in both sentences corrects this situation. In either case, the acceptability of (66a) corresponds to the acceptability of (66b), so the deviance of (66a) in isolation can also be attributed to the inconsistency of contrasting anaphorically related elements.

It appears, then, that the relationship between stress and anaphora is quite simple: anaphora leads to a reduction in stress, except when the stress is contrastive. Notice, now, that this relationship is in fact merely a particular instance of a more general phenomenon, viz., that stress is reduced on items which do not introduce new information. For example, consider the contrast between (67a) and (67b). (examples due to Chomsky).

(67) (a) Hard work matures people.
(b) Hard work matures teaching assistants.

The normal stress pattern for (67a) is with the main stress on *matures*; the normal stress pattern for (67b) is with the main stress on *teaching*. The usual rules for assigning stress (see Chomsky and Halle (1968)) would make the correct prediction for (67b), but would predict that (67a) should receive its main stress on *people*. The reason the stress pattern of (67a) is not as predicted is that *people* provides no new information, and hence receives reduced stress. That is, since it would normally be assumed that discussions of hard work and maturity are about people, the word *people* is de-emphasized through stress reduction. Contrastive stress, however, may be given to *people*, as (68) shows.

(68) Hard work matures PEOPLE, but not MULES.

Cases like these are clearly very closely related to the cases involving anaphora. In fact, whatever mechanism reduces stress in examples like (67a) can also be utilized to account for the interaction between stress and anaphora.[22] More examples of the same phenomenon are alluded to below in Chapter 6.

How are these observations relevant to the problem of ordering the pronominal anaphora rule? Aronoff (1971) proposes that there is a destressing rule for anaphors and uses the interaction of this rule with the Nuclear Stress Rule (which was shown by Bresnan (1971a) to be cyclic) in constructing an apparent ordering paradox. Without going into the details of Aronoff's argument, it is evident that his approach is insufficiently general, for it is clear that the destressing of anaphors should not be separated from the destressing of other redundant elements (that is, elements bearing no new information). If, however, the destressing rule is to reduce stress on all redundant elements, then it is clearly not an ordinary phonological rule expressible in the usual *Sound Patterns of English* formalism. Rather, it is some sort of a constraint on discourse, involving the interaction of semantics and phonology. Further, it seems to be an excellent candidate for a linguistic universal, for it is highly plausible that the primary function of stress is to mark the relative importance of elements in a discourse. Elements bearing no new information would naturally require no emphasis. Given the novel and probably universal character of this destressing rule, then, there is little reason to suppose that it should be possible to order the rule with respect to the other rules of the grammar.[23] Depending on the formulation of the destressing rule, almost any ordering for it seems to be possible. Thus, there appears to be very little reason to believe that considerations of stress bear on the ordering of (31).

3.5 Briefly, then, the following conclusions regarding the ordering of (31) have been reached: (i) there are no grounds for separating (31) into two or more rules and requiring them to apply at different levels; (ii) (31) must apply cyclically (at or near the end of the transformational cycle), post-cyclically, or last-cyclically (at or near the end of the last cycle); and (iii) there is some reason to believe that (31) applies cyclically, although the evidence is far from conclusive.

4. *Conclusion*

This ends my discussion of pronominal anaphora. Since much of Part I has consisted of critiques of arguments and claims in the literature and since many discussions have been rather inconclusive, it might be helpful at this point to summarize the more important conclusions arrived at so far.

(A) Deriving anaphoric pronouns transformationally from full NP's is an untenable approach.

(B) Anaphoric pronouns and reflexives should be handled by different sorts of mechanisms.

(C) The interpretive approach to pronominal anaphora has advantages over the lexical substitution approach.

(D) Existing formulations of the conditions on the pronominal anaphora rule are close, but not quite correct.

(E) There are few reliable arguments for the ordering of the pronominal anaphora rule, although it can be shown that it must apply no earlier than late in the transformational cycle.

Part II will concern itself with other anaphoric relations and will argue for a heterogeneous conception of linguistic theory. Conclusion (A) above will figure prominently in my arguments, as will some of the lesser points which emerged in the defense of (A)-(E).

NOTES

[1] I do not mean to imply that this is a comprehensive survey of the literature on this subject. It is emphatically not.

[2] Actually, there are some problems with number agreement. In particular, a pronoun with split antecedents must be plural, even if each of its antecedents is singular. Further, some plural pronouns may have a single indefinite antecedent. (i) and (ii) illustrate these difficulties.

(i) *John* told *his wife* that *they* had been evicted.

(ii) John bought *a Veg-o-matic*, after seeing *them* advertised on TV.

[3] No examples are given in which first or second person pronouns serve as anaphors, because if such pronouns ever do serve as anaphors, they must be fully identical with their

antecedents, which makes it impossible to tell that an anaphoric relationship holds at all. I take no stand here on the question of wether first and second person pronouns may serve as anaphors.

⁴ The notion of "pronimence" is not defined by Lakoff, but he assumes that it can be formalized and argues for its inclusion in linguistic theory on the basis of the contrast between (i) and (ii).

    (i) *John's house, he always talks about it.

    (ii) John's house, Mary says that he always talks about it.

The alternative to (8) adopted below does not involve this notion. Lakoff also adds to (8) that the pronoun must "have the appropriate stress level." Since anaphora is usually dependent on stress (see Akmajian and Jackendoff (1970) and below), and since Lakoff fails to specify what "appropriate" means, this condition will be ignored for the moment. Chomsky (personal communication) has pointed out that sentences like (iii) are counterexamples to (8) as stated.

    (iii) John claims that he is a genius.

Thus, in addition to its ad hoc character, (8) fails to account for the facts. The crucial point in Lakoff's proposal, however, is that it is the subject-nonsubject distinction which is crucial in (9), and it is this point which is argued against below (but cf. Reinhart (1974)).

⁵ Helke (1970) uses the term "sentential phrase" to mean S's and NP's with the internal structure of sentences. This term and "cyclic node" might not be equivalent, since there is evidence to indicate that AP might be a cyclic (see Bowers (1969) and Selkirk (1970)), although AP is trivially not a sentential phrase as characterized above. It will be seen below that neither term is quite appropriate in (4), so I shall not concern myself here with the question of whether both are needed.

⁶ Except for the variation among speakers, it appears that the condition in question could be formulated in terms of the notion "is superior to" (Chomsky (1971)). A is superior to B if every major category dominating the minimal major category dominating A dominates the minimal major category dominating B. (14) could perhaps be replaced by (i).

    (i) An NP may not be the antecedent of a pronoun if the pronoun is to the left of and superior to the NP.

⁷ Witten (1970) also recognizes the falsity of (6). In its place he proposes that left-to-right anaphora between an indefinite NP and a definite pronoun is impossible if the pronoun commands the NP but the NP does not command the pronoun. Notice, however, that this proposal fails to account for the deviance of (7a, c, and e). Further, reversing the positions of pronoun and antecedent in (15a & b) provides counterexamples to Witten's suggestion, as does (i).

    (i) The man who lost something couldn't find it.

Notice, finally, that the impossibility of reversing pronouns and antecedents in (15d & e) does not support Witten's proposal, since the constraint involved has to do with the distribution of any, rather than with anaphora, as (ii) and (iii) show.

    (ii) *The fact that any businessman is being sued should worry me.

    (iii) *The girl who any bridegroom to be is going to marry can upset John.

⁸ It would be more accurate to say that NP's admit of degrees of determinateness, depending on how much information is provided regarding the identity of possible referents for the antecedent. This is illustrated by (i), in which increased specificity of the antecedent improves right-to-left anaphora.

    (i) Although it made a loud noise, John didn't hear
$$\left\{\begin{array}{l} \text{*something.} \\ \text{?*some car.} \\ \text{??a car.} \\ \text{?a passing car.} \\ \text{a certain car.} \end{array}\right.$$

I am grateful to Julius Moravcsik for pointing this fact out to me.

⁹ Ken Hale (personal communication) has pointed out that (i) and (ii) appear to violate (17).

    (i) If you ask for it politely, you can have an ice cream.

(ii) If you really want *it*, you can have *a lollipop*.

A number of possible accounts of the non-deviance of these sentences suggest themselves. For example, one might claim that the underlined NP's in (i) and (ii) are not really anaphorically related to the pronouns. The existence of sentences like (iii) and (iv) supports this claim.

(iii) If you ask for it politely, you can go swimming.

(iv) If you really want it, I will sing for you.

[10] Any readers who might be uncomfortable because of the lack of precision concerning the new terminology would do well to survey the literature on specificity, for the meaning of the term "specific" appears to be equally imprecise. Not the least of the numerous causes for confusion regarding specificity is that different authors seem to mean very different things by it. Although existing lack of clarity regarding specificity does not, of course, justify further unclarity, it can be seen from the above discussion that whatever the proper criterion in (17) is, it is closely related to specificity. Hence, a clear and precise reformulation of (17) probably depends on a better understanding and definition of specificity than now exists.

[11] Example (9f) is a manifestation of an entirely different constraint. See Appendix II.

[12] I do not wish to imply that this constraint is a function of memory limitations. I am simply pointing out that it involves a feature which figures crucially in problems of performance, but not at all, so far as is known, in competence.

[13] Notice, by the way, that Lakoff's inclusion of the notion of "prominence" in (8) probably requires that (8) be considered a condition on linguistic performance as well. In fact, if the subject-nonsubject distinction is dropped from (8) (as it must be) and "prominence" is defined in such a way as to account for (28), then Lakoff's proposal can probably be made into a terminological variant of (30).

[14] $\triangle$ is treated as if it were a pronoun for the purposes of this discussion — see Chapter 6.

[15] One reason I am not going into the arguments for the ordering of Equi is that I find none of them very compelling.

[16] A cyclic ordering of the pronominal anaphora rule would entail that, in the derivation of a sentence like (i) from (ii), the pronominal anaphora rule would have to apply on the S_1 cycle, but not on the S_2 cycle.

(i) How fond of the girl *John* kicked yesterday Mary thinks *he* is.

(ii) $[_{s_1}$ Mary thinks $[_{s_2}$ he is how fond of the girl $[_{s_3}$ John kicked yesterday $]s_3]s_2]s_1$.

This is how Jackendoff (1969, 1972) proposes to derive such examples. This derivation would be inconsistent with Chomsky's (1971) principle of strict cyclicity, given here as (iii).

(iii) No cyclic rule can apply to a domain dominated by a cyclic node A in such a way as to affect solely a subdomain of A dominated by a node B which is also a cyclic node.

Whether (iii) is tenable and, if so, whether it applies to anaphora rules are questions I do not want to go into here. I merely wish to note that if (iii) does apply to anaphora rules, then (i) shows that the pronominal anaphora rule is not cyclic.

[17] (ii) appears to be an exception to this, for the indicated anaphoric relation is clearly impossible.

(i) Mary thinks the girl who kicked *John* secretly loves *him*.

(ii) **him*, Mary thinks the girl who kicked *John* secretly loves.

In this case, however, there are reasons for the deviance having nothing to do with ordering. Topicalized phrases always require heavy stress, whereas anaphoric elements generally require reduced stress. As a result, (ii) might be excluded because of the impossibility of providing the pronoun with an appropriate stress level.

[18] If, as Emonds (1970) suggests, Extraposition is done "backwards" and last-cyclically, then (53b) and (55a) are irrelevant to the argument here. However, (54b) and (55b) suffice to establish my point.

[19] Of course, some account of the non-ambiguity of (51) and the deviance of (53b) and (54b) is required. I strongly suspect that the relevant factor is non-structural, for there seems to be a general prohibition against right-to-left anaphora across the equative *be* (a similar observation is made by Postal (1971)). Thus (i) is impossible, just as (53b) and (54b) are, although it is very unlikely that any transformation like pseudocleft formation is involved in the derivation of (i).

(i) *The photograph which *he* cherishes most is the photograph *John* took of his mother.

Just what the underlying reason for this prohibition is, I do not pretend to understand.

[20] Actually, Witten's proposal seems to be rather more complex, but if I understand what he says, it does involve the untenable claim that pronominal anaphora with indefinite NP's is determined in deep structure.

[21] Capitals indicate contrastive stress.

[22] Actually, this mechanism can only account for the reduction of stress on anaphors. If it is in fact true that the stress on antecedents also gets reduced, then some other mechanism is required to handle this fact.

[23] Of course, the same might be said of (31). That is, anaphora rules appear to be quite different from other rules, and they are probably largely universal. Yet I have argued above that (31) is crucially ordered with respect to some rules. There are, however, no comparable facts to indicate that the destressing rule in question is ordered, except, perhaps, for its interaction with the Nuclear Stress Rule.

PART II

Other Anaphoric Relations

Chapter 5

THE ESSENTIAL UNITY OF ANAPHORA

In Chapter 1 I stated my intention of showing that the various relations I have been calling anaphoric should be handled by a distinct, narrowly constrained category of rules. The remainder of this monograph will be devoted to presenting arguments in support of this claim. My case will be built primarily on two kinds of evidence: first, that different anaphora rules share a significant set of properties which are not characteristic of other types of rules; and second, that anaphora rules are immune to certain universal constraints on other categories of rules. This chapter consists essentially of an enumeration of these pieces of evidence. Subsequent chapters will discuss what sort of mechanisms the grammar must employ if anaphoric relations are to be treated uniformly.

1. *Shared Properties*

1.1 The most obvious property common to different anaphoric relations is some version of the precede-command condition. That is, it is generally true that anaphors may precede their antecedents only if the antecedents are no more deeply embedded than the anaphors.[1] This has been observed frequently in the literature (e.g., Ross (1967a) and Postal (1972b)), and it is illustrated in examples (1)-(8).

(1) (a) *John* dropped out after *he* tried LSD.
     (b) After *John* tried LSD, *he* dropped out.
     (c) After *he* tried LSD, *John* dropped out.
     (d) **He* dropped out after *John* tried LSD.

(2) (a) John tried LSD after Bill did.[2]
     (b) After Bill tried LSD, John did.
     (c) After Bill did, John tried LSD.
     (d) *John did after Bill tried LSD.

(3) (a) John *tried LSD* after Bill had *done so*.
     (b) After Bill had *tried LSD*, John *did so*.

    (c) After Bill had *done so*, John *tried LSD*.

    (d) *John *did so* after Bill had *tried LSD*.

(4) (a) John believes *that Bill takes LSD*, although no one else believes *it*.

    (b) Although no one else believes *that Bill takes LSD*, John believes *it*.

    (c) Although no one else believes *it*, John believes *that Bill takes LSD*.

    (d) *John believes *it* although no one else believes *that Bill takes LSD*.

(5) (a) John will *take LSD* if Bill does *it*.

    (b) If Bill *takes LSD*, John will do *it*.

    (c) If Bill does *it*, John will *take LSD*.

    (d) *John will do *it*, if Bill *takes LSD*.

(6) (a) John takes LSD, although I don't know why.

    (b) Although John takes LSD, I don't know why.

    (c) Although I don't know why, John takes LSD.

    (d) *I don't know why, although John takes LSD.

(7) (a) John dropped *a capsule of LSD* after Bill took *one*.

    (b) After Bill took *a capsule of LSD*, John dropped *one*.

    (c) After Bill took *one*, John dropped *a capsule of LSD*.

    (d) *John dropped *one* after Bill took *a capsule of LSD*.

(8) (a) John *freaked out*, although *it* wouldn't have happened to Bill.

    (b) Although John *freaked out, it* wouldn't have happened to Bill.

    (c) Although *it* wouldn't have happened to Bill, John *freaked out*.

    (d) *It* wouldn't have happened to Bill, although John *freaked out*.

Observe that while most anaphora rules can apply either right-to-left or left-to-right, there are few, if any, other rules which are bidirectional.[3] For example, Helke's copying rule for deriving reflexives (see Chapter 2, § 3) always places the copies of the relevant NP to the right of that NP. Thus, we can derive (9a), but not (9b).

(9) (a) John talked to Mary about herself.

    (b) *John talked to herself about Mary.

Similarly, tag questions always appear at the end of a sentence, never at the beginning; WH-fronting, Topicalization, and Cleft Sentence formation move items only to the left; and Pseudo-cleft sentence formation moves elements only to the right. This list could be greatly expanded, but these examples will suffice to illustrate the fact that few, if any, grammatical rules other than those I am treating as anaphora rules can apply both left-to-right and right-to-left. The dearth of bidirectional transformations should occasion no great surprise, for the various notations which have been proposed for formulating transformational rules make it extremely cumbersome to formulate bidirectional rules. That is, the available formalisms for writing transformations can express a bidirectional rule only by including two separate structural changes (cf., the statement of Pronominalization by Ross (1967b)). Assuming that linguistic theory includes an evaluation measure for choosing among possible grammars, and assuming (as is generally done) that one important criterion for evaluating grammars is notational economy, we are led to expect that bidirectional transformations will be very rare. This suggests that different notation should be employed for formalizing anaphora rules, since we have just seen that anaphora rules are characteristically bidirectional. Thus, the bidirectionality of anaphora rules lends strong support to the notion that they should be treated as a separate category of rules.

1.2 A second property shared by a variety of anaphoric relations is that they are subject to the Transitivity Condition. This constraint, stated and motivated in Chapter 3, § 4, says essentially that three or more elements may be anaphorically related only if it is possible to establish pairwise anaphoric relations between them. In Chapter 3, I stated the Transitivity Condition as applying to anaphoric relations in general, but my only examples of its operation involved definite pronoun anaphora. (10)-(16) demonstrate the applicability of the Transitivity Condition to other anaphoric relations.[4] (Example (10) is due to George Williams).

(10) *Because Sam didn't _____ until after Mary *joined the party,* didn't want to _____

(11) *Since John wouldn't *do so* unless Bill *tried LSD,* nobody *did so.*

(12) *Although I had done *it* before Hillary *climbed Everest,* nobody believed that I could do *it.*

(13) *The man who had always wanted *one* because his father had owned *a Stanley Steamer* finally found *one* for sale.

(14) *People who won't accept *it* unless someone proves *that Nixon is guilty* are having more and more trouble denying *it.*

(15) *Since I can't figure out who with _____ unless someone tells me how *Bill escaped,* I won't venture a guess as to why _____ .

(16) *When *it* happened to Bill after John *freaked out*, *it* happened to Mary, too.

In addition to providing strong independent evidence for the Transitivity Condition, these facts support the claim that anaphoric relations constitute a linguistically significant class. The Transitivity Condition is a non-trivial constraint whose formulation requires reference to the notion "anaphoric relation." Linguistic theory must allow us to isolate this category of relations if we are to know when the Transitivity Condition applies. Hence, the applicability of the Transitivity Condition to a variety of anaphoric relations lends support to the case for a heterogeneous theory in which anaphora rules constitute a distinct category.

Notice that linguistically significant relations other than anaphora need not be transitive. Consider, for example, the relation of modifier-head. In a phrase like *imitation fur coat*, *imitation* modifies *fur*, *fur* modifies *coat*, but *imitation* does not modify *coat*. Thus, the modification relation is not transitive. Similarly, it is easy to demonstrate that the relation "subject-of" is not transitive: in a sentence like (17), *John* is the subject of *John's refusal to come*, which in turn is the subject of the entire sentence, but *John* is not the subject of the sentence.

(17) John's refusal to come annoyed Mary.

Other linguistic relations are trivially intransitive, such as "directly dominates" or "immediately precedes." These examples show that anaphora differs from at least some other linguistic relations by virtue of its transitivity. Further, those other linguistic relations which are transitive, such as "command" and "dominate" tend to be transitive by virtue of their definitions. This is not true of anaphoric relations; aside from McCawley's analysis of definite pronominal anaphora (which does not generalize to other anaphoric relations — see Chapter 3), no mechanism ever proposed for accounting for any anaphoric relation has entailed that that relation would be transitive. Anaphoric relations seem to be unique among linguistic relations in requiring a constraint like the Transitivity Condition to establish their transitivity. Thus, the applicability of the Transitivity Conditon to different anaphoric relations strengthens the case for utilizing a separate category of rules to deal with them.

1.3 Another property which unites anaphoric relations is their compliance with the constraint given here as (18), which I will refer to as "the Novelty Constraint."

(18) An anaphor may not introduce presuppositions not associated with its antecedent.

Since I do not want to get involved in the controversy over the definition of "presupposition" (see, e.g., Katz (1973) and Stalnaker (1973)), I will limit my use of the term to propositions regarding truth, existence, or uniqueness whose truth is a prerequisite for the assignment of truth value to some sentence.[5]

1.3.1 The clearest applications of the Novelty Constraint are examples of presuppositions of truth, i.e., cases of anaphors with sentential antecedents. Consider first of all the sentences in (19).

(19) (a) John realizes *that Mary is a junkie*, but Bill doesn't
$\left\{ \begin{array}{l} \text{realize} \\ \text{believe} \end{array} \right\}$ *it.*

(b) *John realizes that Mary is a junkie*, but Bill doesn't
$\left\{ \begin{array}{l} \text{realize} \\ \text{believe} \end{array} \right\}$ *it.*

(c) *John believes *that Mary is a junkie*, but Bill doesn't realize *it.*

(d) *John believes that Mary is a junkie*, but Bill doesn't realize *it.*

(e) John believes *that Mary is a junkie*, but Bill doesn't believe *it.*

As Kiparsky and Kiparsky (1970) point out, *realize*, but not *believe*, is a factive predicate, i.e., a verb whose complement is presupposed to be true. In (19a), (19b), and (19d), the antecedent of *it* is a sentence which is either asserted or presupposed to be true, so the indicated anaphoric relations are permitted by the Novelty Constraint. In (19e), neither the pronoun nor the antecedent is presupposed to be true, so the Novelty Constraint is also satisfied. In (19c), however, the antecedent is a sentence which is not presupposed to be true, and the pronoun serves as the complement of a factive. Hence, in (19c) the use of the pronoun introduces the presupposition that Mary is a junkie, in violation of the Novelty Constraint. This accounts for the deviance of (19c). Notice, by the way, that (19c) is acceptable in contexts where the speaker has already indicated that he or she believes Mary to be a junkie. This is just what the Novelty Constraint predicts.

A similar case, but involving a presupposition not induced by factives, is given in (20).

(20) (a) John understands why *Nixon is dishonest*, but Bill doesn't (even) believe *it.*

(b) *John understands why Nixon is dishonest*, but Bill doesn't
    believe *it*.

(c) *John believes that *Nixon is dishonest*, but Bill doesn't
    understand why _____ .

(d) *John believes that Nixon is dishonest*, but Bill doesn't un-
    derstand why _____ .

It is interesting to note that (20) involves phonetically null anaphors, thereby
showing that the Novelty Constraint cannot be restricted to pronominal
anaphora.

1.3.2 That presuppositions of existence cannot be introduces by anaphors is
most clearly shown by examples like (21).

(21) (a) In John's picture of *Mary*, *she* is smiling.
     (b) In John's picture of *her*, *Mary* is smiling.
     (c) *In John's picture of *Mary*, *she* found a hole.
     (d) In John's picture of *her*, *Mary* found a hole.[6]

The complete structural parallelism between (21a) and (21c) shows that
the deviance of (21c) is not the result of structural factors.

In fact, the only difference between (21a) and (21c) which is of any con-
ceivable relevance is that (21a) is about the content of John's picture, but
(21c) is not. The Novelty Constraint makes it possible to exploit this
difference in accounting for the contrast with respect to anaphora. The crucial
fact is that the existence of a picture does not presuppose the existence of
whatever is depicted in the picture. Hence, in (21c), but in none of the other
examples in (21), the use of the pronoun presupposes that Mary exists, while
the use of the antecedent does not. Thus, the Novelty Constraint predicts the
facts in (21).

Similar (though less clear) examples can be constructed using indefinite
pronouns as the anaphors.

(22) (a) In John's story about *Martians*, *one* speaks English.
     (b) *In John's story about *Martians*, *one* found a typo.[7]

Another kind of example in which the Novelty Constraint applies to
presuppositions of existence is illustrated in (23).

(23) (a) *John wants to build *a yurt*, and *it* is green.
     (b) *If Mary had *a son*, she would be unhappy because *he* is not
         cute.
     (c) *Bill will grown *a beard*, and *it* is blond.

Such examples have been discussed at some length in the literature (e.g.,

Baker (1966), Karttunen (1969a), Fodor (1970), Jackendoff (1971)), and a variety of devices have been suggested for dealing with them. While I do not claim to have solved all of the problems connected with such sentences, the Novelty Constraint does serve to rule out these examples; in each sentence the anaphor carries with it a presupposition of existence absent from the antecedent.[8]

1.3.3 My final examples of the applications of the Novelty Constraint are cases involving presuppositions of uniqueness, and the argument in this case is somewhat more involved than in the others. Consider, first of all, examples like (24).

> (24) (a) John thought he had found the solution to the problem.
> (b) John thought he had found a solution to the problem.

Both of the sentences are ambiguous between a transparent and an opaque reading. The opaque readings are the more natural ones, namely, the ones in which it is John who believed that whatever he had found (or thought he had found) solved the problem. Under the transparent readings, on the other hand, it is the speaker who attributes to whatever John he found the property of being a (or the) solution to the problem. This latter interpretation becomes clear in a situation like the following: I tell John that I have misplaced a 3x5 card with formulae written on it; these formulae are a (or the) solution to a problem I had been working on, but I do not tell this to John; John finds a card fitting my description, but it turns out to be the wrong card. In such a case, I could appropriately utter one of the sentences in (24), and the interpretation would be the transparent one. Notice now that both interpretations are still possible in (25).

> (25) John thought that he had found *the solution to the problem*, but Mary believed that she had discovered *it*.

(25) may mean either that John and Mary disagree over who discovered a certain thing, or it may mean that they disagree over which of two different things is the solution to the problem. The former reading is the transparent one, the latter the opaque. Finally, consider (26).

> (26) John thought that he had found *a solution to the problem*, but Mary believed that she had discovered *it*.

(26) is unambiguously transparent; it is not possible to interpret (26) as meaning that John and Mary disagree over which of two things is a solution to the problem. This contrast between (25) and (26) needs to be explained; I will use the Novelty Constraint in explaining it.

Observe that the NP *a solution to the problem* is interpreted specifically under the transparent reading of (24b). That is, if (24b) is interpreted transparently, then *a solution to the problem* is presupposed to have a specific (and hence unique) referent. The use of the indefinite article indicates that the description itself does not suffice to identify the referent uniquely, but the transparent reading does, nevertheless, involve the presupposition that the speaker has a unique referent in mind. No such presupposition is associated with the opaque reading. Since all definite NP's, including definite pronouns, involve presuppositions of uniqueness, it follows that an opaque interpretation of (26) would violate the Novelty Constraint. Since the anaphor presupposes uniqueness, according to the Novelty Constraint, the antecedent must do so too; thus, the antecedent must receive the transparent reading, which is the only one involving a presupposition of uniqueness. In (25), on the other hand, both interpretations are possible, since both anaphor and antecedent are definite (and hence presuppose uniqueness).

1.3.4 We have now seen that the Novelty Constraint is quite well motivated; it holds for a variety of different kinds of anaphora and for a variety of different kinds of presuppositions. In order for it to be statable in anything like the simple form given in (18), anaphors and antecedents must be formally distinguishable classes of entities. Further, anaphors must include phonetically null elements, in addition to definite and indefinite pronouns. The Novelty Constraint provides a further respect in which different anaphoric relations behave uniformly, and thus, it provides another argument for isolating a formally distinguishable class of rules to account for anaphora.[9]

1.4 Still another constraint which applies to a variety of anaphoric relations is stated in (27).

> (27) No Part of the complement of the specifier of a cyclic node may be anaphorically related to the head of that node.[10]

Following Chomsky (1970b), I take the head of S to be the VP and the head of an NP to be the $\overline{\text{N}}$. The specifier of an S is the subject, and of an NP, the determiner. So interpreted, (27) accounts for the ill-formedness of the (b) and (c) portions of (28)-(31).

> (28) (a) A proof that God exists exists.
> (b) *A proof that God exists does.
> (c) *A proof that God does exists.

> (29) (a) Learning that vitamin C improves people's health improve people's health.
> (b) *Learning that vitamin C *improves people's health does so.*
> (c) *Learning that vitamin C *does so improves people's health.*

(30) (a) The fact that LSD causes people to freak out causes people to freak out.

(b) *The fact that LSD *causes people to freak out*

does $\left\{ \begin{array}{l} it \text{ (too)} \\ likewise \\ the\ same\ thing \end{array} \right\}$.

(c) *The fact that LSD does $\left\{ \begin{array}{l} it \text{ (too)} \\ likewise \\ the\ same\ thing \end{array} \right.$

causes people to freak out.

(31) (a) A trainer of horses' horses are generally healthier than mustangs.

(b) *A tariner of *horses'* ones are generally healthier than mustangs.

(c) *The winner of the *game's* one was off today.[11]

In each of the ungrammatical examples, the relative positions of anaphor and antecedent are such that the precede-command condition would allow an anaphoric relation to be established. Since the indicated anaphoric relations are all impossible, (27) is needed.

The point of introducing (27) here, in spite of its ad hoc character, is that it constitutes an additional reason for trying to handle different anaphoric relations uniformly. It is another property common to a variety of anaphoric relations, supporting the idea of postulating a unified category of rules to account for them.

1.5 My final example of a property common to a variety of anaphoric relations is one mentioned briefly by Akmajian (1968). Akmajian observes that the antecedent in an anaphoric relation may contain a negative element not included in the interpretation of the anaphor. (Example (32a) due to G. Lakoff).

(32) (a) *John didn't marry Mary,* even though the fortune-teller had predicted *it.*

(b) John isn't going to Washington, but he won't say why not.

(c) *Nixon won't drop the bomb* in his first term, but *it* might happen in his second term.

(d) ?Although John will trust nobody over 30, Bill will.

(e) John has *no bicycle,* but Bill has *one.*[12]

Similarly, certain adjectival and adverbial modifiers may sometimes be ignored by anaphora rules. This is illustrated in (33)-(37). In each case the interpretation of the anaphor may optionally exclude a modifier of the antecedent. Thus, each of the (a) sentences is ambiguous between a reading synonymous with the (b) sentences and one synonymous with the (c) sentence.

(33) (a) John has a big fancy car, but Bill doesn't have one.
      (b) John has a big fancy car, but Bill doesn't have a big fancy car.
      (c) John has a big fancy car, but Bill doesn't have a car.

(34) (a) John beats Mary because he hates her, and Bill does
           $\left\{\begin{array}{l}\text{it too}\\\text{likewise}\\\text{the same thing}\end{array}\right\}$.
      (b) John beats Mary because he hates her, and Bill beats Mary because he hates her.
      (c) John beats Mary because he hates her, and Bill beats Mary too.

(35) (a) John has been approached by strange women in New York, and it has also happened to Bill.
      (b) John has been approached by strange women in New York, and Bill has also been approached by strange women in New York.
      (c) John has been approached by strange women in New York, and Bill has also been approached by strange women.

(36) (a) I suspect that the DA accidentally suppressed evidence, and even Perry believes it.
      (b) I suspect that the DA accidentally suppressed evidence, and even Perry believes that the DA accidentally suppressed evidence.
      (c) I suspect that the DA accidentally suppressed evidence, and even Perry believes that the DA suppressed evidence.

(37) (a) Yesterday, John jogged a mile in spite of the rain, and today Mary did so.
      (b) Yesterday, John jogged a mile in spite of the rain, and today Mary jogged a mile in spite of the rain.
      (c) Yesterday, John jogged a mile in spite of the rain, and today Mary jogged a mile.[13]

1.6 I have now listed five nontrivial properties, each shared by a variety of anaphoric relations. The existence of such properties is a necessary (though not sufficient) condition for postulating a separate category of rules for dealing with anaphora; to claim that anaphora rules constitute a separate category would be vacuous without a demonstration that something non-trivial unifies the members of this category. If anaphora rules are of a uniform type, then they should share some properties. The preceding discussion has shown that they do.

In order to go beyond this and show that anaphora rules ought to be treated as a separate category, it is necessary to show that anaphora rules do *not* possess some properties characteristic of other types of rules. That is, having argued that anaphoric relations have much in common with one another and should be handled by similar mechanisms, I must now show that anaphora rules differ in crucial respects from other categories of rules. This will complete my argument for postulating a separate category of anaphora rules.

2. *Differences Between Anaphora Rules and Other Rules*

2.0 In the previous section I pointed out one property of anaphora rules which distinguishes them from other rules, namely, their bidirectionality. Further, I argued that the transitivity of anaphora distinguished it from various other linguistic relations. In this section, I will cite several very general constraints on other types of rules which are violated by anaphora rules. This will demonstrate the need to distinguish formally between anaphora rules and other categories of rules.

2.1 Probably the best established set of constraints on transformational rules are Ross' (1967a) constraints on what he calls "chopping rules." Ross states his constraints as applying only to rules which move elements over variables (i.e., rules which can move elements indefinitely far) and which leave behind no trace, but he suggests (Chapter 6) that they are actually somewhat more general than this. In particular, he claims that his constraints also apply to unidirectional deletion rules. This is of great interest in the present context, for many of the anaphoric relations I am concerned with have traditionally been handled by deletion rules (such as VP Deletion and Sluicing). It is my claim that all deletion rules are unidirectional (see § 1.1 above), and that all deletion rules are subject to Ross' constraints. What have traditionally been treated as bidirectional deletion rules are what I call anaphora rules (see Chapter 6 below for a proposal concerning the appropriate mechanism to replace deletion in these instances), and they are not subject to Ross' constraints. Since other anaphora rules (such as the pronominal anaphora rule) are also immune to Ross' constraints, this provides a much more natural way of characterizing the applicability of the constraints. That is, instead of being applicable to movements and unidirectional deletions (but not to anaphora rules and bidirectional deletions), they are applicable to movements and deletions (but not to anaphora rules). Further, if an analysis of movement suggested in Appendix II is correct, then this might be simplified still further. In Appendix II, I suggest that all NP movement rules must leave behind traces, in the form of some sort of anaphoric copy of the moved item. If this suggestion is correct, it might be claimed that there is a deletion rule which eliminates such traces. Under those circumstances, the applicability of Ross' constraints could be restricted to deletion rules alone. In any event, it is clear that my suggestion of treating anaphora rules as a distinct category of rules provides a natural account of the seemingly peculiar correlation between directionality and the applicability of Ross' constraints. A different account of this correlation is proposed by Hankamer (1971), Chapter 4. Hankamer's proposal is not adopted here because it incorrectly predicts that Super Equi (see Chapter 7) will not behave like an anaphora rule.

2.1.1 Since Ross states his constraints in terms of movement rules, I will not quote his statement of them. Rather, I will state them in such a way that they apply to both movements and deletions. The constraints I am concerned wih are the Complex NP Constraint, the Coordinate Structure Constraint, and the Sentential Subject Constraint. They can be stated as follows:

(38) No transformation may (i) move an element A into a position B (without leaving a copy behind), or (ii) delete A under identity with B, if A is in one of the following structures and B is outside that structure:
(a) a sentence dominated by an NP with a lexical head noun (called a "complex NP");
(b) a coordinate conjunction;
or
(c) a sentence serving as the subject of another sentence.[14]

Since Ross (1967a) gives ample evidence for the applicability of these constraints to movement rules, I will limit myself to demonstrating, first of all, that the constraints apply to deletion rules, and, secondly, that they do not apply to anaphora rules. This will serve as a major reason for distinguisting anaphora rules formally from transformations. In order to help the reader see the relevance of my examples to the question of the applicability of these constraints to different categories of rules, I will, wherever appropriate, enclose the structure mentioned in the constraint (viz., the complex NP, the coordinate conjunction, or the sentential subject) in square brackets.

2.1.2 The deletion rules I will consider will be referred to as Comparative deletion, Object deletion, and Relative deletion.[15] I will not state any of these rules, but I will give examples illustrating their operation and showing that their structural descriptions must involve crucial use of variables (i.e., showing that they may delete items under identity with elements which are indefinitely far away).

Comparative deletion is the rule involved in deriving sentences like (39a) from underlying structures like (39b) (see Bresnan (1973) for a detailed discussion of this rule).

(39) (a) John is taller than Bill is.
      (b) John is taller than Bill is tall.

(40) shows that Comparative deletion involves a variable.

(40) John is taller than we thought your mother wanted Bill to turn out to be.

Comparative deletion is unidirectional; the deleted term is always the right-most of the identical terms.[16] (41) shows that Ross' constraints apply to Comparative deletion.[17]

(41) (a) *John is taller than Mary believed [the claim that he is].
      (b) *John is taller than Bill is $\left\{ \begin{array}{l} \text{[long and]} \\ \text{[and long]} \end{array} \right\}$.
      (c) *John is taller than [for Bill to be] would be amazing.[18]

Object deletion is involved in deriving sentences like (42) from structures underlying the sentences in (43).

(42) (a) The soup is ready for you to serve.
      (b) The grass is tall enough to cut.
      (c) John is too smart for us to implicate.

(43) (a) The soup is ready for you to serve it.
      (b) The grass is tall enough to cut it.
      (c) John is too smart for us to implicate him.

Object deletion is unidirectional and involves a crucial variable.

(44) (a) The soup is ready for us to tell Bill to begin to serve.
      (b) The grass is tall enough to try to get someone to cut.
      (c) John is too smart for us to ask you to try to implicate.

(45) shows that the Complex NP Constraint and the Coordinate Structure Constraint apply to Object deletion.

(45) (a) *John is too smart for us to find [evidence to implicate].[19]
      (b) *The soup is ready for Bill to $\left\{ \begin{array}{l} \text{[serve and set the table]} \\ \text{[set the table and serve]} \end{array} \right\}$.[20]

Relative deletion is involved in the derivation of sentences like (46).

(46) John is not the doctor that his father was.

(47) suggests that WH-fronting may not occur in the derivation of sentences like (46).

(47) *John is not the doctor who his father was.

Instead, sentences like (46) are derived by a deletion rule.[21] Relative deletion is unidirectional and involves a crucial variable.

(48) John is not the doctor that his mother once tried to convince us to believe that he is.

(49) shows the applicability of Ross' constraints to Relative deletion.

(49) (a) *John is not the doctor that his mother believed [the claim that he is].
     (b) *John is not the doctor that his father
          $\left\{ \begin{array}{l} \text{[joined the army and was]} \\ \text{[was and joined the army]} \end{array} \right\}$.
     (c) *John is not the doctor that [for you to be] would be won-derful.

These examples suffice to show the generalization of Ross' constraints to deletion rules. (I have ommitted many details — such as explanations of which constraint applies to which example; I trust that the reader will have no trouble filling in such gaps). I will now show that anaphora rules are not subject to these constraints. This will demonstrate the need to distinguish formally between movement and deletion transformations on the one hand, and anaphora rules on the other.

2.1.3 (50) shows that anaphora rules are not subject of the Complex NP Constraint.

(50) (a) *John* believes [the prediction that *he* will win].
     (b) John didn't take LSD, but Bill believed [the claim that he did _____].
     (c) John takes LSD, but I don't know [the reason why ____].
     (d) John didn't *take* LSD, but Mary believed [the claim that he had done *it*].
     (e) [The man who had tried to *do so* twice before] finally suc-ceeded in *climbing Everest.*
     (f) *John has taken LSD,* but most of [the people who know *it*] won't talk about it.
     (g) [The man who had always wanted *one*] finally bought an *okapi.*
     (h) *Mary was raped,* but I don't believe [the claim that *it* happened in Harvard Square].

(51) shows that the Coordinate Structure Constraint is inapplicable to anaphora rules.

(51) (a) *Nixon* seems to believe that [*he* and Agnew] had to cheat to win.

(b) The public realizes that Nixon had *lied*, although Mitchell claims that he $\left\{ \begin{array}{l} \text{[never would \_\_\_\_ and can be trusted]} \\ \text{[is an honest man and never would \_\_\_\_]} \end{array} \right\}$.

(c) I don't know where *the payoff took place*, but I do know [when ____ and that stolen money changed hands].

(d) If Nixon really wants to *tell the truth*, he should [stop beating around the bush and *do it*].

(e) If Mitchell *lied to the committee*, [he *did so* on nationwide television, and he will pay the consequences].

(f) Mitchell claims *Nixon knew nothing*, but [he isn't convincing and I don't believe *it*].

(g) After investigators found *a wiretap* on O'Brien's phone, they [looked for *one* on Mankewitz' and found it].

(h) If *O'Brien's phone can be tapped*, then [nobody is safe and *it* can happen to anyone].

(52) shows that the Sentential Subject Constraint does not apply to anaphora rules.

(52) (a) *Ford* believes that [for *him* to resign] would be a disaster.

(b) Although Ford didn't *resign*, [that many people wanted him to ____] is encouraging.

(c) *Nixon wasn't indicted*, but [why not ____] is still a mystery to me.

(d) Nixon should *resign*, but [for him to do *it* now] would be most uncharacteristic.

(e) [That Dean *did so*] proves that anyone can *tell the truth*.

(f) *Nixon is involved*, but [for him to admit *it*] would show that he has been lying.

(g) Since Mitchell has already told *a lie*, [that he will tell another *one*] is very likely.

(h) *Mitchell was caught lying*, but [that *it* will happen again] is unlikely.

2.1.4 The above examples serve to distinguish anaphora rules from movement and deletion transformations. Ross (1967a), § 1.2.3, proposes still another constraint on transformations which is often referred to as the Right Roof Constraint[22] and which applies not only to movements and deletions, but to copying rules as well. In this section, I will show that anaphora rules are immune to this constraint as well.

The Right Roof Constraint can be stated as follows:

(53) If A precedes but does not command B, then no transformation can
    (a) move an item from A to B;
    (b) copy A in position B; or
    (c) delete B under identity with A.[23]

(53) says essentially that left to right movement, deletion, and copying are blocked by higher sentence boundaries. Some instances of its operation are given below. The constraint blocks the derivation of the (b) examples from the structures underlying the (a) sentences in (54)-(59).

(54) (a) That for John to leave could be disastrous was obvious.
    (b) *That it could be disastrous was obvious for John to leave.

(55) (a) The fact that a man who was wearing a wig came in is significant.
    (b) *The fact that a man came in is significant who was wearing a wig.

(56) (a) That that gangster wouldn't testify has been verified.
    (b) *That he wouldn't testify has been verified, that gangster.[24]

(57) (a) The man who loved Mary killed himself.
    (b) *The man who loved Mary killed herself.[25]

(58) (a) I don't expect the claim that Bill is too fat to entertain him.
    (b) *I don't expect the claim that Bill is too fat to entertain.

(59) (a) The man who says that the box is taller than it is wide is tall.
    (b) *The man who says that the box is taller than it is wide is.

In addition to governing movement, copying, and deletion, there is some reason to believe that the Right Roof Constraint may also govern certain kinds of rules of interpretation. For example, Jackendoff (1972) and Lasnik (1972) both formulate their rules for determining the scope of negation in such a way that they conform to (53). That is, the scope of a negative element is a subset of the material it commands. If (53) is generalized to certain types of interpretive rules, it may be possible to simplify the scope rule. In addition, the rule (see Chapter 2, § 3) which marks non-intersecting reference between two NP's separated only by a verb is subject to the Right Roof Constraint. Otherwise, it would rule out (60a-c) and the interpretation of (60d) in which *the officers* and *the soldiers* have a non-empty intersection.

(60) (a) After *John* slept, *he* went out.

    (b) The fact that the government spies on us upsets me.
    (c) The man who had once helped you betrayed you.
    (d) Our interviewing the soldiers annoys the officers.

Thus, the Right Roof Constraint governs a wide variety of rule types, including several types of transformations and perhaps some types of interpretive rules. It does not, however, apply to anaphora rules.

(61) (a) That *John* was unpopular upset *him*.
      (b) The man who most wanted to win the prize didn't ____
      (c) The fact that John left doesn't explain why ____
      (d) After John *went to New Jersey*, Bill did *it* too.
      (e) The man who *discovered Plutonium* couldn't have *done so* without help.
      (f) The man who says *he hates you* doesn't mean *it*.
      (g) The person who sold me *an Edsel* bought *one* from you.
      (h) If John *was mugged, it* can happen to anyone.

2.2 The above examples show that several constraints proposed by Ross (1967a) serve to distinguish anaphora rules from various other types of grammatical rules, including several types of transformations, plus certain interpretive rules. This supports my claim that anaphoric relations should be accounted for by a category of rules formally distinguishable from other categories. Further evidence of much the same type is provided by noticing the immunity of anaphora rules to the constraints proposed by Chomsky (1971).

Chomsky's system of constraints is so formulated as to render Ross' constraints unnecessary. That is, Ross' constraints are, in a sense, corollaries of Chomsky's. Hence, the examples showing the inapplicability of Ross' constraints to anaphora rules will also show that Chomsky's constraints don't apply to them.[26] Since Chomsky's paper, "Constraints on Transformations" argues at length that his constraints apply to all kinds of transformations and to at least some kinds of interpretive rules, and since Chomsky's system of constraints is quite complex, I will not state them all; nor will I try to justify them. I will merely observe that they also serve to distinguish anaphora rules from other categories of rules which have been studied, thus strengthening the case for a heterogeneous theory.

As an illustration of how Chomsky's constraints support my thesis, let us consider one of his constraints, namely, the Specified Subject Constraint. I choose this constraint because it covers one class of clear cases not dealt with by Ross. Chomsky (1971) states the Specified Subject Constraint as follows:

(62) "No rule can involve X and Y in ......X...... [...Z...-WYU...] where Z is the specified subject of WYU."

The brackets in this formulation are taken to be the boundaries of a cyclic node (NP or S), and the notion "specified subject" includes all lexically filled NP specifiers. Thus, this constraint says that no rule may relate two items if one of them is inside a cyclic node which the other precedes, and the subject of that cyclic node appears between them.

Without considering Chomsky's mechanisms for handling apparent counterexamples to (62), let us examine some examples of its operation. In each case, the operation of a rule is blocked by he presence of a "specified subject." Note that the rules would not be blocked were it not for the specified subjects. That is, the judgements on the relevant examples are reversed if the specified subjects are removed. The reader should convince him or herself of this fact. The Specified Subject Constraint prevents the structures underlying the (a) sentences from being transformed into the (b) examples in each of the following examples.

(63) (a) Bill read John's story about someone.
     (b) *Who did Bill read John's story about.

(64) (a) I don't understand John's analysis of the auxiliary.
     (b) *It is the auxiliary that I don't understand John's analysis of.

(65) (a) Mary admired John's picture of himself.
     (b) *Mary admired John's picture of herself.

(66) (a) John is too ugly for me to buy Mary's picture of him.
     (b) *John is too ugly for me to buy Mary's picture of.

The Specified Subject Constraint also rules (67) ungrammatical.

(67) *John is not the doctor that I heard Mary's stories about.

Further, the Specified Subject Constraint applies to certain interpretive rules. For example, the rule, cited above, marking disjoint reference is prevented from applying by a specified subject.[27] Hence, the sentences in (68) are grammatical.

(68) (a) We looked at John's picture of me.
     (b) You wanted Bill to meet you.[28]
     (c) *John* liked Mary's story about *him*.

Another interpretive rule governed by the Specified Subject Constraint is the rule for the interpretation of reciprocals.[29] In both of the examples in (69), the Specified Subject Constraint prevents *each other* from being associated with *the men*, thus rendering the examples deviant.

(69) (a) *The men admired John's pictures of each other.
     (b) *The men wanted John to photograph each other.

The Specified Subject Constraint applies to the rule for the interpretation of *respectively*, as well. This rule must associate item-by-item two sets of two or more items; if a specified subject intervenes between the two sets, then the rule cannot operate the sentence is deviant.

(70) (a) *John, Bill, and Fred wanted Mary to go to Rome, Paris, and Oslo, respectively.

(b) *Mary, Jane, and Sue admired the photographer's pictures of Tom, Dick, and Harry, respectively.[30]

A final example of the applicability of the Specified Subject Constraint is to the rule for interpreting the scope of negatives. Normally, if a quantifier like *many* follows a negative element, the sentence is ambiguous between a reading in which the quantifier is within the scope of negation and one in which it is outside of it. Thus, a sentence like (71) may mean that there are many theorems whose proofs I don't understand, or that there aren't many whose proofs I do understand.

(71) I don't understand proofs of many of the theorems.

As Lasnik (1971) observes, the Specified Subject Constraint prevents the scope of negation from crossing a specified subject, so a sentence like (72) unambiguously means that there are many of Euclid's proofs that I don't understand.

(72) I don't understand Euclid's proofs of many of the theorems.

(72) cannot mean that there are not many of Euclid's proofs that I do understand. This follows from the Specified Subject Constraint.

The Specified Subject Constraint appears to be extraordinarily well supported. A wide variety of different kinds of rules are subject to it, including several types of transformations and a number of interpretive rules. Observe now that anaphora rules are immune to the Specified Subject Constraint.

(73) (a) *John* likes Mary's portrait of *him*.

(b) A person who *likes dogs* shouldn't read John's book about a man who doesn't ＿＿＿ .

(c) The woman *who left suddenly* didn't want Bill to know why ＿＿＿ .

(d) A man who had always wanted to *climb Everest* bought John's portrait of a man who had actually done *it*.

(e) Every man who has *won the Heisman Trophy* wants his son to *do so* too.

(f) The people who claim *that the earth is flat* loved John's story about a man who proved *it*.

(g) A man who owns *a St. Bernard* bought Mary's picture of *one*.

(h) Your friend *who was mugged* likes Mary's story about how *it* happened.

The Specified Subject Constraint, then, provides yet another distinction between anaphora rules and other rule types. This strengthens further my case for a heterogeneous theory.

3. *Conclusion*

In this chapter I have exhibited a number of properties common to anaphoric relations and a number of respects in which anaphora rules differ from other categories of rules. On the basis of these observations, it seems reasonable to assert that anaphora rules are subject to an entirely different set of constraints from other categories. It seems, in fact, that even the conventional formalism employed in the formulation of other types of rules is inappropriate for stating anaphora rules. The conclusion one is naturally led to is that anaphoric relations should be handled by an entirely novel type of rule.

As I pointed out in Chapter 1, postulating this new type of rule does not have the undesirable result of enriching linguistic theory, since this allows us to impose stronger constraints on other rule types (e.g., the prohibition against bidirectional transformations). Further, § 1 of this chapter showed that the proposed category of anaphora rules is quite narrowly circumscribed. Hence, in opting for heterogeneity here, I am attempting to restrict, not increase, the power of linguistic theory.

In the next chapter, I will attempt to refute some of the arguments purportedly showing that certain anaphoric relations must be handled by deletion transformations. In so doing, I hope to shed some light on the question of the kind of formalism that would be best suited to the task of stating anaphora rules.

NOTES

1 There may be some anaphoric relations which obey additional constraints which obscure this. For example, if Gapping is an anaphora rule (as suggested by Jackendoff (1971a)), then the impossibility of backwards Gapping in English might be taken as counterevidence to my claim. Note, however, that I have not claimed that backwards anaphora is always possible; rather, I am saying that if it is possible, then the precede-command condition will hold. Further, it seems to be the case that most anaphoric relations are bidirectional, so the cases like English Gapping are exceptional.

[2] The underlining of blank spaces used in earlier chapters to indicate the presence of phonetically null anaphors will now be abandoned, except where there might be doubt regarding the location or antecedent of such anaphors.

[3] Dislocation would be an example of a bidirectional rule which is not an anaphora rule, if, contrary to the usual assumptions, it could be shown that the Right and Left Dislocation rules can be collapsed. For an interesting discussion of dislocation, which casts serious doubt on the existence of these rules, see van Riemsdijk and Zwarts (1974).

[4] In each of these examples, the statement of the Transitivity Condition given in Chapter 3, § 4, and repeated here as (i), serves to rule out the sentence if the first of the three underlined elements is substituted for A, the second for C, and the third for B.

> (i) If A, B, and C are elements of a sentence such that A and B are anaphorically related, and B and C are anaphorically related, then the sentence is ungrammatical unless A and C are anaphorically related.

[5] This is clearly too restrictive, since questions and commands may have presuppositions, but cannot be true or false.

[6] These examples were the result of an interesting discussion between Ray Jackendoff and me in the spring of 1971. It was these examples which first suggested the Novelty Constraint to me. Since then, various people have suggested other accounts of (21) to me, and I am no longer certain of the relevance of these examples to the Novelty Constraint. However, the remaining examples in this section leave me convinced of the need for the Novelty Constraint, or something like it.

[7] (22b) is grammatical if a Martian's finding a typo was part of the story; this is not the intended interpretation. Notice, however, that the Novelty Constraint correctly predicts that (22b) would be grammatical under this interpretation.

[8] Notice that I am sidestepping the really difficult issue here, namely, determining which contextual features induce presuppositions of existence. I believe, however, that this problem can be solved using Jackendoff's (1971b) notion of "modal operator." Jackendoff includes these operators in the semantic representation of such items as *want, if,* and *will* ; he introduces a formalism for expressing a relationship between modal operators and NP's which he calls "dependence." I propose that modal operators specify what conditions would have to be fulfilled in order for NP's dependent on them to be assigned referents. For example, the operator *Unrealized,* which Jackendoff associates with *want,* specifies that NP's dependent on it could be assigned referents only if the subject's wants are realized. Presuppositions of existence are always conditional on fulfillment of relevant modal conditions. Under such an interpretation of Jackendoff's proposals, the Novelty Constraint can be taken to require that an anaphor be subject to all of the modal conditions to which its antecedent is subject. Jackendoff (1971b), in addressing the problem of ruling out examples like (23), proposes the following "coreference conditions" :

> (i) If NP_1 and NP_2 are intended to be coreferential, they must be dependent on
>> (a) the same type modal operators (weak form)
>> (b) the same token modal operators (strong form).

The modal operator associated with *want* is subject to (ib), while the operator associated with *will* is subject to (ia), as (ii) shows.

> (ii) (a) ??John wants to build *a yurt,* and I want to live in *it.*
>> (b) Bill will grow *a beard,* and *it* will be blonde.

Jackendoff gives no principled method for determining which coreference condition applies to which modal operator, although he does suggest the following hypothesis : "whenever a modal operator makes a definite claim about the existence of an identifiable referent, the weak condition holds ; whenever a modal operator leaves uncertainty as to the existence of an identifiable referent, the strong condition holds."

I believe that the Novelty Constraint (plus a sufficiently loose interpretation of the notion "modal operator") will make it possible to dispense with the coreference conditions. This is highly desirable, since they are clearly ad hoc, while the Novelty Constraint has ample independent motivation. This area is extremely difficult, but the sort of approach suggested here seems very promising to me.

⁹ Notice that the Novelty Constraint also provides a parallel argument for treating different kinds of presuppositions uniformly, since it applies to at least three kinds of presuppositions.

¹⁰ (27) is clearly unsatisfactory as stated ; it is an ad hoc description of the facts, devoid of any explanatory power. However, since I know of no more enlightening account of the phenomena handled by (27), I must use the formulation of (27) to establish my conclusion. Emmon Bach (personal communication) has pointed out that (i) appears to be a counter-example to (27) as stated.

      (i) John's attempt to *convince me* didn't _____ .

¹¹ The examples in (31) can be ruled out on independent grounds, viz., *one* can never have a possessive determiner, e.g.,

      (i) *Wild *horses* are less healthy than a trainer's *ones*.

      (ii) *The loser's *game* was worse than the winner's *one*.

However, such impossible NP's can ordinarily be made acceptable by deleting *one(s)* :

      (iii) Wild horses are less healthy than a trainer's.

      (iv) The loser's game was worse than the winner's.

Note that this device in no way improves (31).

      (v) *A trainer of horses' are generally healthier than mustangs.

      (vi) *The winner of the game's was off today.

Thus, it seems that (27) is needed to account for (31).

¹² (32e), it will be noticed, is less persuasive than some of the other examples since it is possible that the antecedent of *one* is simply *bicycle*.

¹³ Akmajian suggests that modifiers of the antecedent are ignored if there is an overt contrast between them and the modifiers of the anaphor. I believe that there is a larger generalization (illustrated in (33) - (37)), viz., that modifiers may be optionally ignored by whatever mechanism associates the readings of the antecedents with anaphors, within the limits of semantic compatibility. Notice that this does not seem to hold for phonetically null anaphors, although the judgements are not entirely clear. Thus, the (a) sentences cannot be understood as synonymous with the (b) sentences in (i) and (ii).

      (i) (a) Yesterday, John jogged a mile in spite of the rain, and today Mary did.

         (b) Yesterday, John jogged a mile in spite of the rain, and today Mary jogged a mile.

      (ii) (a) John beats Mary because he loves her, and Bill does too.

         (b) John beats Mary because he loves her, and Bill beats Mary, too.

This difference between null and non-null anaphors will be discussed further in the next chapter.

¹⁴ Ross (1967a) formulates this somewhat differently ; he refers to a sentence immediately dominated by NP which is, in turn, immediately dominated by S. I do not wish to take a stand on the question of whether sentential subjects are always dominated by NP, so I have stated the constraint without referring to any such NP.

¹⁵ The reason I have only three examples is that very few deletions involve crucial use of variables, and it is impossible to consider the applicability of (38) to rules without variables, since such rules would exclude the environments in question even without (38).

¹⁶ Examples like (i) and (ii) are not genuine counterexamples to this claim if we assume that WH-fronting follows Comparative deletion.

      (i) This is the bread than which there is no better.

      (ii) ?Than whom is even Tony taller?

¹⁷ It has at times been suggested (e.g., Chomsky (1971)) that the formation of comparatives involves a movement rule. If independent evidence for this could be found, then Ross' formulation of his constraints strictly in terms of movement rules could account for (41). However, I know of no such evidence. Further, Joan Bresnan (personal communication) has observed that there is evidence against postulating a movement rule for comparatives. This evidence consists of the fact that Comparative deletion may delete left branches of NP's,

although (as Ross (1967a) observed) these may never be moved by movement rules. This is illustrated in (i) and (ii).

    (i) John gave more of my money to the WCTU than he gave of your money to the ASPCA.

    (ii) *How much did John give of your money to the ASPCA?

¹⁸ Notice that it is perfectly possible for the subject of a comparative clause to be sentential, as (i) shows.

    (i) For Nixon to tell the truth would be more amazing than for Ford to lie.

This indicates that the Sentential Subject Constraint is needed in order to rule out (41c).

¹⁹ Object deletion only deletes the objects of infinitival verbs, so examples like (i) do not suffice to show the applicability of the Complex NP Constraint to Object deletion.

    (i) *John is too smart for us to find evidence which will implicate.

²⁰ It is not possible to test the applicability of the Sentential Subject Constraint to Object deletion, for the relevant examples are ruled out on independent grounds. As noted in footnote 19, Object deletion only applies in infinitival complements, and, as (i) shows, infinitives may not have sentential subjects which are themselves infinitives.

    (i) *The grass is tall enough for (for) us to cut (it) to be dangerous.

Since (i) is ungrammatical irrespective of whether Object deletion applies, it cannot serve as evidence for deciding whether the Sentential Subject Constraint is applicable to Object deletion.

²¹ I will not speculate here on the form of the rule, although a plausible guess might be that the pronoun *one* is deleted under anaphora with *the doctor*. Notice that it is implausible to suggest that WH-fronting does occur in such examples, but is followed by obligatory deletion of the WH-word. This follows from the fact that prepositions, which may normally accompany a fronted WH-word (see Ross (1967a)), never occur clause initially when the relative pronoun has been deleted.

    (i) (a) John is not the doctor for which his mother hoped.
        (b) *John is not the doctor for his mother hoped.
        (c) John is not the doctor his mother hoped for.

This follows automatically from an analysis of examples like (46) or (ic) which derives them directly by deletion, without the intermediate application of WH-fronting, but it would require an ad hoc constraint in a theory postulating the intermediate stage. Notice, by the way, that similar considerations suggest that (ii) is derived directly by deletion, without the application of WH-fronting.

    (ii) John saw the man I met.

This follows from (iii).

    (iii) (a) John saw the man to whom I was talking.
         (b) *John saw the man to I was talking.
         (c) John saw the man I was talking to.

²² This terminology is due to Grosu (1972).

²³ Pseudo-cleft sentence formation is not a genuine counterexample to (53), if (53) is interpreted as constraining rules whose formulation would allow but not require them to perform operations. In fact, the ungrammaticality of (i) might be taken as support of (53) (cf. a similar point made by Chomsky (1971)).

    (i) *That what he ate is a secret was a steak.

²⁴ Notice the contrast between Left dislocation, which is not covered by (53), and Right dislocation, which is.

    (i) That gangster, we have verified that he wouldn't testify.

²⁵ Note that Chomsky's (1965) Insertion Prohibition, which I (following Helke (1970)) used in Chapter 2 to eliminate the usual "simplex sentence" condition on Reflexivization will not rule out (57b). Thus, (57) does support the Right Roof Constraint.

²⁶ This is highly oversimplified; in fact, the relationship between Ross' and Chomsky's constraints is considerably less direct than these remarks suggest. I think it is nevertheless

true that my examples showing the immunity of anaphora rules to Ross' constraints also suffice to show their immunity to Chomsky's.

27 As I stated this rule in Chapter 2, § 3, it would never apply to environments covered by the Specified Subject Constraint, so its failure to apply in such contexts is questionable evidence for the constraint. Perhaps the point should be formulated as follows : if the constraint holds, then the statement of the rule can be generalized to these contexts.

28 In all of the previous examples of the Specified Subject Constraint, the "specified subjects" have been specifiers of NP's. Chomsky (1971) gives may more examples in which the specified subjects are subjects of clauses, but these cases have been omitted here because they are covered by other constraints discussed above, specifically the Insertion Prohibition and the Complex NP Constraint.

29 This rule is discussed in great detail by Fiengo and Lasnik (1973). Chomsky (1971), following Dougherty (1970), handles these examples by means of a transformation of "*Each movement*" ; some problems for this analysis are pointed out by Fiengo and Lasnik, who suggest an interpretive analysis in its place. I should comment, by the way, on Fiengo and Lasnik's characterization of the reciprocal rule as an anaphora rule. What they mean is that reciprocals must be assigned antecedents in order to be interpreted. Thus, in terms of function, the reciprocal rule shares much with anaphora rules ; in terms of formal properties, however, it clearly does not belong to the category of rules I am considering under the title "anaphora rules". Recall that the rule for handling reflexives also performs a function closely related to that of anaphora rules ; as I argued in Chapter 2, § 3, however, that rule is not an anaphora rule.

30 There appears to be considerable variation in the judgements of sentences involving *respectively*, but (70) represents the most common reactions.

Chapter 6

AN ALTERNATIVE TO DELETION

In the last chapter I showed that different anaphoric relations share a number of properties and hence should be accounted for formally in a uniform manner. Further, I argued that anaphora rules differ in a number of respects from other categories of rules. Of particular interest is the conclusion that anaphora cannot be handled by deletion transformations — even in cases in which the anaphor is not realized phonetically. This is important because it is quite widely accepted that null anaphors must be the result of deletion under identity. Hence, it is now necessary to exhibit a workable alternative analysis.

Opinions regarding non-null anaphors are a good deal more mixed. Existing proposals include deletion under identity, generalization of McCawley's lexical substitution approach (see Chapter 3), generalization of Pronominalization (see Chapter 2), or an interpretive approach. It will come as no surprise that my analysis is closest to the latter. My primary reason is the following. Chapters 2, 3, and 5 show that Pronominalization, lexical substitution, and deletion are all untenable approaches to at least some anaphoric relations. Since Chapter 5 argues that anaphora should be handled uniformly, it follows that none of these three approaches should be used for *any* anaphoric relations. In other words, only the interpretive approach offers any hope of being adequate for all kinds of anaphora.[1] Pronominalization and lexical substitution both fail to account for definite pronominal anaphora (Chapters 2 and 3), and deletion is an unsatisfactory approach for reasons given in Chapter 5. Hence, the interpretive approach offers the best hope of accounting for anaphora uniformly.

The first attempt to work out an interpretive analysis of anaphoric relations other than definite pronominal anaphora was by Akmajian (1968). Much of the criticism directed towards interpretive theories has focussed on the inadequacies of this analysis, so in trying to construct an adequate analysis, it will be instructive to consider the shortcomings of Akmajian's proposal Therefore, the next section is devoted to an exposition of aspects of Akmajian's analysis and a review of the criticisms directed against it. I will then propose an analysis which is close to Akmajian's but is not subject to the criticisms directed against it.

1. *The Nonexpansion Hypothesis and Its Shortcomings*

1.1 The Nonexpansion Hypothesis

The essential idea behind Akmajian's proposal is to generalize an interpretive analysis of definite pronominal anaphora to other anaphoric relations. In the case of non-null anaphors like *do so, do it*, indefinite pronouns, etc., this is quite straightforward: the range of anaphors to which anaphora rules are applicable is broadened somewhat, and the range of constituent types which may serve as antecedents is also broadened, so that it includes at least S and VP, in addition to NP. Then certain provisions must be made for the fact (discussed in Chapter 5, § 1.5) that portions of the antecedent may be ignored in assigning a reading to the anaphor. Basically, however, the generalization from ordinary pronominal anaphora to these other cases is quite simple, thanks largely to the near identity of the conditions governing different anaphoric relations (see Chapter 5, § 1).

In extending this approach still further to cover the cases usually handled by VP deletion or Sluicing (see Ross (1969)), the problem is that there appears to be no anaphor in the relevant sentences. The natural solution, which I have more or less assumed by employing the term "null anaphor," is to generate anaphors with no phonetic realization. This is the tack taken by Akmajian (1968). In keeping with other research along similar lines, he represents his null anaphor by the symbol △. Certain non-terminal nodes (including at least VP, S, and NP) would then be permitted to go unexpanded, exhaustively dominating △. As with other anaphors, △ would be associated with an antecedent under appropriate conditions, and the reading of the antecedent would determine the interpretation of △. Finally, surface structures with uninterpreted △'s would be deemed semantically anomalous.

One feature of this proposal has come under heavy attack: to my knowledge, it is the only feature of this approach which has been seriously criticized. I refer to the fact that the null anaphor △ has no internal structure. Critics of Akmajian's proposal have demonstrated that a variety of syntactic and semantic processes must refer to elements internal to the missing constituents. This shows that what I have been calling null anaphors must have internal structure at some level of their derivations.[2]

I will refer to the idea that null anaphors consist simply of △ — i.e., that the nodes S and VP dominating null anaphors do not get expanded any further — as "the nonexpansion hypothesis." In the next section I will enumerate the arguments which have been advanced ostensibly in favor of handling these cases by means of deletion under identity, showing that they are all, in fact, only arguments against the nonexpansion hypothesis.

1.2 Shortcomings of the Nonexpansion Hypothesis

Ross (1969) presents a number of arguments showing that the missing strings in examples like (1) are relevant to some purely syntactic phenomena, from which he concludes that there must be a transformation of Sluicing, deleting under identity the material following the WH-word in embedded questions.

(1) John heard someone out back, but he doesn't know who.

Some of Ross's arguments involve unjustified assumptions about the form a non-deletion theory would have to take.[3] These arguments will not be considered here. The others will be very briefly summarized.

1.2.1 First of all, the fact, illustrated in (2), that case marking seems to apply within the missing clause of sentences like (1) is inexplicable if the nonexpansion hypothesis is accepted.

(2) (a) Ralph is going to invite somebody from Kankakee, but they
don't know $\left\{ \begin{array}{l} \text{who} \\ \text{whom} \end{array} \right\}$.

(b) Somebody from Kankakee is going to be invited, but they
don't know $\left\{ \begin{array}{l} \text{who} \\ \text{*whom} \end{array} \right\}$.

This distribution of data follows from a deletion analysis, Ross observes, if deletion follows case marking.

1.2.2 Secondly, Ross points out that the distribution of data in (3) follows immediately from (4) if Sluicing is a transformation, but is difficult or impossible to reconcile with the nonexpansion hypothesis.

(3) I know he has a picture of somebody, but I don't know
$\left\{ \begin{array}{l} \text{who} \\ \text{of whom} \\ \text{*a picture of whom} \end{array} \right\}$.

(4) (a) I don't know who he has a picture of.
(b) I don't know of whom he has a picture.
(c) *I don't know a picture of whom he has.

1.2.3 Similarly, Ross' transformation of Sluicing relates (5) to (6), whereas the nonexpansion hypothesis would make them unrelated.

(5) Bill is planning to do away with one of his inlaws, but I don't
know $\left\{ \begin{array}{l} \text{*with which} \\ \text{which} \end{array} \right\}$.

(6) (a) I don't know which of his inlaws Bill is planning to do away with.

   (b) *I don't know with which of his inlaws Bill is planning to do away.

1.2.4 Finally, if Sluicing is a transformation, it is possible to explain the difference between (7a) and (7b) in terms of the facts in (8) and (9).

(7) (a) She was dancing but I don't know $\left\{ \begin{array}{l} \text{with whom} \\ \text{who with} \end{array} \right\}$.

   (b) He would report me under some circumstances but I can only guess $\left\{ \begin{array}{l} \text{under which} \\ \text{*which under} \end{array} \right\}$.

(8) (a) I don't know with whom she was dancing.

   (b) I don't know who she was dancing with.

(9) (a) I can only guess under which circumstances he would report me.

   (b) *I can only guess which circumstances he would report me under.

The nonexpansion hypothesis fails to distinguish between (7a) and (7b).

1.2.5 Ross (1969) also presents (10) as evidence against the nonexpansion hypothesis (and in favor of a transformation of VP deletion), pointing out that it is generally accepted that such occurrences of *there* are transformationally inserted and that number agreement must take place in the second clause before *there* is inserted.

(10) Some people think there are no such rules, but there $\left\{ \begin{array}{l} \text{are} \\ \text{*is} \end{array} \right\}$.

How, Ross asks, is it possible to make the correct predictions in (10), unless the second clause has a plural subject at the point where number agreement takes place? But if this subject is present in deep structure, then it seems that a deletion rule is needed to account for its disappearance.

1.2.6 Grinder and Postal (1971) argue for VP deletion and against the non-expansion hypothesis as well, on the basis of facts like (11).

(11) (a) *John doesn't have a car, and it is a convertible.[4]

   (b) John doesn't have a car, but Bill has a car, and it is a convertible.

   (c) John doesn't have a car, but Bill does, and it is a convertible.

The anomaly of (11) is due to the fact that *it* has no antecedent. If the nonexpansion hypothesis were correct, then one would expect (11c) to be ill-formed for exactly the same reason. On the other hand, a transformation of VP deletion could account for the well-formedness of (11c) by relating it to (11b). This argument is called "the missing antecedent argument."

2. *An Alternative*

The arguments above all show that a theory employing deletion rules to account for at least some anaphoric relations is to be preferred over one incorporating the nonexpansion hypothesis. However, in a theory with transformations of Sluicing and VP deletion, the kinds of mechanisms utilized to account for different kinds of anaphora must be different (given that pronominal anaphora does not involve deletion). This makes it difficult or impossible to account for the similarities among different kinds of anaphora noted in Chapter 5. Moreover, it was seen in Chapter 5, § 2, that a number of constraints governing other deletion rules fail to apply to VP deletion and Sluicing; in a theory including these transformations, the criteria for applying these constraints must be considerably complicated. It is hence worth considering whether it might be possible to account for the various anaphoric relations without utilizing either deletions or the nonexpansion hypothesis.

Since the nonexpansion hypothesis seems to be untenable, it seems reasonable to propose instead that null anaphors have all the structure of their antecedents, lacking only phonetic material.[5] More specifically, suppose that lexical insertion is always optional (an assumption which is made on other grounds in much current research — see, e.g., Jackendoff (1969), Emonds (1970), or Grinder (1971a)). This makes it possible to generate structures with all of their normal syntactic properties, but lacking any phonological or semantic material. If the anaphora rule or rules are allowed to associate such an empty structure with an antecedent, then the reading of the antecedent can be associated with the empty nodes. Surface structures containing uninterpreted empty nodes would be regarded as semantically anomalous. For an anaphora rule to associate two structures, they would have to be nondistinct (in some sense which must include near identity of the structures[6] but obviously does not include identity with respect to lexical insertion). Thus, the structure of (12a) will be interpreted like sentence (12b), but (13) is anomalous since the VP can have no antecedent.[7]

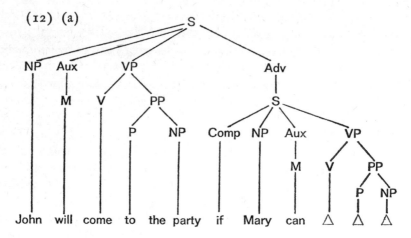

(12) (a)

(b) John will come to the party if Mary can come to the party.

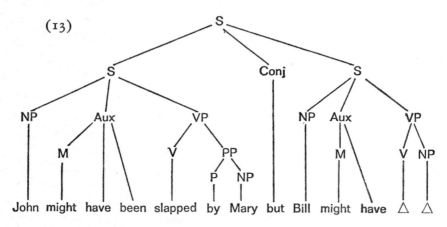

(13)

Such an analysis will be referred to as "the empty structures hypothesis."

The empty structures hypothesis, to repeat, involves generating anaphors which look just like their antecedents, except that lexical insertion need not have taken place. Deletion is unnecessary, since the lexical material which would be deleted is never inserted. In order to account for the meaning of such sentences, however, empty structures must be associated with appropriate antecedents ; this is accomplished by anaphora rules with the properties discussed in Chapter 5.

If the anaphora rules in question are also allowed to pair two structures both of which are lexically filled, then the rule which reduces stress on anaphors (alluded to in Chapter 4) can be utilized to account for the lack of stress on strings like the second occurrence of *come to the party* in (12b).

A natural objection to this proposal is the following: if anaphora assignment may apply either to empty or to nonempty structures, then what blocks the generation of (14a) from a structure like (14b)?

(14) (a) *John will come to the party if Mary can to the.

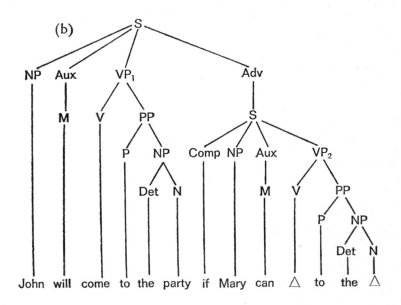

The answer is that the anaphora rule involved must be formulated so that it would have to associate the entire VP's of the two clauses. Then a rule which assigns the reading of the antecedent to the anaphor could optionally apply. If it does not apply, then the uninterpreted empty nodes render the structure anomalous. If, on the other hand, the reading of VP$_1$ is assigned to VP$_2$, then the reading of VP$_2$ contains the semantic material corresponding to the words *to* and *the* twice. It is plausible to rule out such redundancy as semantically anomalous.[8]

The anaphora rules which the empty structures hypothesis postulates would be very similar to the one needed to account for pronominal anaphora. The primary difference appears to be that these rules require a relatively complex non-distinctness condition on the anaphors and antecedents, in place of agreement in person, number, and gender. This similarity supports the empty structures hypothesis, for it offers hope of treating different anaphoric relations uniformly.

Notice now that none of the objections to the nonexpansion hypothesis summarized earlier applies to the empty structures hypothesis. The missing antecedent argument, for example, is inapplicable, since the antecedent would not be missing, but just lexically empty. Similarly, the facts illustrated in

(2)-(10) are handled in this analysis just as they are in a deletion analysis. § 1.2 demonstrates that phonetically null anaphors must, at some stage of their derivations, have the same structure as their antecedents; the question of whether lexical insertion ever occurs in those structures is independent of the evidence presented so far.

It is interesting to note, by the way, that the empty structures hypothesis requires less drastic modifications of the standard theory than the non-expansion hypothesis. Under the nonexpansion hypothesis, nodes like S and VP which ordinarily do not directly dominate terminal symbols must be allowed to directly dominate a dummy element (say $\triangle$) which serves as a phonetically null anaphor. That is, the nonexpansion hypothesis requires the otherwise unmotivated phrase structure rules S $\rightarrow$ $\triangle$ and VP $\rightarrow$ $\triangle$. No new phrase structure rules are needed under the empty structures hypothesis, since preterminal nodes are assumed to dominate $\triangle$ prior to lexical insertion anyway. All that is required is that lexical insertion be optional.

3. *Further Arguments for the Empty Structures Hypothesis*

I have argued above that linguistic theory can be made more restrictive if the transformations of VP deletion and Sluicing do not exist, and their work is done instead by interpretive rules operating on empty structures. In addition to this general metatheoretical argument against the deletion analysis, there are some minor technical difficulties in the deletion approach which the empty structures hypothesis avoids.

3.1 One of these difficulties has already been touched upon in the discussion of the Transitivity Condition in the last chapter. Consider structures like those in (15).

(15) (a) [S₁ [S₂ Because Sam didn't join the party until after [S₃ Mary joined the party]], James didn't want to join the party].

(b) [S₁ [S₂ Since I can't figure out how Bill escaped unless [S₃ someone tells me when Bill escaped]], I won't venture a guess as to why Bill escaped].

Under a deletion analysis, VP deletion and Sluicing are both subject to the precede-command condition. Therefore, the structures in (15) could be transformed into the structures in (16), and then into the ill-formed sentences in (17).

(16) (a) [S₁ [S₂ Because Sam didn't until after [S₃ Mary joined the party]], James didn't want to join the party].

(b) [S₁ [S₂ Since I can't figure out how unless [S₃ someone tells me when Bill escaped]], I won't venture a guess as to why Bill escaped].

(17) (a) *Because Sam didn't until after Mary joined the party, James didn't want to.
(b) *Since I can't figure out how unless someone tells me when Bill escaped, I won't venture a guess as to why.

The normal operation of VP deletion and Sluicing would derive the ungrammatical surface structures in (17) from the well-formed underlying structures in (15). In order to exclude (17), a deletion theory would have to be augmented by some as yet undiscovered constraint.

The empty structures hypothesis, on the other hand, allows us to use an independently necessary principle, viz., the Transitivity Condition, to rule out (17). In each example, a null anaphor both precedes and commands an item with which it must be anaphorically related, according to the Transitivity Condition; since this is impossible, the examples are ungrammatical.

3.2 Another difficulty encountered by the deletion approach is that of ordering the transformation of VP deletion. Most investigators have, I think, assumed that it must be a very late rule. However, this assumption entails certain difficulties. For one thing, VP deletion would have to precede *Do support*, the rule which inserts *do* into the auxiliaries of sentences with stranded tense markers (cf. Chomsky (1957) and Akmajian and Wasow (1975)). This order is necessary to account for the presence of *do* in examples like (18).

(18) John plays tennis whenever Mary does.

Tense is stranded in (18) only because of the absence of an overt VP in the second clause. Since the insertion of *do* is contingent on the stranding of tense, under a deletion analysis, *Do* support cannot apply until VP deletion has.

There are some reasons for believing that *Do* support cannot be post-cyclic or last-cyclic. If it were, its operation in sentences like (18) would violate Chomsky's Insertion Prohibition (see Chapter 2, § 3), given here as (19).

(19) "[N]o morphological material... can be introduced into a configuration dominated by S once the cycle of transformational rules has already completed its application to this configuration."

Similarly, a post or last-cyclic ordering of *Do* support violates Chomsky's (1971) principle of strict cyclicity, given here as (20).

(20) "No rule can apply to a domain dominated by a cyclic node A

in such a way as to affect solely a subdomain of A dominated by a node B which is also a cyclic node."

If either (19) or (20) is correct, then *Do* support cannot be post or last-cyclic. Further, Bresnan's (1971b) arguments for ordering contraction rules — including the rule responsible for contracting *not* — at the end of the syntactic cycle suggest that *Do* support should precede the end of the S_2 cycle in examples like (21).

(21) [S_1 John says [S_2 that you don't like turtles S_2] S_1].

If Bresnan is correct, then unless *Do* support in (21) takes place on the S_2 cycle, contraction must be formulated in such a way that *n't* may be attached directly to tense. Such a counterintuitive formulation is avoided if *Do* support is cyclic. Accepting this ordering of *Do* support, we are forced to conclude that VP deletion could not be a post-cyclic or last-cyclic rule either, since, as we observed above, VP deletion would have to precede *Do* support.

Now consider (22).

(22) [S_1 [S_2 The man [S_3 who claimed he didn't have a car S_3] actually did S_1], and [S_4 it was a convertible S_4] S_1].

Since the pronominal anaphora rule cannot apply pre-cyclically (see Chapter 4), it follows that *it* in (22) cannot be associated with an antecedent until the S_1 cycle. We have just seen, however, that if VP deletion exists, then it should apply no later than the S_2 cycle. If this is so, then *it* in (22) could not be associated with an antecedent until after the application of VP deletion had eliminated its antecedent. In other words, unless VP deletion is ordered post-cyclically or last-cyclically, the missing antecedent argument applies. But we have just seen that VP deletion could not be so ordered. Thus, a theory with VP deletion runs into an ordering paradox, given plausible assumptions about *Do* support.

This paradox is avoided under the empty structures hypothesis, since the "missing" antecedent is never really missing, but just phonetically null. In my theory, there is nothing to prevent the pronominal anaphora rule from applying after the VP anaphora rule in the derivation of (22).

3.3 Observe that if the Insertion Prohibition holds, then (23)(=(18)) provides an even more direct argument against VP deletion.

(23) [S_2 John plays tennis [S_1 whenever Mary does S_1] S_2].

Since VP deletion is assumed to delete under identity, it could not apply in (23) until the S_2 cycle (since the antecedent VP is not included in the S_1 cycle). The subsequent operation of *Do* support to S_1 would then violate the Insertion Prohibition.

Notice, by the way, that it is not tenable to try to escape this argument by ordering **VP** deletion pre-cyclically, for, as (24) shows, VP deletion must follow Passive, which is known to be a cyclic rule.

(24) John hoped that he would be arrested by the police, but
$$\left\{ \begin{array}{l} \text{he wasn't} \\ \text{*they didn't} \end{array} \right\}.$$

Hence, if VP deletion exists, *Do* support must violate the Insertion Prohibition in the derivation of (23).

3.4 Another argument for the empty structures hypothesis is provided by some facts first noted by Ross (1969). These facts are illustrated by (25).

(25) (a) John accused a man who teaches at an Ivy League university, but I don't know which university.

(b) *John accused a man who teaches at an Ivy League university, but I don't know which university he accused a man who teaches at.

(25b) is ungrammatical because its derivation involves fronting *which university* out of the complex NP, *a man who teaches at a university*, thereby violating Ross' (1967a) Complex NP Constraint (see Chapter 5, § 2.1.2). Under a deletion analysis, the derivation of (25a) would require something close to (25b) as an intermediate stage. That is, the derivation of (25a) requires that the Complex NP Constraint be violated, so it ought to be ungrammatical as well. The fact that it is not creates a problem for a deletion analysis. Ross (1969) suggests that this problem can be handled by a derivational constraint, and Chomsky (class lectures, 1970) has proposed a different mechanism for handling such cases.[9]

While Ross' and Chomsky's accounts of (25) will work, such artifacts are unnecessary under the empty structures hypothesis. The Complex NP Constraint prohibits chopping only from an NP with "a lexical head noun," and this certainly excludes empty structures. That is, Ross' original formulation of the Complex NP Constraint allows the extraction of an NP from a lexically empty relative clause like the one in (25a), but not from lexically filled relatives like (25b). Hence, under the empty structures hypothesis, we are led by Ross' formulation of his constraints to predict just the judgements illustrated in (25).

Note that a similar argument holds for the Specified Subject Constraint. Since an empty node cannot, under reasonable assumptions, be a "specified subject," it follows that extractions from empty NP's should be possible where they are impossible from the filled counterparts. That this is indeed the case is demonstrated by (26).

(26) Bill likes John's pictures of some contestants, but I don't know
$$\left\{ \begin{array}{l} \text{which contestants} \\ \text{*which contestants Bill likes John's pictures of} \end{array} \right\} .$$

Thus, as Ross (1967a) and Chomsky (1971) state their constraints, the empty structures hypothesis makes correct predictions where deletion analyses do not (without modification).[10]

3.5 A final problem for deletion theories, but not for the empty structures hypothesis, consists of examples like (27).

(27) (a) John isn't going to Washington, although I don't know why
          not.

     (b) John will go if not Bill.

     (c) John loves Mary, although not Mary John.

In such examples, the auxiliary is missing and the word *not* appears in clause-initial position instead of in the auxiliary. The word *not* may not appear initially in clauses with an overt auxiliary, except as part of certain phrases such as *not many, not long ago,* etc.

   In a deletion theory, one might try to capture this fact by blocking the transformation placing *not* into the auxiliary (cf. Chomsky (1957), Klima (1964), Lasnik (1972)) when the auxiliary has been deleted. Unfortunately, this creates an ordering paradox. The placement of *not* must occur cyclically, if Bresnan's (1971b) analysis of contraction or Chomsky's (1971) principle of strict cyclicity (see § 3.2 above) is to be maintained; further *Do* support would violate the Insertion Prohibition if Negative placement were post-cyclic or last-cyclic (see § 3.2). However, as I argued above, VP deletion[11] could not occur in examples like (27b) until the matrix cycle. The same is true of Sluicing and Gapping in (27a) and (27c)[12]; this follows from the fact that Passive, a cyclic rule, precedes both, as (28) shows.

(28) (a) John was mugged, but he doesn't know $\left\{ \begin{array}{l} \text{by whom} \\ \text{*who} \end{array} \right\} .$

     (b) John was hit by Bill, and $\left\{ \begin{array}{l} \text{Fred by Pete} \\ \text{*Pete Fred} \end{array} \right\} .$

Negative placement would take place in the examples of (27) prior to the application of Sluicing, VP deletion, or Gapping. Hence the application of Negative placement cannot be made contingent on the non-application of these deletion rules. Put another way, he auxiliary will still be present when Negative placement applies, so it is not simply absence of the auxiliary that blocks Negative placement.

   Instead, in order to account for (27), a deletion theory must make Negative placement optional. Then, in order to rule out examples like (29), it must include a surface structure constraint to the effect that sentences with initial *not* must lack an auxiliary (or begin with phrases like *not many, not long ago, etc.*).

(29) (a) *Not John is going to Washington.
     (b) *Not Bill will go.
     (c) *Not Mary loves John.

The empty structures hypothesis needs no such ad hoc device. Rather, Negative placement is so formulated that *not* can be inserted only into lexically filled auxiliaries (and that it is obligatory when the auxiliary is lexically filled).

Notice, by the way that under the empty structures hypothesis, the fact that (30) is a synonymous alternative to (27a) follows immediately from the fact, noted in Chapter 5, § 1.5, that anaphors may optionally differ from their antecedents by a negative element.

(30) John isn't going to Washington, although I don't know why.

Under a deletion theory, the synonymy of (27a) and (30) is as peculiar and unaccountable a fact as the existence of (27a).

Notice also that the two theories make different predictions regarding comparatives. The deletion theory predicts that comparatives should behave like the elliptical structures in (27). Hence, under the deletion theory, the grammaticality of (31a) suggests that (31b) should be possible.

(31) (a) John hit more pitches than Bill didn't (hit).[13]
     (b) *John hit more pitches than not Bill.

My theory, however, is that comparatives are formed by deletion under identity, whereas the examples of (27) are instances of empty structures (i.e., null anaphors). According to my analysis, Negative placement in comparatives will obligatorily take place before Comparative deletion, and (31b) cannot be derived. Therefore, (31) is an automatic consequence of my approach and an anomaly under the deletion theory.

3.6 The empty structures hypothesis, then, is to be preferred over a theory incorporating deletion transformations of VP deletion and Sluicing for two reasons: first of all, it makes possible the uniform treatment of anaphora argued for in Chapter 5; and secondly, it avoids several messy problems besetting the deletion theory.

4. Non-null Anaphors

The interpretive approach to pronominal anaphora can be generalized to all non-null anaphors in quite a straightforward manner. Problems analogous to those which led me to adopt the empty structures hypothesis in place of the nonexpansion hypothesis do not arise. The generalization is effected simply by specifying what types of constituents may serve as antecedents for each anaphor. As we saw in the last chapter, the conditions governing different anaphoric relations are remarkably similar.[14] So there should be little doubt at this point as to how we would handle these non-null anaphors.

Natural as the interpretive approach appears in the present context, the bulk of the literature dealing with the phenomena in question (see, e.g., Lakoff (1970a) or Ross (1967a)) assumes that the derivation of non-null anaphors involves either deletion or replacement under identity. It might, therefore, be a good idea to present some arguments showing the superiority of the interpretive approach over the transformational approach for these non-null anaphors.

The most obvious and strongest argument for an interpretive approach is the need, demonstrated in Chapter 5, for a uniform treatment of anaphora. That is, if *do so, do it*, etc. are derived transformationally, but ordinary anaphoric pronouns are not, then how do we account for the striking similarities in their behavior? In particular, if these elements are transformationally derived, then why don't the relevant transformations obey Ross' (1967a) or Chomsky's (1971) constraints?

In addition to this general argument, there are a number of specific difficulties encountered by the transformational theory but not by the interpretive theory.

Akmajian (1973) and Chomsky (1969) argue that if deletions or replacements are to be limited either to constituents or continuous strings, then certain anaphoric elements cannot be derived by deletion or replacement. The examples in (32) illustrate this point, with the bracketed phrases representing the items presumed to have been deleted or replaced (32a) due to G. Lakoff).

(32) (a) Goldwater won in the West, but it couldn't have happened in the East. [Goldwater won]

   (b) Although nobody knows it, John beats his wife every night. [John beats his wife every night]

   (c) John punched Bill in the nose, but he wouldn't have done it to Pete. [punched... in the nose]

   (d) The bouncer threw John out because he was making too much noise, but he did it to Pete because of the length of his hair. [threw... out]

(e) We may manage to eliminate water pollution, but we'll never do it with air pollution. [manage to eliminate]

(f) These shoes could be repaired with epoxy, but it can't be done with bubble gum. [these shoes... repaired]

(g) Two years ago, Nixon defeated McGovern in California, but he couldn't do so today. [defeat McGovern in California]

(h) John hoisted Mary up into a tree and poured paint on her, and I'd like to do $\left\{ \begin{array}{c} \text{likewise} \\ \text{the same} \end{array} \right\}$ with Jane. [hoist... up into a tree and pour paint on her]

Akmajian and Chomsky point out that none of the bracketed expressions in (32) are single constituents and that many of them are not even continuous strings. For this reason, they claim, if the anaphors in (32) are derived by deletion or replacement then it will be difficult or impossible to specify what sorts of items may be deleted or replaced by a transformation. Such a specification is desirable in order to maximize the restrictiveness of linguistic theory.

Akmajian (1973) proposes that examples like (32) should be handled by a surface structure interpretive principle. This principle would associate with each anaphor the reading of another constituent, minus the reading of those elements in contrast. For example, in (32h), the reading of the anaphor turns out to be the reading of the first conjunct, minus *John* and *Mary,* which are the two items in contrast.[15]

Ross (1969) and Leben (1970) have countered this argument by showing that a suitable relaxation of the notion of "identity" leads to plausible underlying structure for examples like (32), without necessitating abandonment of the transformational approach. Although consideration of the details of this proposal would involve going too far afield, it should be observed that Ross and Leben do not succeed in providing any basis for choosing between the transformational and interpretive approaches to such examples; rather, they show that the transformational theory cannot be ruled out simply because of sentences like (32).

Ross (1969) does attempt to provide an argument for choosing the deletion approach. The structure of his argument is the following: (33) shows that "sloppy identity" is a necessary part of linguistic theory, so long as Sluicing is a deletion rule; with sloppy identity it is possible to handle cases like those in (32) without Akmajian's interpretive principle (i.e., with deletions); therefore, if Sluicing can be shown to be a deletion, then the interpretive principle need not (and hence should not) be included in the grammar, and the examples of (32) should be treated as deletion under sloppy identity.

(33) Bob knows how to crane his neck, but I don't know how.

Ross then presents the arguments of § 1.2 to try to show that Sluicing is a
deletion rule. Quite apart from the fact that none of the arguments of § 1.2
applies to the empty structures hypothesis, the above argument fails to be
convincing because it is possible to argue in a perfectly analogous manner that
sloppy identity should *not* be a part of linguistic theory. The argument is the
following: *it* in (34) may be interpreted to mean the second man's paycheck;
this shows that the rule associating a pronoun with the reading of its antecedent — a rule which cannot be a deletion — may in some cases ignore anaphoric relations within the antecedent; since this is just like the phenomena
sloppy identity is meant to handle, we should try to account for these phenomena in the same way, viz., not in terms of conditions on deletion, but
in terms of conditions on copying semantic material.

(34) The man who gave *his paycheck* to his wife was wiser than the
       man who gave *it* to his mistress.

The arguments above boil down to the idea that where there are two possible
mechanisms for accounting for certain facts, if one mechanism can be shown
to be necessary in some cases, then the other mechanism should be abandoned.
Ross claims to have shown sloppy identity to be necessary, and I argue that
the interpretive mechanism is necessary. It would seem to follow that both
are needed. Recall, however, that one crucial step in Ross' argument was
faulty, namely the demonstration that Sluicing is a deletion. Thus, it appears
that sloppy identity is not needed after all. This conclusion predicts that
genuine deletions require strict identity. This prediction is borne out. Thus,
(35), which involves the syntactic deletion rule of Comparative deletion,
lacks the sloppy reading (i.e., it unambiguously means that Bill lost John's
books.

(35) John lost more of his books than Bill lost.

(This example is due to Emmon Bach).[16]

Another argument against the transformational approach is provided by
considering examples like (36a), which would be derived from (36b).

(36) (a) Although nobody believes *that John is a junkie, it* is true.
       (b) Although nobody believes that John is a junkie, that John is
            a junkie is true.

If such a derivation of (36a) were possible, then a completely parallel derivation of (37a) from (37b) would be possible.

(37) (a) *Although nobody believes that *John is a junkie, it*.
       (b) Although nobody believes that John is a junkie, John is a
            junkie.

The complete parallelism between (36) and (37) would make it difficult to account for the deviance of (37a) in a transformational theory. Under an interpretive analysis, the explanation is very simple: *it* is an NP and (37a) would therefore require the nonexistent phrase structure rule S → Adv NP. Thus, the interpretive approach avoids what looks like a difficult problem for the transformational approach.

A final argument against deriving non-null anaphors by deletion or replacement has to do with a peculiar property of a dialect of English spoken in parts of Massachusetts. In this dialect, a semantically empty *not* is added in certain instances where the anaphor *so* is used. For example, speakers of this dialect would use the sentences in (38) to mean what speakers of the majority dialect of American English would mean by the same sentences without the negative elements.

> (38) (a) John will go to the movies tonight, and so won't Mary.
>   (b) You have brown hair, and so don't I.

If a deletion or replacement transformation is involved in the generation of (38), then either the negative element is present in the underlying structure, or it is inserted by the transformation inserting *so*. In the former case, the underlying structures of (38) would correspond to the sentences in (39).

> (39) (a) John will go to the movies tonight, and Mary won't go to the movies tonight.
>   (b) You have brown hair, and I don't have brown hair.

Thus, the required transformation would have to affect the meaning of the sentence in a radical and unprecedented manner. Alternatively, it might be argued that the negative element is transformationally inserted together with *so*. If this is the case, however, the fact that *not* ends up in the auxiliary and behaves just like ordinary negative elements (except semantically) is rendered purely accidental. Further, the fact that *not* contracts in (38) is incompatible with such an approach, since *not* would not be inserted until the last cycle, whereas contraction occurs cyclically (Bresnan (1971b)). Thus, the dialect in which (38) occurs cannot be plausibly described in a transformational theory. It seems unlikely that this dialect difference would involve the replacement of a transformation by an anaphora rule, so the argument against the transformational approach in the Massachusetts dialect supports the contention that deletion is not involved in the standard dialect.

5. *Differences Between Null and Non-null Anaphors*

One consequence of the proposals put forward in this chapter is that there is a crucial difference between null and non-null anaphors, namely, that the former have internal structure, but the latter do not. That is, under the empty structures hypothesis, null anaphors are phonetically empty duplicates of their antecedents, whereas non-null anaphors are simple lexical items with no internal structure.[17] This difference manifests itself in a number of ways, supporting the analysis proposed here.

First of all, as Bresnan (1972b) points out, the missing antecedent argument does not apply to non-null anaphors. This is illustrated by some of Bresnan's examples.

(40) (a) *My uncle didn't buy anything for Christmas, so my aunt did it for him, and it was bright red. [it=something]

(b) *My uncle has never ridden a camel, but his brother finally managed it, although it was lame. [it=camel]

(c) *Jack didn't get picked off by throw to first, but it happened to Bill, and it singed his ear. [it=throw to first]

Notice also that *it* is not the only non-null anaphor exempt from the missing antecedent argument.

(41) *My uncle has never ridden a camel, but his brother finally did so, although it was lame. [it=camel]

These examples are ungrammatical because, in each case, the necessary antecedent of *it* is missing. In the place of the VP which would have contained the antecedent there is simply an anaphor with no internal structure. The analysis proposed in this chapter predicts that non-null anaphors will differ from null anaphors in this way.[18]

My analysis also predicts that other arguments against the nonexpansion hypothesis will fail to carry over to non-null anaphors. As noted above, Ross (1969) observed that the applicability of *There* insertion to null anaphors (illustrated in (10), repeated here) shows that these anaphors have internal structure.

(10) Some people think there are no such rules, but there are.

Under my analysis, since non-null anaphors do not have internal structure, *There* insertion should be inapplicable to them, and there should be no sentences corresponding to (10) with non-null anaphors.

In order to test this prediction directly, it would be necessary to construct a VP which can be the antecedent of the non-null anaphor *do so* and whose main verb allows *There* insertion to apply. I have been unable to discover such a construction. I have, however, found a slightly more complex case which tests the same phenomenon. Consider example (42).

(42) In the spring, certain trees *tend to be blooming*, and in the summer, others *do so*.

It seems that VP's with the main verb *tend* may serve as antecedents for *do so*. Further, *tend* requires the application of *It* replacement. Hence, if *There* insertion applies on the complement of *tend*, the surface subject of *tend* will be *there*. Such manipulations would not, of course, be possible within an unstructured anaphor, and this serves as a means of distinguishing empty structures from simple anaphors. My analysis predicts that *there* may be the subject of an empty VP whose antecedent's main verb is *tend*, but that *do so* may not have *there* as its subject under any circumstances. This prediction is borne out, as (43) shows.

> (43) (a) In the spring, there tend to be certain trees blooming, and in the summer there do, too.
>
> (b) *In the spring there *tend to be certain trees blooming*, and in the summer there *do so*, too.

(43a) is possible because *there* can be inserted into a lexically unfilled structure, subsequently getting raised by *It* replacement. No comparable derivation is possible in (43b), since *do so* is a base generated VP, and *do* does not permit *There* insertion.

Other evidence distinguishing null from non-null anaphors is given by Leben (1970). For example, (44) shows that non-null elements may differ from their antecedents with respect to passivization, while (45) shows this not to be the case for phonetically null anaphors.

> (44) (a) Angela's phone was tapped by FBI agents, and they tried to do it to me, too, but failed.
>
> (b) ?The cup was finally won by the Australians after trying to do so for 20 years.

> (45) (a) *My phone was tapped by the FBI, but the CIA wouldn't.
>
> (b) *The cup was finally won by the Australians after trying to for 20 years.

These facts would follow immediately from a theory which included the empty structures hypothesis instead of the transformation of VP deletion, but which treated forms like *do so* and *do it* as simple anaphors, not associated with any empty structures. This is because null anaphors would have to match their antecedents node by node, whereas the non-null anaphors would simply be associated with a single non-terminal node (such as VP).[19]

Further, Leben points out that (46a) is ambiguous, while (46b) is not.

> (46) (a) Kennedy always expected to be assassinated, but I never expected it.
>
> (b) Kennedy always expected to be assassinated, but I never did.

(46a) may mean either "I never expected Kennedy to be assassinated" or "I never expected to be assassinated," but (46b) has only the latter interpretation. If *it* in (46a) were part of an empty structure corresponding to the infinitive in the first clause, then (46a) and (46b) should be synonymous. If, on the other hand, *it* is assumed to be a simple pronoun, whose antecedent is [S △ be assassinated],[20] the interpretive principle outlined by Akmajian (1973) will correctly predict two readings for (46a).[21]

In sum, there are several differences between null and non-null anaphors which lend support to my hypotheses about their structures.

6. *Conclusion*

On the basis of the arguments in this chapter and the previous one, we can divide the phenomena traditionally handled by deletion or replacement transformations into three categories. First are the true deletions (such as Comparative deletion): these are unidirectional rules and obey the constraints proposed by Ross (1967a) and Chomsky (1971). Second are null anaphors, traditionally assumed to be the output of deletion transformations: null anaphors differ from non-null anaphors in that they have internal structure, to which syntactic and semantic rules may refer; they differ from true deletions in that the rules associating them with antecedents are bidirectional, immune to Ross' and Chomsky's constraints, and subject to a number of constraints characteristic of anaphora rules. Finally, there are the non-null anaphors: these have no internal structure and are governed by bidirectional anaphora rules immune to the constraints on other types of rules. The facts presented in this chapter and the previous one show that these three cases must be distinguished formally.

The analysis presented here effects this tripartite division as follows. First of all, a heterogeneous theory is adopted, in which anaphora rules may be distinguished as a separate category from other rule types, in particular from deletion and replacement transformations (but also from other types of interpretive rules). This category of rules is subject to different constraints from other categories. Secondly, the empty structures hypothesis makes the necessary distinctions between null and non-null anaphors.

No other analysis I have heard of makes the needed distinctions among these three types of phenomena. Further, I do not see how it would be possible to do so in a natural manner without adopting a heterogeneous theory of grammar.

NOTES

1 I should reiterate what I said in Chapter 3 about my use of the term "interpretive". I use this term to describe any theory in which anaphors are present in deep structure and are associated with antecedents by rules operating on derived structures. As is evident from my discussion in the previous chapter, I do not wish to claim that anaphora rules form a natural class with other categories of rules which I or others may refer to as interpretive (such as the rules for interpreting quantifiers and negatives). On the contrary, as I have said repeatedly, I consider anaphora rules to be an entirely separate rule type.

2 The critics I refer to (viz., Ross (1969) and Grinder and Postal (1971)) incorrectly conclude from their observations that null anaphors must be the result of deletion under identity. § 2 of this chapter shows how both deletion and their arguments can be avoided.

3 Specifically, Ross argues at length against a "straw man" analysis in which no anaphor is generated at all. The only such analysis whose existence I know of is Frieden's (1970). Since I consider such an approach untenable (for a variety of reasons, including those Ross mentions), I will not go into it.

4 I am only interested here in the non-specific interpretation of *a car*. If *a car* is interpreted specifically, then, (11a) is probably acceptable.

5 Jerry Katz first suggested this approach to me.

6 Full identity is not needed, since they may differ with respect to the presence of a negative element (see Chapter 5, § 1.5).

7 These diagrams are oversimplified in that (among other shortcomings) they do not show the syntactic features on the empty nodes. These features must match with those on the corresponding nodes of the antecedent.

8 Those negatives and modifiers which may be ignored for the purposes of anaphora (see Chapter 5, § 1.5) are, of course, not counterexamples to this account of (14).

9 Chomsky's proposal was that clauses containing violations of the Complex NP Constraint (or of his alternative to it) be marked with $\#$ (where surface structures containing $\#$ are deemed ungrammatical). Then the deletion rule could eliminate $\#$, along with the rest of the clause, and the difference between (25a) and (25b) is accounted for.

10 Unfortunately, this argument is weakened considerably by the fact that the Coordinate Structure Constraint and the Sentential Subject Constraint as stated ought to apply to empty structures, as well as to filled ones. Yet, my judgement is that examples lige (i) and (ii) do not sound nearly as bad as they should.
    (i) ??John is talking to Bill and someone, but I don't know who.
    (ii) ?John says that for me to meet someone would be very dangerous, but he won't say who.

11 Actually, (27b) is not an instance of simple VP deletion, since the auxiliary is gone, too. It is possible, therefore, that this argument does not apply to VP deletion. It does, however, apply to Sluicing.

12 This is the only argument I know of for treating Gapping as an anaphora rule. I know of no arguments against such a treatment, however.

13 (31a) shows that it is false to claim (as it sometimes has been) that comparatives exclude negatives.

14 I do not exclude the possibility that there may be additional, less general conditions on some anaphoric relations; for example, some of the conditions on pronominal anaphora discussed in Chapter 4 do not generalize to other anaphoric relations. I am claiming that all anaphoric relations should be handled by very similar rules, not that they can all be handled by a single rule.

15 If the notion of contrast is associated with contrastive stress, then Akmajian's principle cannot adequately account for (32b), since *John beats his wife* is probably not a constituent, but *Although nobody knows it* is not in contrast. This can be handled by the modification

of Akmajian's principle proposed in chapter 5, § 1.5, viz., that modifiers may optionally be ignored without contrast. In (32b), of course, the modifier (viz., the adverbial clause) *must* be ignored, since otherwise the interpretation of *it* leads to an infinite regress.

[16] Essentially the same argument is given by Bach, Bresnan, and Wasow (1974). Notice that although Comparative deletion does not allow sloppy identity, Comparative ellipsis (see Bresnan (1974)) does, as (i) shows.
 (i) John lost more of his books than Bill did.
This correlates with the fact that Comparative ellipsis, but not Comparative deletion may operate right-to-left, as in (ii).
 (ii) More men than women got jobs.

[17] Of course, a theory could be constructed in which non-null anaphors are themselves merely parts of larger, otherwise empty structures. For example, sentence (i) might possibly have a surface structure something like (ii).
 (i) John took LSD before Bill had done so.

(ii)

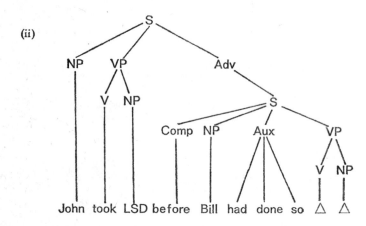

If such an analysis were correct, it would follow that the arguments for preferring the empty structures hypothesis to the nonexpansion hypothesis would also apply in sentences with non-null anaphors. It will be seen below that this is not the case. Moreover, such an analysis is highly implausible for syntactic reasons. For one thing, this would be the only case in English where *have* and *do* appear in the same auxiliary (although they may cooccur if either one is a main verb). If, however, *do so* is made part of the VP, then it ruins the necessary symmetry of the two VP's.

[18] Postal (1972b) has disputed Bresnan's version of this argument, but Bresnan (1972b) has answered Postal's criticisms quite convincingly.

[19] Note that a completely parallel account of the facts mentioned in Chapter 5, footnote 13 can be given. That is, null anaphors cannot ignore modifiers on their antecedents because this would leave the corresponding modifiers on the anaphors without an interpretation.

[20] For arguments indicating that Equi is an anaphora rule, i.e., that this is the appropriate structure, see Chapter 7.

[21] As for (46b), the empty structures hypothesis can handle it, if it is assumed (as it apparently must be — cf. Jackendoff (1972), Chapter 5) that verbs are marked in the lexicon for their control properties. Then the main verb of the empty VP in (46b) must share with *expect* the property of requiring its complement's subject, if empty, to be anaphorically related to the matrix agent. Formally, this would be a result either of the nondistinctness requirement obtaining between anaphor and antecedent (if the relevant feature is syntactic), or of the copying of the semantic material from the antecedent into the anaphor (if the feature is semantic).

Chapter 7

THE STATUS OF EQUI

0. *Introduction*

So far, very little has been said about Equi. There is an extensive literature on missing complement subjects, most of it assuming that a deletion-under-identity rule is involved. An interpretive alternative to this approach has been worked out in some detail by Jackendoff (1969, 1972). The main purpose of the present chapter is to evaluate the relative merits of these two approaches.

The task of deciding what kind of a rule Equi is has been complicated somewhat by several recent papers (Grinder (1970, 1971), Kimball (1971), Partee (1973), Tavakolian (1973)) suggesting that it may be necessary to postulate distinct rules to account for different cases of missing complement subjects. Tavakolian (1973) suggests that at least the following three cases must be distinguished: (i) missing subjects of infinitives which are controlled by (i.e., understood to be identical to) NP's in the next higher clause; (ii) missing subjects of infinitives controlled by NP's which are further away; and (iii) missing subjects of gerunds. For convenience, type (i) will be referred to as "classical Equi," type (ii) as "super Equi," and type (iii) as "gerundive Equi."

I will not go into the arguments that have been given for dealing with these three cases separately. It will be seen below that some arguments regarding the theoretical status of Equi fail to apply to all three cases. This in itself is sufficient reason for making these distinctions in the present context. My goal in this chapter is not to solve all of the many difficult problems connected with missing complement subjects, but, rather, simply to determine whether the rules involved should be deletion transformations or anaphora rules, or, perhaps, a mixture of the two. For this reason, I will skirt a number of important issues and assume without argument certain conclusions which have been established to my satisfaction elsewhere in the literature.

1. *Two Approaches to Equi*

Before attempting to choose between deletion and interpretation, I will sketch briefly the salient features of each approach. This should prove useful in deciding between them.

1.1 The deletion theory is quite straightforward. It asserts that complement subjects are present in underlying structure and that they can be deleted under identity with other NP's in the same sentence. Some attention has been given to the problem of specifying precisely what the necessary identity condition is (see Postal (1970b)), and it is widely agreed that identity of reference is involved. Far more research has been devoted to what has come to be referred to as the "control problem," viz., under identity with which NP's may a given complement subject be deleted? Some of the complications involved in the control problem are illustrated in (1)-(3).

(1) (a) John told Mary to buy a hat.
    (b) John promised Mary to buy a hat.

(2) (a) John asked Mary to leave.
    (b) John asked Mary when to leave.

(3) (a) After getting up, Mary called John.
    (b) After getting up, John was called by Mary.

In each of these examples, the controller in the (a) sentence is *Mary* and in the (b) sentence is *John*. The change in control is a function of different factors in these three cases, so it is evident that the control problem can have no simple solution. To date, no entirely satisfactory solution to the control problem has been found. In my opinion, the most promising work has been that of Jackendoff (1972, Chapter 5); since that work assumes an interpretive approach, its relative success is a reason for abandoning the deletion theory. Nevertheless, researchers who adopt the deletion approach have not felt it necessary to justify their use of a deletion transformation in dealing with these phenomena. Hence, their work deals almost exclusively with issues which are tangential to our concern here, namely the choice between approaches.

1.2 In contrast, Jackendoff has attempted to justify his decision to adopt an interpretive approach. His reasons, however, are primarily methodological; that is, his theory of grammar does not allow the operation of a syntactic transformation to be contingent on identity of reference, as a deletion approach to Equi would require. Since I reject this methodological argument (see Chapter 2, § 4.3), it will be necessary for me to find other grounds on which to base my decision.

Jackendoff's analysis of Equi consists essentially of the empty structures hypothesis applied to missing complement subjects.[1] Under his theory, complement subjects may be empty, if lexical insertion fails to apply to them.

Empty complement subjects will be assigned antecedents by an anaphora rule. Verbs are lexically marked for control properties; that is, the lexical entry for a verb will indicate which NP's in the sentence the subject of the complement may be anaphorically related to, if that subject is empty. The NP's are identified in these lexical markings in terms of what Jackendoff (following Gruber (1965)) calls "thematic relations." Since it is not my purpose here to consider the control problem, I will not go into this matter of lexically marked control properties any further; the interested reader should consult Jackendoff (1972), Chapter 5. For our purposes, all we really need to know about Jackendoff's system is that he generates empty NP's in complement subject position and assigns antecedents to them by means of an anaphora rule.

2. Choosing Between the Theories

2.1 Turning now to the problem of deciding which of the two approaches sketched above is to be adopted, let us examine first the question of what sorts of considerations might enter into our decision. In other words, do the theories make different predictions, and, if so, what are the differences?

One obvious test to use in choosing between deletion and anaphora is discussed at length in Chapter 5, § 2. It is argued there that deletions are subject to a variety of constraints to which anaphora rules are immune. Hence, the applicability of Ross' (1967a) and Chomsky's (1971) constraints is one important criterion for choosing between the two approaches to Equi.

Similarly, directionality may serve as a criterion for distinguishing transformations from anaphora rules: the latter are characteristically bidirectional, whereas other categories of rules (in particular, deletions) are unidirectional. The directionality of Equi may therefore be a clue as to its status.

Another consideration which could help us to decide is the question of whether Equi is optional or obligatory. It turns out, as we shall see below, that at least some types of Equi may be either optional or obligatory, depending on the matrix verb. Assuming that verbs must be lexically marked with respect to the obligatoriness of Equi, then the two theories must employ rather different devices in order to accomplish this marking. In the case of the deletion theory, individual verbs would be assigned rule features (see Lakoff (1965)); that is, a verb whose complement obligatorily undergoes Equi would be marked with a feature [+Equi], indicating that the normally optional rule of Equi is obligatory for sentences with this matrix verb. Under the interpretive theory, obligatoriness of Equi would be marked with a subcategorization feature indicating that the complement subject must be empty. That is, the lexical entries for the verbs would contain a feature $[+ \underline{\quad\quad} [_S [_{NP} \triangle] \, X]]$, indicating that lexical insertion is forbidden in the subjects of complements to these verbs. This will have the desired effect, since empty nodes must be given an interpretation, in order for the sentences in which they appear to be grammatical. Since the need for rule features is dubious (see Chapter 1, § 3), this difference immediately suggests that the interpretive theory is to be adopted, if possible. There is, however, a more interesting and substantial consequence of the different devices the two theories employ in this connection. The feature [+ Equi] in the deletion theory requires Equi to apply if its structural description is met; but when the complement subject is distinct from any other NP in the sentence the rule would be inapplicable. Hence, under the deletion theory, the complements to verbs requiring Equi would allow surface structure subjects, so long as these subjects were distinct from NP's in controller positions. In the interpretive theory, on the other hand, obligatory Equi is effected by making complement subjects obligatorily empty. This means that no lexical insertion may take place in the affected complement subjects. Hence, under the interpretive theory, the complements to verbs requiring Equi would never allow surface structure subjects. This provides a concrete test for choosing between analyses.

A final difference between the theories which might provide a basis for choosing is the fact that the deletion theory entails that, after Equi has applied, the affected complements are truly subjectless, lacking even an NP node in subject position. In contrast, the empty subject postulated by the interpretive theory remains throughout the derivation. Hence, the behavior of late rules with respect to subjectless complements might provide evidence for choosing between the theories.

2.2 Evidence

2.2.1 Let us first consider gerundive Equi. It is well known that gerundive Equi is bidirectional. This is illustrated in (4).

> (4) (a) Losing the race upset John.
> (b) John regretted losing the race.

This immediately suggests that gerundive Equi should be handled by an anaphora rule, i.e., that the interpretive approach is to be preferred.

Unfortunately, the evidence regarding the applicability of Ross' and Chomsky's constraints to gerundive Equi is considerably less clear. Speakers vary significantly in their judgements of the relevant examples. (The parenthetical expressions following the examples indicate the constraint involved).

> (5) (a) ?John accepted the conclusion that perjuring himself had endangered Mary. (Complex NP Constraint).[2]
> (b) ?John tried both honesty and perjuring himself. (Coordinate

Structure Constraint).[3]
- (c) Perjuring himself upset John. (Sentential Subject Constraint).
- (d) ??John obeyed the State's laws against perjuring himself. (Specified Subject Constraint).

With the exception of (5c), none of these is quite good enough to support the interpretive theory nor bad enough to support the deletion theory, so Ross' and Chomsky's constraints are not much help deciding which approach to take to gerundive Equi.

The interpretive theory receives strong support from considerations of obligatoriness and optionality. A number of verbs, including *abhor, celebrate, consider, curse, discuss, dislike, preclude, protest, resent,* and *welcome,* take gerundive complements whose subjects may optionally be missing. The complement subjects may or may not be identical to some other NP in the sentence.

(6)

John $\begin{Bmatrix} \text{abhored} \\ \text{celebrated} \\ \text{considered} \\ \text{cursed} \\ \text{discussed} \\ \text{disliked} \\ \text{precluded} \\ \text{protested} \\ \text{resented} \\ \text{welcomed} \end{Bmatrix}$ $\begin{Bmatrix} \text{(a) winning the prize.} \\ \text{(b) } his \text{ winning the prize.} \\ \text{(c) Mary's winning the prize.} \end{Bmatrix}$

Other verbs, including *attempt, avoid, begin, continue, deny, disavow, eschew, resist,* and *try* take subjectless gerundive complements. Their complements may not have lexically filled subjects; neither anaphoric pronouns nor full NP's may appear as subjects of their complements.[4]

(7)

John $\begin{Bmatrix} \text{attempted} \\ \text{avoided} \\ \text{began} \\ \text{continued} \\ \text{denied} \\ \text{disavowed} \\ \text{eschewed} \\ \text{resisted} \\ \text{tried} \end{Bmatrix}$ $\begin{Bmatrix} \text{(a) perjuring himself.} \\ \text{(b) *} his \text{ perjuring himself.} \\ \text{(c) *Mary's perjuring herself.} \end{Bmatrix}$

The intrepretive analysis of gerundive Equi makes the correct predictions here; the deletion analysis, in contrast, predicts that examples like (7c) should be grammatical. Under the deletion analysis, the verbs in (7) are marked [+ Equi]. This forces Equi to apply where its structural description is met, thus accounting for (7b), but it does not account for the ill-formedness of (7c), in which Equi is inapplicable, for lack of identity between the complement subject and a controller.[5] The interpretive theory, on the other hand, rules out (7b) by assigning to the verbs in question the feature [+ ―― [$_S$ [$_{NP}$ $\triangle$] X]]; this forbids lexical insertion into the complement, thereby preventing the generation of (7c) at the same time.[6] The contrast between (6) and (7) therefore serves as a strong argument for the interpretive approach to gerundive Equi.

The last argument I know of bearing on the theoretical status of gerundive Equi has to do with the interpretation of negation. The argument is not terribly compelling, for it is predicated on two rather controversial assumptions. The first assumption is that the scope of negative elements is determined no earlier than at the end of the transformational cycle; that is, I assume that the interpretive rule for negation is either cyclic, following all cyclic syntactic transformations, or post-cyclic. This assumption is based on the work of Jackendoff (1969, 1972) and Lasnik (1972), both of whom argue for its correctness. My second assumption is that Ross' (1967a) proposed convention of "tree pruning" is correct, i.e., that non-branching S-nodes are automatically removed from phrase structure trees. As I already remarked, neither of these assumptions is universally accepted,[7] so the argument based on them is very provisional. However, since it is not a critical argument for me, I will not attempt to justify these assumptions.

Putting aside such reservations for the moment, let me sketch the argument. It is widely agreed that the scope of negation may include only items commanded by the negative element. In other words, the scope of negation includes only material in the same clause as or "lower" clauses than the negative element. If the pruning convention is correct, then a deletion rule of Equi should cause command relations to change: by removing the subject of a complement clause, it leaves an S-node exhaustively dominating VP, and therefore subject to pruning. Hence, the deletion theory of Equi will make different predictions about the scope of negation from the interpretive theory.

Let us now look at some specific examples. Consider, first of all, sentence (8) (originally due to G. Lakoff).

(8) George doesn't beat his wife because he loves her.

This sentence has two readings, one synonymous with (9a), the other with (9b).

(9) (a) Not because he loves her does George beat his wife.

(b) Because he loves her, George doesn't beat his wife.

In the reading of sentence (8) synonymous with (9a), the adverbial clause, *because he loves her*, is inside the scope of negation; in the other reading, it is outside. Now consider (10).

(10) George considered not beating his wife because he loves her.

If gerundive Equi were a deletion rule, then its operation would cause pruning, putting *not* in the matrix clause. Hence, *not* would command the adverbial, and (10) would allow a reading in which the adverbial is inside the scope of negation, viz., a reading synonymous with (11).

(11) Not because he loves her did George consider beating his wife.

However, (10) has no such reading: it cannot be interpreted to mean the same as (11). This suggests that the gerund phrase in (10), *not beating his wife*, is still immediately dominated by S at the level at which the scope of negation is determined. Given our assumption that scope of negation is determined either post-cyclically or at the end of the cycle, it follows that the scope of *not* in (10) would have to be determined after the operation of all transformational rules to (10); in particular, the determination of scope of negation would follow a deletion rule of Equi. Therefore, under our assumptions, if gerundive Equi were a deletion rule, then (10) could be synonymous with (11).

Under an interpretive analysis, of course, the relevant S node does branch, so pruning would never take place, and the scope of negation in (10) could not include the adverbial.

We see, then, that under certain plausible (but controversial) assumptions, the deletion approach to gerundive Equi leads us to predict wrongly that (10) will have a reading synonymous with (11). Since the interpretive theory does not make this prediction, the fact that the prediction is not borne out supports the interpretive approach.

All of the arguments I have been able to discover bearing on the choice between treating gerundive Equi as a deletion or anaphora rule support the latter alternative. The deletion approach appears to create syntactic, semantic, and methodological difficulties which do not arise in the interpretive theory. Gerundive Equi, then, appears to be an anaphora rule, and not a deletion rule.

2.2.2 Let us now turn our attention to super Equi, viz., missing infinitival subjects whose controllers are not in the next clause up the tree. Grinder (1970) first discussed these cases, proposing a deletion analysis. Kimball (1971) argued that Grinder's Super Equi transformation should be replaced by a rule deleting dative phrases, i.e., phrases of the form *to NP* or *for NP*.

That is, Kimball claims that a sentence like (12a), which Grinder derives from something like (12b) by Super Equi, should be derived from something like (12c), with classical Equi deleting him_1 under identity with him_2, and Dative deletion deleting him_2 under identity with *John*.

(12) (a) John claims that it would be distasteful to perjure himself.
   (b) *John* claims that it would be distasteful for *him* to perjure himself.
   (c) *John* claims that it would be distasteful to him_2 for him_1 to perjure himself.

Grinder (1971) attempts to refute Kimball's analysis. Which (if either) analysis is correct is of no great import for our purposes, for either Super Equi or Dative deletion could be reformulated as an anaphora rule. Hence, we can ask whether such a reformulation is desirable without having settled the dispute between Grinder and Kimball.[8] However, since the dative phrases Kimball postulates are not in the same clause with the missing complement subjects, we must be careful to construct our arguments in such a way that they will apply to either analysis. With this caution in mind, let us turn to the arguments bearing on the decision between the deletion and interpretive approaches to super Equi.

Observe, first of all, that super Equi is bidirectional.

(13) (a) John was angry because it was necessary to perjure himself.
   (b) Because it was necessary to perjure himself, John was angry.
   (c) John was annoyed that it was impossible to protect himself.
   (d) That it was impossible to protect himself annoyed John.

This suggests that super Equi should be analyzed as an anaphora rule.

Ross' and Chomsky's constraints provide additional support for the interpretive approach. Super Equi appears to be immune to all of the constraints, with the possible exception of the Right Roof Constraint.

(14) (a) John resented the fact that it was necessary to perjure himself. (Complex NP Constraint)
   (b) John remarked that time was short and that it was impossible to extricate himself quickly. (Coordinate Structure Constraint)
   (c) That it was necessary to perjure himself upset John. (Sentential Subject Constraint)
   (d) ?The fact that John was implicated was no reason to perjure himself. (Right Roof Constraint[9])
   (e) John ignored Mary's admonition not to perjure himself. (Specified Subject Constraint)

On the basis of the criteria developed in Chapter 5, then, super Equi would appear to be best treated as an anaphora rule.

Unfortunately, our test based on obligatoriness is inapplicable, since super Equi appears to be optional in all cases. The argument based on the interpretation of negatives, however, does carry over to super Equi, on the assumption that Kimball is wrong, i.e., that there are no missing dative phrases (only missing complement subjects) in the relevant examples.

(15a) is ambiguous between readings synonymous with (15b) and (15c), just as (8) was ambiguous.[10]

> (15) (a) George claims that it isn't necessary to beat his wife because he loves her.
>
> (b) George claims that it is not because he loves her that it is necessary to beat his wife.
>
> (c) George claims that it is because he loves her that it isn't necessary to beat his wife.

The deletion theory of super Equi would predict that pruning should occur in (16a), allowing a reading synonymous with (16b); the interpretive theory would allow no such reading.

> (16) (a) George claims that it is necessary not to beat his wife because he loves her.
>
> (b) George claims that it is not because he loves her that it is necessary to beat his wife.

The impossibility of this interpretation of (16a) lends some support to the interpretive approach.

Thus, with super Equi, as with gerundive Equi, what evidence there is supports the adoption of an interpretive approach.

2.2.3 Preliminary as my conclusions regarding the status of gerundive and super Equi are, they are based on substantially stronger evidence than I have been able to discover in connection with classical Equi. My only really unequivocal piece of evidence regarding classical Equi is the fact that it is bidirectional.

> (17) (a) It would disgust John to cover himself with butter.
>
> (b) To cover himself with butter would disgust John.[11]

This supports an interpretive analysis of classical Equi.

The test based on Ross' and Chomsky's constraints is only partially applicable, since the restricted environment of classical Equi excludes the environments necessary for testing the applicability of some of the constraints. The Complex NP Constraint, for example, could never apply to classical Equi

for the simple reason that classical Equi only applies to subjects of the complements to main verbs of the clause containing the controller, whereas the
Complex NP Constraint could only apply if the missing subject were contained in a complex NP not containing the controller. These two environments are mutually exclusive. The only two constraints whose environments
do not automatically exclude classical Equi are the Coordinate Structure Constraint and the Sentential Subject Constraint. Unfortunately, even limiting
ourselves to these two constraints, the results we get on this test are not
entirely unequivocal.

(18) (a) ?John wants very much to exonerate himself and for you
           to believe his story. (Coordinate Structure Constraint)

      (b) To perjure himself would never occur to John. (Sentential
           Subject Constraint)

Similar ambiguity arises in connection with the test based on obligatoriness
or optionality of Equi. At first glance, classical Equi seems to be always
obligatory (with those verbs with allow classical Equi at all).

(19) (a)

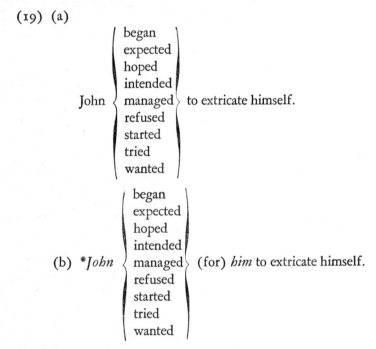

There is, however, an independent reason for excluding (19b), namely, the
constraint (given in Chapter 2 as (41) and discussed in Chapter 2, § 3)
requiring NP's separated only by a verb (plus an optional preposition) to
have non-intersecting reference. Hence, (19b) is not really evidence for the

obligatoriness of classical Equi. This complicates somewhat the application of this argument to classical Equi — but it does not make it impossible.

Notice that the verbs in (19) fall into two classes: those allowing complement subjects and those whose complements are always subjectless.[12]

(20)

(a) John $\begin{Bmatrix} \text{expected} \\ \text{hoped for} \\ \text{intended for} \\ \text{wanted} \end{Bmatrix}$ Mary to extricate herself.

(b) *John $\begin{Bmatrix} \text{began} \\ \text{managed} \\ \text{refused} \\ \text{started} \\ \text{tried} \end{Bmatrix}$ (for) Mary to extricate herself.

Under the interpretive analysis, the verbs in (20a) optionally allow lexical insertion into their complements' subjects, whereas the verbs in (20b) prohibit lexical insertion in this position.[13] Thus the interpretive approach accounts quite naturally for the existence of both classes of verbs illustrated in (20). The deletion theory of classical Equi, in constrast, cannot account for the existence of verbs like (20b), except by means of the extensions of that theory noted in footnote 5. It seems, therefore, that the interpretive approach to classical Equi provides a more satisfactory account of the existence of verbs like those in (20b) than does the deletion approach.

The argument based on the scope of negation and tree pruning carries over without significant modification to classical Equi. If classical Equi were a deletion rule, then its operation would cause pruning, and negative elements in infinitives would command adverbials in the matrix clause. As with the other types of Equi, a deletion analysis of classical Equi therefore predicts incorrectly that (21a) can have a reading synonymous with (21b).

(21) (a) George wants not to beat his wife because he loves her.
(b) Not because he loves her does George want to beat his wife.[14]

Under the interpretive analysis pruning does not take place, so this incorrect prediction is avoided. As before, the interpretive analysis appears slightly preferable.

Another argument can be constructed along similar lines using the rule for the interpretation of reciprocals discussed by Fiengo and Lasnik (1973). This rule must be ordered after classical Equi, for the rule of Pseudocleft sentence formation precedes the reciprocal rule but follows Equi. This can be seen from the following examples.

(22) (a) John wants to save himself.
      (b) What John wants is to save himself.

(23) (a) A spitz and a chow attacked each other.
      (b) *What attacked each other were a spitz and a chow.

(22) shows that classical Equi precedes Pseudocleft sentence formation; if pseudocleft sentences were formed before classical Equi applied, (22b) could not be derived, for the structural description of classical Equi would not be met. If classical Equi applies first, however, then (22b) can be derived from (22a) by Pseudocleft sentence formation. By the same token, the ill-formed-ness of (23b) shows that the reciprocal interpretation rule follows Pseudo-cleft sentence formation; if the reciprocal rule applied first, then (23b) could be derived from the well-formed (23a). Hence, assuming linear ordering of rules, the reciprocal rule must follow Equi.

Now consider the following examples.

(24) (a) *John and Bill expected Mary to entertain each other.
      (b) Mary expected John and Bill to entertain each other.

(25) (a) *John and Bill told Mary to entertain each other.
      (b) Mary told John and Bill to entertain each other.

(26) (a) John and Bill promised Mary to entertain each other.
      (b) *Mary promised John and Bill to entertain each other.

The judgements in (26) are the reverse of those in (24) and (25). This correlates with the fact that *promise* differs from most other verbs in that its subject is always the controller, even if an object is present. (24)-(26) indicate that the complement subject of such sentences must be plural or have a plural controller, in order for the interpretation of *each other* to be possible.

This means that the reciprocal rule must have available to it information regarding the number of the complement subject. If classical Equi is formu-lated as a deletion rule, this leads to an ordering paradox. On the one hand, the reciprocal rule must have available to it information which is eliminated by Equi (viz., information about the number of the complement subject); this forces us to order Equi after the reciprocal rule. On the other hand, we know that the reciprocal rule must follow classical Equi.

Under the interpretive analysis, this problem does not arise, for the empty complement subjects will be marked for number.[15] This allows the reciprocal rule to refer to the number of the complement subject; its ordering relative to classical Equi is irrelevant, since an interpretive Equi would not affect the presence of the feature indicating number.

Thus, facts like (24)-(26) support an interpretive approach to classical

Equi.[16] In fact, all of the arguments I have been able to discover concerning the status of classical Equi support an interpretive approach.

3. *Conclusion*

The evidence I have been able to adduce, while admittedly not over-whelming, is certainly consistent: every argument I have discovered bearing on the status of the various kinds of Equi favors the interpretive approach over a deletion theory. This is consistent with my initial observation that work within the interpretive theory has produced the most promising pro-posals to date for dealing with the control problem.

Much more work needs to be done on the question of missing complement subjects, for there remain many knotty problems to be solved in connection with them. My purpose in this chapter has merely been to decide between two possible methods of approaching these problems. The conclusion the evidence points to is clear: Equi should be formulated as an anaphora rule, subject to the constraints applicable to anaphora rules and immune from the known constraints on other categories of rules.

NOTES

[1] This is a slightly misleading way of putting the matter, since Jackendoff's work on Equi predates the empty structures hypothesis. In fact, the latter was modelled after the former. Moreover, Jackendoff's work on Equi goes into considerably more detail than work on the empty structures hypothesis.

[2] Other examples involving the Complex NP Constraint are worse.
　　(i) ?*John insulted the woman who had favored perjuring himself.
Perhaps the ungrammaticality of (i) results from the fact (pointed out to me by Noam Chomsky) that it violates the Specified Subject Constraint, as well as the Complex Noun Phrase Constraint.

[3] I have no explanation for the difference between (i) and (ii), which might be taken as involving the Coordinate Structure Constraint.
　　(i) *John* resented *his* and Mary's being left out.
　　(ii) *John resented and Mary's being left out.

[4] I am indebted to Robert Fiengo for pointing facts like these out to me.

[5] Proponents of the deletion theory have proposed ways of dealing with (7). Perlmutter (1968) suggests that a deep structure constraint requires identity between the subject and complement subject of verbs such as those in (7), thus ruling out (7c). Lakoff (1965) suggests instead that these verbs are "positive absolute exceptions"; that is, he proposes that lexical entries for these verbs contain features which require that they fit the structural description of and undergo the transformation of Equi. In other words, Lakoff proposes marking the ungrammaticality of examples like (7c) in the lexicon. These proposals are clearly ad hoc extensions of the deletion theory intended to account for (7c). The interpretive theory, in contrast, automatically predicts that examples like (7c) will be deviant for the same reason that examples like (7b) are.

[6] The existence of examples like (i) is a serious problem for this analysis, since it is the derived subject (not the deep structure subject) of the complement which is empty here.

(i) John tried to be interviewed by a reporter.

It has been pointed out to me by Joan Bresnan that such examples cease to be a problem if it is assumed that lexical insertion is cyclic, occuring at the beginning of each cycle. I know of no reason to reject such an analysis, although I have not explored the matter in detail. Notice, incidentally, that (i) is also a problem for any analysis which proposed to generate the complements in (7) as subjectless VP's. Similar comments hold of (ii).

(ii) John tries to be easy to understand.

[7] Actually, the claim that the interpretation of negatives takes place late is less controversial than it might at first seem, for the existing generative semantic treatments of negation (especially Lakoff (1969)) postulate derivational constraints which involve levels close to surface structure. I believe that the present argument can be maintained even under Lakoff's analysis. Of course, Lakoff would undoubtedly reject the conclusion that the facts in question support an interpretive analysis.

[8] Partee (1973) and Tavakolian (1973) point out that all of Grinder's (1971b) examples in his attempted refutation of Kimball's analysis involve gerunds. Kimball's arguments with respect to infinitival complements have thus gone unanswered.

[9] (14d) shows the immunity of super Equi to the Right Roof Constraint only under the assumption that a dative phrase (as well as a complement subject) is missing. If we reject the dative analysis (i.e., Kimball's reanalysis of super Equi), then the missing element (viz., the infinitival subject) is not in a higher sentence than its controller. Since the various forms of Equi (aside from Kimball's reanalysis) account only for missing *complement* subjects, they cannot be tested for the applicability of the Right Roof Constraint.

[10] There are undoubtedly several other interpretations of (15a) which need not concern us here.

[11] Tavakolian (1973) points out that sentences like (17b) are impossible without a modal, as (i) shows.

(i) *To cover himself with butter disgusted John.

Tavakolian suggests that this indicates that backwards classical Equi is possible only in sentences with modals. However, sentences (ii) and (iii) suggest that Equi is not a factor in the deviance of (i).

(ii) For Bill to cover himself with butter would disgust John.

(iii) *For Bill to cover himself with butter disgusted John.

Rather, I suspect that the need for a modal in sentences with initial infinitival complements is a function of the semantic content of the *for-to* complementizer (see Bresnan (1972a)).

[12] I ignore here the questions of whether Raising into object position exists and, if so, where it applies. The important point here is that some verbs give evidence of allowing lexically filled complement subjects in underlying structure, but others do not.

[13] Alternatively, the verbs in (20b) might take bare VP complements. There are difficulties entailed by both of these analyses, such as accounting for the existence of examples like (i).

$$\text{(i) John} \left\{ \begin{array}{l} \text{began} \\ \text{managed} \\ \text{refused} \\ \text{?started} \\ \text{tried} \end{array} \right\} \left\{ \begin{array}{l} \text{to appear to be happy} \\ \text{to be heard (??by the audience)} \end{array} \right\} .$$

The approach mentioned in footnote 6 seems to me to be the most promising solution to this problem.

[14] This argument can be circumvented by supposing that the negative in the infinitive is not part of the complement VP. In this case, the presence of the negative would block pruning. Notice however that such a way out would not be very plausible for (i), which behaves exactly like (21a) with respect to the relevant phenomenon.

(i) George tries to not beat his wife because he loves her.

15 Although I have not explicitly said so up to now, an interpretive analysis of Equi, in conjunction with Helke's analysis of reflexivization as a copying rule (see Chapter 2, § 3) requires that empty NP nodes include features of person, number, and gender. Otherwise, such examples as (i) would be indistinguishable from (ii).

    (i) John wanted to help himself.

        I enjoy gnashing my teeth.

        John thinks it is important to protect himself.

    (ii) *John wanted to help yourself.

        *I enjoy gnashing our teeth.

        *John thinks it is important to protect herself.

Generating syntactic features independently of (or prior to) lexical insertion is certainly no novelty (cf. Chomsky (1965) or Postal (1966)), and does not appear to pose any particular problems.

16 A completely parallel argument could be constructed using the rule for interpreting *respectively* in place of the reciprocal rule, if there is a good argument that *respectively* interpretation must follow classical Equi. Since I know of no such argument, I have not presented the *respectively* examples.

Chapter 8

CONCLUSIONS

1. *Summary*

Aside from providing a critical review of portions of the existing literature on anaphora — especially pronominal anaphora — my purpose in writing this monograph is to put forward an extended argument for a heterogeneous theory of language — that is, a theory in which grammars consist of a number of distinct components, each of which can perform only a narrowly circumscribed set of operations. In particular, I have argued that anaphora rules constitute one of these components.

The crux of my argument for such a theory is presented in Chapter 5; there I enumerate a number of properties of anaphora rules which establish their similarity to one another and their distinctness from other types of rules which have been studied. Supporting evidence is presented in Chapters 3, 4, and 6, where I discuss a number of the conditions necessary for an adequate treatment of anaphora. In Chapter 3 I show that one of these conditions is that anaphors be present in deep structure, and in Chapter 6 I show that this may be maintained even for phonetically null anaphors if we allow lexically empty syntactic structures to be generated. Given these conditions, the only existing work on anaphora which could possibly provide an adequate account is the work of interpretivists, although, as I have repeatedly pointed out, I reject the notion that anaphora rules and other kinds of interpretive rules constitute a natural class.

My motivation for presenting this argument, and my reason for advocating a heterogeneous linguistic theory is my concern with what Chomsky has referred to as "the fundamental problem of linguistic theory," namely developing a theory restrictive enough to account for the ease and speed with which children acquire language, yet rich enough to be consistent with the variety of existing natural languages. The greatest shortcoming of generative grammar has been its failure to come closer to solving this fundamental problem. It is my hope that a sufficiently well worked out heterogeneous theory might succeed where the more homogeneous theories of the past have failed.

Observe that this stand commits me to the position that the constraints on the various categories of rules which a heterogeneous theory postulates reflect the properties of the innate linguistic faculty of human beings. If these constraints were not assumed to be innate, then their existence would in no way help us to explain children's succeess at language acquisition. In other words, a theory which limits the class of possible human languages only explains language acquisition if it is assumed that children learning languages can ignore the possibility that the languages they are learning are not members of this class. If the constraints are to explain language acquisition, they must facilitate learning by eliminating some logically possible hypotheses; but in order to do this, the constraints must be available to the child. From this (plus the fact that they are not consciously known) it follows that they must be manifestations of innate mechanisms.

If the constraints on the various components of a heterogeneous theory have an innate basis, then they must be universal. In particular, my remarks commit me to the position that the properties I have identified as being characteristic of anaphora rules must be universal.[1] Of course, this is a claim which must ultimately be checked against evidence from languages other than English. Even in the absence of such independent confirmation, however, there is reason to believe that many of the conditions governing anaphora may be universal. Specifically, it has been pointed out by Witten (1970) that traditional grammar books and courses of instruction in foreign languages almost never include anything about anaphora. Certainly, conditions like the precede-command condition, the Transitivity Condition, and the Novelty Constraint are never mentioned — much less the immunity of anaphora to other constraints. Since observance of these conditions is essential to proper use and understanding of anaphoric expressions, and since mastery of anaphora is a crucial aspect of learning a language, the failure of language instruction texts to discuss them is all the more noteworthy. The natural conclusion to draw is that properties of anaphora are not mentioned in grammar books because nobody ever thought it necessary to mention them; and this could only be the case if anaphora rules for different languages are extremely similar. In short, the fact that anaphora rules are not given in language instruction manuals or courses supports the idea, to which my position commits me, that the properties of anaphoric relations and the constraints governing anaphora rules are largely universal.

2. *Form vs. Function*

By taking such a strongly nativist position and viewing linguistic research as an attempt to understand the innate basis of language acquisition, I have naturally been led to emphasize form over function. Postulating innate mechanisms in order to account for language acquisition is motivated in large part by the formal complexity of languages, so attempts to specify manifestations of these mechanisms naturally tend to concentrate on structural properties of language.

This has certainly been the case in the present monograph. The properties I cite in arguing for the unity and distinctness of anaphora have no obvious functional basis, and I feel no obligation to try to provide one. It is by no means clear how — or indeed even whether — the precede-command condition or the Novelty Constraint, for example, facilitate efficient communication, but assuming that they are universal can help us to account for the mystery of language acquisition. The question of whether all structural properties of language have a functional explanation is one which I feel linguists are at present unprepared to answer; but it is independent of the "fundamental problem." I can see no justification for dogmatic insistence that the form of language must be explicable in terms of its function (cf. Lakoff (1973) or Premack (1972)).

It is largely for this reason that I have avoided the terms "coreference" and "ellipsis" which most generative grammarians use in connection with the phenomena I have been discussing. While definite pronouns do function as indicators of coreference, so do reflexives and reciprocals; but despite this similarity of function, there are strong reasons for handling these phenomena in formally different ways (see Chapter 2, § 3). Similarly, though empty VP's and deleted comparatives may both serve to reduce redundancy, there are strong reasons for distinguishing between the types of devices employed in accounting for them (see Chapter 5). Further, emphasizing function makes it difficult or impossible to handle diverse kinds of anaphors uniformly, for some represent "coreference" and others represent "ellipsis." In fact, ordinary definite anaphoric pronouns may serve two distinct functions, namely, indicating identity of sense, as in (1a) (due to Karttunen), or indicating identity of reference, as in (1b).

(1) (a) The man who gave *his paycheck* to his wife was wiser than
           the man who gave *it* to his mistress.
     (b) *Every true patriot* honors *his* country's flag.

In (1a), the most natural interpretation is that *it* refers to the second man's paycheck, whereas *his paycheck* refers to the first man's; the pronoun *it* appears instead of a repetition of the phrase *his paycheck*, but it does not share the reference of the first occurrence of that phrase. In (1b), on the other hand, the pronoun cannot be replaced by a repetition of its antecedent, for the sentence makes no claims about whether patriots honor the flags of other patriots' countries. It would, however, be a mistake to argue that two separate kinds of devices are needed in order to account for these different functions of pronominal anaphora; this would make it impossible to capture the fact that the assignment of antecedents to pronouns seems to be essentially independent of their function (however, see Chapter 4, § 2.2).

I am not, of course, denying that there are significant generalizations about function, nor that it is important to consider them. Rather, I am asserting that form and function are two largely independent considerations in linguistics, and that to assume that every formal property has a functional basis can obscure important generalizations. Only by ignoring the functions of anaphora have I been able to treat the problem of identifying possible antecedents independently of the question of how the meanings of anaphor and antecedent are related. But the variety of ways in which the meanings may be related obscures the fundamental unity of different anaphoric relations. I hope that future work may account for the differences in function as well as the similarities of form. In order to account for language acquisition, however, a theory of language must exploit these formal regularities.

3. Formalization

With all this talk about formal properties of language, my critics will undoubtedly say, isn't it peculiar that my rules, constraints, and generalizations have been stated informally in ordinary language, and not formalized in some rigorous mathematical notation?

The best reply to this line of criticism, it seems to me, is to quote from a talk given by Jerome Letvin at Hampshire College in the spring of 1973: "Premature formalization," he said, "is like pornography in the hands of a two-year old." Of course, it would be easy to invent notational conventions for stating anaphora rules or constraints on them, but to do so would be a meaningless exercise unless the notation itself helped to reveal previously hidden regularities in the structure of language. A useful formalization embodies a theory, so certain theoretical insights necessarily precede the development of notational conventions.

The prime example of an enlightening use of notation is in phonological theory. Phonologists spend a large part of their energy on exploring the consequences of various notational conventions and proposing modifications in their formalism which will better bring out the fundamental generalizations about language. Over the years, this has proved to be a very worthwhile activity, providing a good deal of insight into the sound patterns of languages.

In syntax and semantics, in contrast, there has been a steady drift away from stating rules formally and discussing notational conventions. I believe that there is good reason for this trend. Our understanding of the structure and functions of language is in such a primitive state of development that insistence on rigorous formalizations would be premature. This is not to deny that it is always necessary to be as explicit and precise about one's claims as possible. However, it is my opinion that few of the notational systems for syntax or semantics proposed by linguists in recent years (e.g., those in Chomsky (1957), Katz & Fodor (1963), or Lakoff (1970b)) have provided us with much insight into the structure of language.[2] Hence, I do not regard the move away from formalization in syntax and semantics as a bad thing. Nor do I feel it necessary to apologize for the lack of formalization in the present work. Rather, I regard this monograph as part of the groundwork necessary for the development of a formalism adequate for the representation of anaphora. And I would, of course, welcome any notational proposals which shed light on the nature of anaphoric relations.

4. A Speculation

In closing, I would like to consider one final question. If my conclusions in this monograph are correct, then anaphoric relations are governed by rules whose formal properties are radically different from those of any other kind of grammatical rule which has been studied within the framework of generative grammar. It is striking, for example, that there are constraints which seem to govern every known type of rule except anaphora rules (see Chapter 5, § 2). It is natural to ask why anaphora rules are so different. What gives anaphora its distinctive character, relative to other known categories of rules?

I do not pretend to have a complete answer to this question. Indeed, as my discussion of form and function above indicates, I believe that the ultimate answer may come from neurophysiology — that is, that the final answer may be that anaphora's uniqueness reflects something about the structure of the human nervous system. However, there is one fact about anaphora that sets it apart from almost all else which has been studied by generative grammarians, and which hence might be responsible for its apparent uniqueness. I refer to the fact that anaphora is in large part a discourse phenomenon. Whereas such well-studied phenomena as word order or scope of negation and quantifiers are restricted to single sentences, all of the anaphoric relations discussed here may involve elements not in the same sentence. Compare, for example, VP anaphora and Comparative deletion: the antecedent of one speaker's empty VP may be in another speaker's sentence, but Comparative deletion is restricted to a single speaker's sentence. Thus, the exchange in (2) is perfectly normal, but the exchange in (3) constitues an interruption.

(2) Speaker A: John might be leaving soon.
    Speaker B: He can't be.
(3) Speaker A: John might be leaving sooner.
    Speaker B: Than you think.

(2) consists of two sentences with an anaphoric relation (actually two)

holding between them; (3) is an anomalous situation because it consists of a single sentence spoken in parts by two speakers. However, this is the only possible interpretation of (3), because deletions are restricted to single sentences. Thus, the superficial similarity of VP anaphora and Comparative deletion as two instances of ellipsis is deceptive, since one is a discourse phenomenon, while the other is restricted to single sentences.

Notice that even Equi may be a discourse phenomenon at times.

(4) Speaker A: John will lie in court tomorrow.
     Speaker B: To perjure himself would be a mistake.

The apparent uniqueness of anaphora rules, then, might just be a function of the fact that they are the only discourse rules which have been studied in any detail. Whether the distinctive properties of anaphora rules are shared by other rules of discourse must await further research. But it will not surprise me if they are.

NOTES

[1] I could of course be wrong about the universality of some particular property or properties, without having to change my basic position, but I am committed to the position that at least many of the properties discussed in Chapter 5 are universal to anaphora rules.

[2] I am not saying that none of the above works provides us with insight; it is the notational proposals in these works which fail to impress me.

Appendix I

THE BACH-PETERS PARADOX AND KARTTUNEN'S ARGUMENT

Karttunen (1971) discusses sentences like (1) in some detail.

(1) The pilot who shot at it hit the mig that chased him.

He shows that, contrary to the prevailing view, (1) does have a finite source in a grammar including a Pronominalization transformation which replaces a full NP by a pronoun under suitable conditions of identity. This follows from Karttunen's observation that (1) can be derived from a structure like (2) in the indicated manner.

(2)

NP_1 pronominalizes NP_2
NP_6 pronominalizes NP_4[1]

The only innovation in such a derivation consists of allowing NP_6 (or NP_3 — see footnote 1) to pronominalize NP_4. The argument that (1) proved the nonexistence of Pronominalization was based on the assumption that only NP_5 could serve as the antecedent for *him*. But, as Karttunen notes, this assumption is totaly arbitrary and unwarranted.

Having thus disposed of one argument against Pronominalization[2], Kart-tunen goes on to observe that (1) can also be derived from (3).

(3)

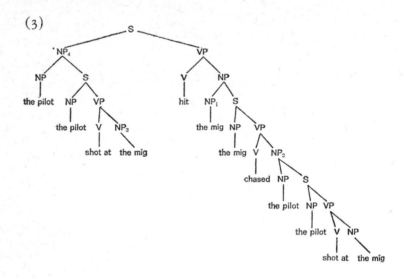

NP$_4$ pronominalizes NP$_2$
NP$_1$ pronominalizes NP$_3$

(2) and (3), he says, "are different structures and, presumably, are associated with different meanings," and this "commits us to the view that (1) is ambiguous" (pp. 160-161). He then proceeds to argue quite plausibly that such an ambiguity does, in fact, exist.

Since alternative approaches to anaphora (such as those of Jackendoff (1969) or McCawley (1970)) do not predict the existence of this ambiguity, Karttunen concludes that (1) provides an argument *for* rather than *against* the transformation of Pronominalization.

Karttunen ends his article on a slightly less positive note, however, for he observes that (1) can also be derived from (4) as indicated.

If (1) "is derivable from three seemingly quite different deep structures, one would expect it to be, not two, but three ways ambiguous. But apparently there is no such third interpretation" (p. 178). Kuroda (1971) argues that a third reading for (1) can, in fact, be distinguished, and that Karttunen's analysis does, therefore, provide an argument for the existence of a Pro-nominalization transformation.

Accepting Kuroda's factual claims,[3] I will show that Karttunen's analysis predicts too many ambiguities for (1). I will further show how an interpretive approach to anaphora can provide a very natural account of the facts.

(4)

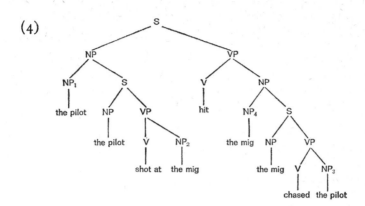

NP₁ pronominalizes NP₃
NP₄ pronominalizes NP₂

A crucial assumption in Karttunen's paper is that every deep structure underlying a given surface structure corresponds to a distinct reading. That is, if a surface structure S can be derived from n different deep structures, then S is at least n ways ambiguous. Without this assumption, it would not be possible to say that the existence of multiple deep structures for (1) predicts that it is ambiguous. But the fulfillment of this prediction is Karttunen's sole reason for advocating the transformational derivation of pronouns. Hence, if it can be demonstrated that Karttunen's analysis allows (1) to be derived from too many different deep structures, then his entire argument collapses.

(5) is constructed from (2) by attaching relative clauses to the two most deeply embedded occurrences of *the pilot*. These extra relative clauses are prevented from appearing in surface structure by applying Pronominalization two extra times. Thus, we now see that (1) has at least four different deep structures under Karttunen's analysis.

In a perfectly parallel fashion, extra relative clauses can be attached to (3) to provide yet another source for (1).

Notice now that this procedure of attaching relative clauses can be iterated. That is, it can be applied to (5) and (6), thereby providing still more deep structures for (1). For example, (7) is constructed from (5) in this manner.

In fact, what I have sketched is an algorithm for constructing new deep structures for (1). Since this algorithm applies to its own output, it follows that Karttunen's analysis allows (1) to be derived from infinitely many deep

Consider (5).

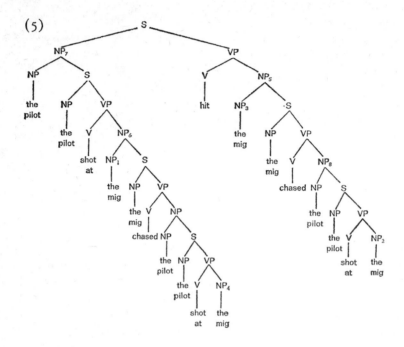

(5)

NP₁ pronominalizes NP₂
NP₃ pronominalizes NP₄
NP₅ pronominalizes NP₆
NP₇ pronominalizes NP₈

structures. Hence, Karttunen would be forced to predict incorrectly that (1) has infinitely many distinct readings.

It is thus clear that (1) fails to provide an argument for the existence of a transformation of Pronominalization.

How, then, is the ambiguity of (1) to be accounted for? In this section I will show how a rather simple-minded approach to the interpretation of pronouns assigns to (1) just the readings described by Kuroda.

In what follows, I will assume that anaphoric pronouns are present in deep structure (i.e., that there is no Pronominalization transformation), and that the grammar of English contains rule for associating these pronouns with appropriate antecedents. Further, I will assume that the interpretation of anaphoric pronouns is determined by another rule, which utilizes information about antecedency. There is nothing about these assumptions which is un-

(6)

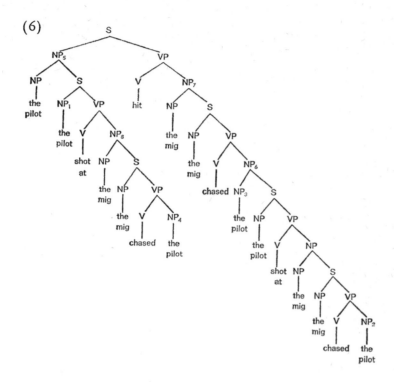

NP₁ pronominalizes NP₂
NP₃ pronominalizes NP₄
NP₅ pronominalizes NP₆
NP₇ pronominalizes NP₈

usual, except the idea that the interpretation of pronouns and the assignment of antecedents might be distinct problems.

The rule assigning antecedents to pronouns will be referred to as "the anaphora rule." It stipulates that an NP may serve as the antecedent for a given pronoun if they agree in certain features (e.g., gender and number) and if certain structural relations obtain between them. These structural relations will be something like the usual precede-command condition included in the various formulations of Pronominalization (see Chapter 2).

The rule which assigns interpretations to pronouns will be referred to as "the semantic rule." It simply assigns the reading of the antecedent to the pronoun. When the antecedent is referential (in the sense of Donellan (1966)), this reading will include a referential index or some other device for indicating coreference.

(7)

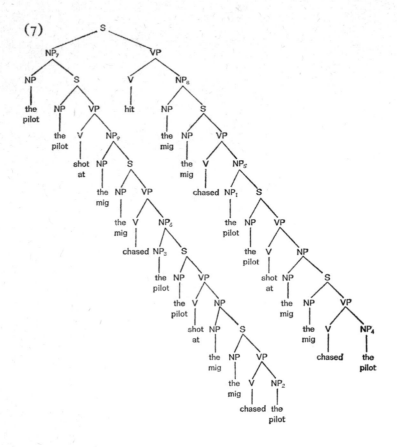

NP₁ pronominalizes NP₂
NP₃ pronominalizes NP₄
NP₅ pronominalizes NP₆
NP₇ pronominalizes NP₅
NP₈ pronominalizes NP₉

Applying the anaphora rule to (1), now, there is no natural way to prevent the simple NP's *the pilot* and *the mig* from serving as antecedents of *him* and *it*, respectively. Thus, the anaphora rule yields the four possible combinations of pronouns and antecedents for (1) given in (8).

(8) (a) *The pilot* who shot at *it* hit *the mig* that chased *him*.

(b) *The pilot* who shot at *it* hit *the mig that chased him*.

(c) *The pilot who shot at it* hit *the mig* that chased *him*.

(d) *The pilot who shot at it* hit *the mig that chased him*.

Now the semantic rule is applied to each of the structures in (8). Since the purpose of the semantic rule is to assign interpretations to anaphoric pronouns, the rule will always be applied in such a way as to eliminate pronouns from the structure. If the application of the semantic rule fails to eliminate the pronouns from a structure, then this structure is marked as semantically anomalous, because it contains uninterpreted pronouns. The results of applying the semantic rule to (8) are given in (9).[4]

(9) (a) The pilot who shot at the mig hit the mig that chased the pilot.

   (b) The pilot who shot at the mig that chased the pilot hit the mig that chased the pilot.

   (c) The pilot who shot at the mig hit the mig that chased the pilot who shot at the mig.

   (d) The pilot who shot at the mig that chased him hit the mig that chased the pilot who shot at it.

As noted above, (9d) must be judged anomalous, This leaves (9a-c) as interpretations for (1). Notice now that (9a) is isomorphic to (4), (9b) is isomorphic to (2), and (9c) is isomorphic to (3). Thus, the readings provided by the simple rules suggested here correspond perfectly to the readings Kuroda identified for (1).

Observe that the algorithm described in part 2 for generating spurious readings cannot be duplicated in the present system because the anaphora rule operates only on *syntactic* structures. Hence, the pronouns in (9d) cannot be assigned antecedents, and no structures corresponding to (5), (6), or (7) can be generated.

Thus, it seems that Karttunen (1971) is wrong in claiming that the ambiguity of (1) provides evidence against an interpretive approach to anaphora. On the contrary, a simple interpretive approach accounts for the data quite easily, whereas a traditional analysis incorporating a Pronominalization transformation does not.

NOTES

[1] Karttunen actually proposes that NP_3 should pronominalize NP_4. This seems objectionable to me on two grounds: first, there is no evidence to indicate that relative pronouns are derived from full NP's identical to the heads of the relatives; and second, even if relative pronouns are derived from full NP's, it seems probable that they are transformed into their surface forms cyclically, thus rendering Karttunen's derivations impossible. Using NP_6 instead of NP_3, however, does not affect Karttunen's argument in any way.

[2] There are many others. See Chapter 2.

[3] In my dissertation, I argued that one of the readings Karttunen assigns to (1) is not a normal interpretation of (1). For present purposes, I will not question the data as given by Karttunen and Kuroda. Should my earlier interpretation of the facts be correct, the proposal in this appendix can be modified to produce the right results.

[4] Technically, the structures in (9) should be semantic structures rather than just surface strings, but since little is known about how semantic structures should be represented, I have simply used strings which preserve the relevant features of the semantic structures in question.

Appendix II

POSTAL'S WH-CONSTRAINT

o. *Introduction*

The purpose of this appendix is to consider some very interesting data which are unaccounted for by the mechanisms discussed elsewhere in this monograph. The facts in question were first noted by Postal, who has proposed several different (but closely related) analyses of them. The structure of the chapter will be as follows: (i) the relevant data will be presented and discussed; (ii) an analysis of them will be proposed and its consequences explored; and (iii) the analysis proposed here will be compared with Postal's most recent analysis of these data.

1. *The Facts*

Consider the contrast between the (a) and (b) sentences of (1) and (2).

(1) (a) *Who* said Mary kissed *him?*
    (b) **Who* did *he* say Mary kissed?

(2) (a) *The man who* said Mary kissed *him* was lying.
    (b) **The man who he* said Mary kissed was lying.

Since it was concluded in Chapter 4 that WH-fronting applies before the pronominal anaphora rule, there is nothing in the preceding chapters that accounts for the deviance of (1b) and (2b).

Further, as Postal (1970a) argues, the contrast in (1) and (2) cannot be accounted for by any constraint statable in terms of deep structure or surface structure.[1] (3) and (4) (in which the (a) and (b) sentences presumably have the same deep structures) show that deep structure does not suffice to account for such contrasts.

(3) (a) *Who* fed *his* dog?
    (b) **Who* was *hid* dog fed by?

(4) (a) *Who* did Mary talk to about *his* sister?
    (b) ?*Who did Mary talk about *his* sister to?

The inadequacy of a surface structure constraint to account for this phenomenon is demonstrated by the fact that relatives with the WH-word deleted in surface structure behave similarly.

(5) (a) *The man* Mary talked to about *his* sister is a friend of mine.
(b) ?*The man Mary talked to *his* sister about is a friend of mine.

In addition, the contrast in question cannot be a function of whether the pronoun is a subject, nor of the relative proximity of pronoun and antecedent (cf. Chapter 4, § 2.3), for in (6), the pronoun is both an object and far from the WH-word.

(6) *Who did your favorite second cousin tell *him* I had seen?

Rather, the correct generalization in all these cases (as has been observed by several people) is that such sentences are grammatical whenever the WH-word is fronted from a position to the left of the pronoun.

Given this generalization, there are two sorts of analyses which immediately suggest themselves. On the one hand, one could formulate a constraint blocking anaphora between WH-words and pronouns whose relative positions had been reversed by WH-fronting. Such a solution will be referred to as a "cross-over solution." On the other hand, one could apply the pronominal anaphora rule prior to WH-fronting in these cases. Both approaches entail serious difficulties.

Notice first that since the pronominal anaphora rule has been shown to apply after WH-fronting (Chapter 4, § 3.2.1), it follows that the cross-over approach requires the pronominal anaphora rule to refer to a previous stage of the deerivation, i.e., the pre-WH-fronting structure. Thus, the cross-over solution requires a derivational constraint. Furthermore, such an analysis would not differentiate between cases in which the pre-fronting position of the WH-word is less deeply embedded than the pronoun and cases in which it is not. For ease of reference, cases of the former sort will be called *weakly crossed sentences*, and those of the latter type, *strongly crossed sentences*.[2] The sentences in (7), however, demonstrate that such a differentiation is necessary, for although weakly crossed sentences would violate a cross-over constraint, they are far less deviant than strongly crossed sentences. ((7a) from *Remembered Death* by Agatha Christie, Pocket Books, p. 58; (7b) from *Travels with My Aunt* by Graham Greene, Bantam Paperback, p. 190; and (7c) from *Murder in Retrospect* by Agatha Christie, Dell, p. 108).

(7) (a) He was the type of *man* with *whom his* work would always come first.
(b) On December 23rd, the postman brought *a large envelope which*, when I opened *it* at breakfast shed a lot of silvery tinsel into my plate.

(c) He was the kind of *man who* when *he* loses *his* collar stud bellows the house down.

(d) ?How many *copies of Aspects* does your friend who collects *them* own?

(e) ?*Which well-known actor* did the policeman who arrested *him* accuse of being drunk?[3]

It seems, then, that the cross-over solution to the problem posed by (1) and (2) cannot be maintained. There remains, therefore, the possibility of applying the pronominal anaphora rule before WH-fronting. The difficulty with this idea is that, as (8) shows, the pronominal anaphora rule must be allowed to apply after WH-fronting.

(8) (a) *He* finally married one of the women *Bill* had been dating.

(b) Which of the women *Bill* had been dating did *he* finally marry?

Applying the anaphora rule both before and after fronting would not alleviate the problem, for (1) requires that certain anaphoric relations be blocked prior to WH-fronting, whereas (8) requires that other anaphoric relations not be blocked so early. It might be suggested that anaphora assignment applies both before and after WH-fronting, but that WH-words may not be marked for anaphora once they have been fronted. This would account for all the data presented so far, and it seems plausible to claim that WH-words, when put into complementizer position (see Chomsky (1971)), lose the ability to enter into anaphoric relations with pronouns. Formally, this could be accomplished by depriving WH-words in complementizer position of their NP status. Unfortunately, such a solution fails because of sentences like (9).

(9) (a) *Who* killed Cock Robin, and why did *he* do it?

(b) If I knew *who* stole the jewels, I would turn *him* in.

In these examples, WH is fronted on a cycle in which the pronoun is not even included, so the indicated anaphoric relations cannot be marked prior to WH-fronting. Such examples show that in some cases, WH-words must be marked for anaphora after fronting.

Thus, it seems that (1) and (8) entail a genuine ordering paradox.

2. *An Analysis*

2.1 The Trace Proposal

That there is an escape from this apparent paradox was pointed out by Peter Culicover (personal communication). Culicover suggested that WH-fronting could be formulated so that a phonetically null copy of the WH-word is left behind in its pre-fronting position. By the arguments of Chapter 2, § 4, this copy would necessarily be anaphorically related to the WH-word. Hence, if the WH-word itself enters into an anaphoric relation with the pronoun, then by the Transitivity Condition (Chapter 3, § 4), the copy and the pronoun must enter into an anaphoric relation. If this relation is blocked, then the sentence is deviant. It therefore follows that WH-words' behavior with respect to anaphora should be just what it would be if they were in their pre-fronting positions. This consequence is discussed in the next section.

This analysis (which I will refer to as the trace analysis) is illustrated in (10).

(10) (a) [S₁ He said [S₂ Mary kissed someone S₂] S₁].
      (b) [S₁ *Who* did he say [S₂ Mary kissed $\triangle$ S₂] S₁].

The transformation of WH-fronting converts a structure like (10a) into one like (10b). Now, if *who* and *he* in (10b) are to be allowed to enter into an anaphoric relation, the Transitivity Condition requires that $\triangle$ and *he* also be anaphorically related. Consequently, the resultant sentence will be ungrammatical for the same reason that (11) is.

(11) *He* said Mary kissed *someone*.

Notice that this proposal does not block (8b), since the trace left by WH-fronting will be anaphorically related to *which of the women John dated*, not to *John*, so that the Transitivity Condition does not apply.

One immediate objection to such an analysis is the following: if, as an earlier chapter suggested, empty nodes are to be treated by the anaphora rules just like pro-forms, then there is no reason why *he* may not serve as the antecedent for $\triangle$, in which case the relevant anaphoric relation would always be possible. So some means must be found to keep *he* from serving as the antecedent of $\triangle$.

This can be accomplished formally simply by marking the trace left behind by WH-fronting with some feature (e.g., -pro) which distinguishes them from pronouns. This does not prevent these traces from having the WH-words as their antecedents, for this anaphoric relation is marked by the rule of WH-fronting, and, as was shown in Chapter 2, copying rules may produce anaphoric relations forbidden by the anaphora rules.

The analysis suggested above appears at first to be quite ad hoc. In fact, it amounts to a weakening of the standard requirement that the rules of a grammar be simply ordered. There are, however, some reasons (beyond the arguments given above) to believe that it may be correct.

The first of these reasons is that a number of other researchers (Chomsky (1971), Perlmutter (1972), Selkirk (1972)) make very similar proposals for independent reasons. Consideration of these other reasons for adopting the trace analysis would take us too far afield, but their existence lends plausibility to what at first appears to be a rather dubious analysis.

Chomsky (1971) also points out that other movement transformations behave exactly like WH-fronting with respect to the phenomena that led him to postulate traces. This led him to suggest that movement rules universally leave behind traces. This is an attractive suggestion, for a theory in which all movement transformations must leave behind traces is certainly more restrictive (i.e., compatible with fewer grammars) than one in which only some such rules do.[4]

If all movement rules leave behind traces, then other movement rules should interact with pronominal anaphora in much the same way as WH-fronting.

That is, paradigms like (1) and (2) ought to exist in cases involving movement transformations other than WH-fronting. That such paradigms do, in fact, exist is shown by (12).

(12) (a) It was *John* that said Mary kissed *him*.
      (b) *It was *John* that *he* said kissed Mary.[5]

Notice, by the way, that (12) cannot be accounted for by ordering Cleft sentence formation after the pronominal anaphora rule, because of examples like (13).

(13) (a) *He* finally married the woman *Bill* had been dating.
      (b) It was the woman *Bill* had been dating that *he* finally married.

Thus, Chomsky's proposal to require all movement transformations to leave behind a trace receives support from (12).

Topicalization behaves much like Cleft sentence formation, thereby providing further support for Chomsky's proposal. (14) shows that the pronominal anaphora rule must be allowed to apply after Topicalization, and (15) shows that the paradigm of (1) generalizes to Topicalization.

(14) (a) *He* loves the woman *John* married.
      (b) The woman *John* married, *he* loves.
(15) (a) *John*, Mary claims said Jane kissed *him*.[6]
      (b) *John*, Mary claims *he* said Jane kissed.

Further supporting evidence involves the rules of Tough movement and It-replacement. Both of these rules were shown to follow the pronominal anaphora rule in Chapter 4, § 3.2.1. One would therefore predict that the marginal[7] sentences in (16) could be made fully grammatical by applying Tough movement and Subject raising.

(16) (a) ??It was easy for *his* brother to help *John*.
      (b) ??It seems to *his* brother that *John* is unhappy.

That this expectation is not borne out is shown in (17).

(17) (a) ?*John* was easy for *his* brother to help.
      (b) ??*John* seems to *his* brother to be unhappy.[8]

These facts follow immediately from an analysis which requires Tough movement and It-replacement to leave behind a trace, since the trace may be anaphorically related to a pronoun only if the NP could have been, had it not been moved. (Recall that the Transitivity Condition requires that the trace be marked for anaphora whenever the moved NP is).

2.2 Some Consequences

The most obvious prediction this analysis makes is that all strongly crossed sentences are ungrammatical. This prediction is fully borne out for all speakers, as is evidenced by the complete agreement among informants regarding (1b), (2b), (12b), and (15b). Similarly, this analysis correctly predicts that a preposed NP can always serve as the antecedent of a pronoun to the right of its pre-fronting position, as, e.g., in (1a), (2a), (12a), and (15a).

In weakly crossed sentences, the analysis suggested above predicts that an anaphoric relation is possible only if the antecedent is determinate. Since there is a good deal of individual variation regarding the possibility of right-to-left anaphora (and hence regarding determinateness — cf. Chapter 4, § 2.2), the trace analysis correctly predicts that reactions to weakly crossed sentences will differ widely as well. Further, it predicts a correlation between judgements regarding right-to-left anaphora and judgements regarding weakly crossed sentences.

For movements other than WH-fronting, such a correlation can easily be seen to exist.

(18) (a) A man who had heard *it* before interrupted *Bill's story*.
      (b) ?*A man who had heard *it* before interrupted *someone's story*.

(19) (a) It was *Bill's story* that a man who had heard *it* before interrupted.
      (b) ?*It was *someone's story* that a man who had heard *it* before interrupted.

(20) (a) *Bill's story*, a man who had heard *it* before interrupted.
      (b) ?*Someone's story*, a man who had heard *it* before interrupted.

In the case of WH-fronting, the situation is a bit more complex, for it is not *a priori* clear how to assign determinateness to WH-words. Chomsky (1964) argues that WH-words in questions are derived from "unspecified indefinites." If this is correct, then these words are indeterminate, and should yield ungrammatical weakly crossed sentences. In fact, it appears that questions beginning with *who, whose,* or *what* behave just like the corresponding declarative sentences with *someone, someone's,* or *something.* Thus, the examples in (21) are just about as bad as those in (22).

(21) (a) ?*Who did the woman *he* loved betray?
    (b) ?*Whose story did a woman who had met *him* before interrupt?
    (c) ?*What did the man who lost *it* need to find?

(22) (a) ?*The woman *he* loved betrayed *someone.*
    (b) ?*A woman who had met *him* before interrupted *someone's* story.
    (c) ?*The man who lost *it* needed to find *something.*

Weakly crossed questions involving *which* and *how many* sound a good deal more natural, as do the corresponding declaratives.

(23) (a) ?*Which picture* did the man who painted *it* refuse to sell?
    (b) ?*How many dachshunds* does your friend who breeds *them* own?

(24) (a) ?The man who painted *it* refused to sell *one picture.*
    (b) ?Your friend who breeds *them* owns *many dachshunds.*

This is consistent with the claim that it is the determinateness of the antecedents which is relevant in such cases, for the intuitive characterization of the determinateness given in Chapter 4, § 2.2 would lead one to expect that forms like *which picture* and *how many dachshunds* would be more determinate than forms like *who* and *what*. This corresponds to the fact that NP's like *one picture* and *many dachshunds* are more likely to be interpreted specifically than NP's like *someone* and *something.*

If the antecedent is separated from the WH-word by a preposition, then the sentences are still better, both in their interrogative forms and in their declarative forms.

(25) (a) Which of *John's teachers* do the people who know *them* all respect most?
    (b) How many of *the demonstrators* did the police who arrested *them* beat up?

(26) (a) The people who know *them* all respect one of *John's teachers* most.

(b) The police who arrested *them* beat up many of *the demonstrators*.

It is quite likely that some readers will disagree with the judgements assigned in (18)-(26). This is not surprising, for there seems to be a great deal of variation among speakers with respect to determinateness.[9] It is, however, striking that speakers tend to give the same response to the interrogative sentences as to the corresponding declaratives. Thus, though the data themselves may be rather marginal, the correlation that emerges from them seems reasonably clear. This is strong supporting evidence for something akin to the proposal in this appendix.

Do similar correspondences hold for relative clauses? At first it might seem that the answer to this question is "no" because of contrasts like (27).

(27) (a) ??Mary pities *the man who* the woman *he* loved betrayed.

(b) The woman *he* loved betrayed *the man*.

It is, however, not implausible to suggest that a simple NP like *the man* in (27b) differs from the head NP of a relative clause with respect to determinateness. If such a difference can be justified, then facts like (27) can be accounted for without having to abandon the idea under consideration.

Unfortunately, it is very difficult to find an independent criterion for judging the determinateness of relative pronouns. A plausible guess would be that a relative pronoun is determinate just in case the relative clause is non-restrictive.[10] This proposal is not tenable, however, because of sentences like (28) (due to Paul Kiparsky).

(28) (a) The mushroom that I'm talking about still grows in Kashmir.

(b) A beaver who has any self-respect builds dams.

Nevertheless, some speakers do feel that weakly crossed relative clauses are better if they are non-restrictive.

(29) (a) ?*I just met *the doctor who* the patients *he* treats detest.

(b) ?I just met *Dr. Morgan, who* the patients *he* treats detest.

(c) ?*Mary wants to meet *a man who* the policeman who arrested *him* said was innocent.

(d) ?Mary wants to meet *a certain man, who* the policeman who arrested *him* said was innocent.

(e) ??Everyone avoids *the city which* even the people who live in *it* can't stand.

(f) Everyone avoids *the City, which* even the people who live in *it* can't stand.

Unfortunately, these judgements are quite uncertain and subject to considerable individual variation.

In general, then, it appears to be rather difficult to test the proposal in this appendix on weakly crossed relative clauses. There is, however, one fact concerning relatives which does support this analysis. Larry Horn (personal communication) has noticed that right-to-left anaphora from indeterminates is often possible in environments containing *even* or *only*.[11] This is illustrated in (30).

(30) (a) ??The man who designed *it* can understand *a computer*.
     (b) Only the man who designed *it* can understand *a computer*.
     (c) ??If you are looking for *it*, you'll never find *a unicorn*.
     (d) Even if you are looking for *it*, you'll never find *a unicorn*.

Avery Andrews (personal communication) has observed that *even* and *only* also improve some weakly crossed relative clauses. This is demonstrated by (31) ((31b) due to Joan Bresnan).

(31) (a) ??I have *a friend who* those who know *him* well can appreciate.
     (b) I have *a friend who* only those who know *him* well can appreciate.
     (c) ?John owns *a machine which* the man who designed *it* can't understand.
     (d) John owns *a machine which* even the man who designed *it* can't understand.

Whatever the underlying reason for this property of *even* and *only*, it seems clear that the phenomena illustrated in (30) and (31) are closely related. The analysis suggested in this chapter captures this fact by treating weakly crossed sentences as instances of right-to-left anaphora. Thus, (30) and (31) provide support for this analysis.

3. *Postal's Analysis*

Postal's most recent analysis of the problems considered in this chapter suggests that weakly and strongly crossed sentences should be handled in rather different ways. The remainder of this chapter will consider the mechanisms Postal proposes, and compare them with the analysis described in § 2.

3.1 The Two-Rule Proposal

To account for strongly crossed sentences, Postal orders his pronominal anaphora rule before such movement rules as WH-fronting, Cleft sentence formation, and Topicalization. Specifically, Postal (lecture at MIT, January, 1972) proposes that pronominal anaphora should be marked "at the end of the first covering cycle," i.e., at the end of the first cycle including both the anaphor and the antecedent. He argues that this entails that it will always apply before WH-fronting, Topicalization, and certain other movement rules. In order to account for sentences like (8b), (13b), and (14b), Postal proposes a second pronominal anaphora rule, applying after all of these movement transformations, which allows anaphoric relations to be established between definite pronouns and NP's to their left, so long as the NP does not command the pronoun.

This analysis has the same basic effect as the trace proposal, viz., it finds a way around the strict ordering of the movement rules with respect to the pronominal anaphora rule. There are, nevertheless, differences between the two analyses.

The most important difference is that the trace proposal predicts that movement transformations may sometimes reduce the number of possible pronoun-antecedent pairs, whereas Postal's analysis predicts that this is not the case. The former prediction appears to be somewhat more accurate, as (32) shows.

(32) (a) Bostonians who know *the police* believe that many of *them* are on the take.

(b) ??How many of *them* do Bostonians who know *the police* believe are on the take?

(c) Those people who had encountered *the gang* always recognized the sheriff's picture of *them*.

(d) ??The sheriff whose picture of *them* those people who had encountered *the gang* always recognized was ultimately gunned down.

(e) *The members of the band* all thought one of *them* was a fugitive from justice.

(f) ??It was one of *them* that *the members of the band* all thought was a fugitive from justice.

(g) ??One of *them, the members of the band* all thought was a fugitive from justice.[12]

To account for such facts, Postal's two-rule proposal would have to be augmented by still another constraint blocking sentences like (32b), (32d), (32f), and (32g). The analysis suggested in § 2, on the other hand, makes just the right predictions here.

Another difference between the trace analysis and the two-rule proposal is that Postal's second anaphora rule applies only to NP's which do not command the relevant pronouns. The trace analysis, on the other hand, restricts anaphoric relations only for NP's which leave behind a trace, i.e., for NP's mentioned by movement rules (cf. § 3.2.2 below). Thus, Postal would predict that sentences like (33b) are impossible, whereas the trace proposal correctly permits them.

(33) (a) *He likes many of John's teachers.
      (b) How many of John's teachers does he like?[13]

It seems, then, that the evidence, while not overwhelming, tends to support the trace analysis of § 2 over Postal's two-rule proposal.

3.2 The WH-Constraint

Postal (1972a) suggests that the derivational constraint given here as (34) is part of the grammar of one dialect of English.

(34) Mark as ill-formed any derivation in which:
      (i)   there are two nominal constituents, A and B, in the input structure of a WH-movement rule, where:
            (a) A is a pronoun
            (b) B is a WH form[14]
            (c) A is to the left of B
            and:
      (ii) the corresponding constituents of A and B in the output structure of the WH-movement rule, call them A' and B', respectively, are alligned such that B' is to the left of A' and:
      (iii) in the Semantic Representation, A and B (or more precisely, their corresponding elements) are marked as stipulated coreferents.[15]

Postal calls (34) "the WH-Constraint."

The effect of the WH-Constraint is to mark as ill-formed all weakly or strongly crossed questions and relative clauses. Since strongly crossed sentences are ungrammatical for independent reasons, the WH-Constraint is actually relevant only to weakly crossed sentences. Postal's claim is that, in his dialect, all weakly crossed questions and relatives are ungrammatical.

Although it would obviously be presumptuous to contradict anyone's claims about his own judgements of grammaticality, in this case it seems that Postal's dialect is exceedingly rare. Whole some weakly crossed questions and relatives are rejected by many speakers, others appear to be acceptable to virtually everyone. There are a great many borderline cases, and wide variation exists among speakers. For example, few (if any) speakers reject (35a), most speakers reject (35b), and reactions to (35c) are extremely mixed.

(35) (a) This is the kind of *article which* even the person who wrote *it* doesn't understand.

(b) **What* did the man who needed *it* lose?

(c) *?Which councilman* did the woman *he* was dating vote against?

Postal's analysis allows for only two dialects: the one with the WH-Constraint and the one without it. The real situation is certainly far more complex than that. Postal might perhaps postulate that there are other dialects with modified versions of the WH-Constraint, but it is far from obvious what form this modification would take.

On the other hand, Postal could say that the variation among speakers is a function of the variation regarding right-to-left anaphora. This would be consistent with everything he says, and it would be an automatic consequence of his ordering of the pronominal anaphora rule with respect to WH-fronting. Notice, however, that such an approach renders highly questionable the need for the WH-Constraint in the first place. If Postal's dialect does indeed reject all weakly crossed questions and relatives, it could simply be stipulated that, for Postal, all WH-words are indeterminate. It would follow that weakly crossed questions and relatives are ungrammatical in his dialect, and the WH-Constraint would no longer be needed. Such an alternative would be preferable to the WH-Constraint in several ways. First, it would correlate the individual variation regarding weakly crossed questions and relatives with the individual variation regarding determinateness. Secondly, it would eliminate the need for a rather lengthy and apparently ad hoc derivational constraint. Thirdly, it would permit weakly and strongly crossed sentences to be treated uniformly.

3.2.1 Postal (1970a, 1972a) argues against any analysis constructed along these lines. His argument is based on the fact that, under certain circumstances, WH-words in questions do not get fronted. He observes that the WH-constraint predicts that such sentences would differ considerably from ordinary questions with respect to possible anaphoric relations. The analysis suggested above, on the other hand, would predict that the fronting of WH-words does not affect the possible anaphoric relations. Postal gives a number of examples which allegedly support the prediction of the WH-constraint.

These examples fall into two groups: those in which Postal's factual claims are very questionable,[16] and those in which intonational factors provide an explanation for the facts. Examples of the latter type consist of what Postal calls "incredulity question clauses" and "legalistic question clauses." Incredulity question clauses are formed by replacing words or phrases in the immediately preceding sentences with WH-words, and assigning these WH-words extra heavy stress and, in Postal's words, "a special sharply rising intonation." Legalistic question clauses, according to Postal, "seem natural only in the mouths of courtroom attorneys, police investigators, and quiz program announcers," and are characterized by falling intonation. Examples of these are given in (36).

(36) (a) Nixon appointed who to the Supreme Court?
     (b) The person you saw was walking in which direction?

In many cases, certain anaphoric relations in incredulity question clauses and legalistic question clauses seem far more natural than in the corresponding ordinary questions. Thus, in (37)-(40), the (a) sentences seem much better than the (b) sentences.

(37) (a) The newsman who criticized *him* later belted *which official?*[17]
     (b) ??*Which official* did the newsman who criticized *him* later belt?

(38) (a) Finding out *he* won surprised *which candidate?*
     (b) ?*Which candidate* did finding out *he* won surprise?

(39) (a) Mr. Jones, for $ 100,000, the man who appointed *him* later said *what Secretary of State* was an imbecile?
     (b) ?*What Secretary of State* did the man who appointed *him* later say was an imbecile?

(40) (a) Remembering you are under oath, the witness who claimed he had never seen *it* was walking towards *what building?*
     (b) ?*What building* was the witness who claimed he had never seen *it* walking towards?

    The key fact about such examples is that the intonation and context indicate that the questioner knows the answer, and is trying to elicit this answer from his listener. Thus, it would not be implausible to say that the underlined NP's in the (a) sentences are determinate (i.e., specific). If this is the case, then the non-deviance of the (a) sentences is no problem for the analysis defended here. As for the marginality of the (b) sentences, this can be attributed to the fact that the normal contexts and intonation patterns for these sentences do not force a specific interpretation of the underlined NP's. In fact, if the (b) sentences occur in the same contexts (e.g., after the initial phrases of (39a) and (40a)) and with the same intonation patterns as the (a) sentences, then there is no difference with respect to possible anaphoric relations. Thus, the data in (37)-(40) do not support the WH-constraint over the analysis defended here.

In the remaining examples Postal presents in defense of the WH-constraint, his data are extremely questionable, at best. They consist of questions containing more than one WH-word. In these cases, only one WH-word may be fronted, and the WH-constraint predicts that the other WH-words in the sentence may serve as antecedents to pronouns on their left. Specifically, the WH-constraint predicts a difference in acceptability between the (a) and (b) sentences in (41) and (42).

(41) (a) ?Which columnist reported *her* victory to *which actress'* father?

(b) ?To *which actress'* father did Joseph Alsop report *her* victory?

(42) (a) ?What company had *his* wife spy on *what well-known industrialist?*

(b) ?*What well-known industrialist* did General Motors have *his* wife spy on?

In these cases, Postal's claims to the contrary notwithstanding, there is little or no difference, so the analysis defended here makes the right prediction, but the WH-constraint does not.[18]

3.2.2 Another argument in favor of the WH-Constraint might be constructed on the basis of examples like (43).

(43) (a) *He* hung *Bill's* gold-plated cast of Barbara Streisand's nose on the wall.

(b) *Whose* gold-plated cast of Barbara Streisand's nose did *he* hang on the wall?

(c) ?*Bill's* gold-plated cast of Barbara Streisand's nose, *he* hung on the wall.

(d) ?It was *Bill's* gold-plated cast of Barbara Streisand's nose that *he* hung on the wall.

The difference between WH-fronting and other NP preposing transformations illustrated in (43) could be argued to be a reflex of the WH-Constraint. A little reflection, however, indicates that this is not the case. The most obvious defect in the claim that (43) supports Postal's position is that his reanalysis incorrectly predicts that all of the examples in (43) should be equally deviant (since *Bill* commands *he* in both (43c) and (43d)). Furthermore, the intuitions given in (43) are not subject to the same individual or dialectical variations as the WH-constraint. That is, speakers who are perfectly willing to accept weakly crossed sentences like (7) will nonetheless recognize the contrast in (43). For such speakers, Postal would have to say that the

WH-constraint operates selectively — a rather unsatisfactory conclusion, especially in the absence of a principle for determining in which cases it does operate.

A further reason for suspecting the claim that (43) supports the WH-constraint is that (43c) and (43d) are acceptable only if *Bill* receives very weak stress. In each case, if *Bill* is the item being focused, then the indicated anaphoric relation is impossible. Since in (43b) *whose* must necessarily be the focus, it appears that the contrast in (43) ought to be explained in terms of anaphoric relations involving the focused element, rather than through an ad hoc device like the WH-constraint.

One way of capturing facts like (43) in the analysis presented here would be to stipulate that, in cases of what Ross (1967a) terms "pied piping," the NP mentioned in the structural description of the movement transformation leaves behind a trace, and the entire NP which actually gets moved does too. Specifically, in (43b), since the fronting rule mentions only the WH-word, the trace left behind will be something like (44).

(44)

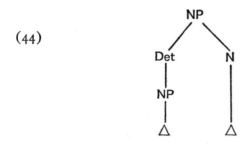

Therefore, both *whose* and *whose gold-plated cast of Barbara Streisand's nose* will be able to enter into only those anaphoric relations which would have been possible from their pre-fronting positions. This analysis also provides an account of the correlation between stress and anaphora in (43c) and (43d). From the rather plausible assumption that Cleft sentence formation and Topicalization should be formulated as rules fronting the focused element, it follows that the indicated anaphoric relations in (43c) and (43d) will be impossible just in case *Bill* is the NP mentioned by the rule, i.e., just in case *Bill* is the focus. Since the stress indicates the focus, the relevance of stress in these examples is explained.

Another case in which WH-fronting appears to behave differently from other fronting rules is given in (45).

(45) (a) ??*Whose* mother did the girl *he* married insult?
(b) *John*'s mother, the girl *he* married insulted.
(c) It was *John*'s mother that the girl *he* married insulted.

Since (45) does exhibit the variation characteristic of the WH-constraint, and since stress does not affect the judgements in (45), this contrast might at first be taken as support for Postal's reanalysis against the position taken here. There is, however, a perfectly straightforward explanation for (45), namely that *whose* tends to be interpreted indeterminately, whereas *John* is determinate. This explanation is supported by the fact that (45b) and (45c) become at least as bad as (45a) if *someone* is substituted for *John*.

4. *Summary*

It was shown early in this chapter that an ordering paradox involving the pronominal anaphora rule and WH-fronting could be duplicated using several other NP movement rules. It was seen that these paradoxes could be resolved either by modifying the notion of movement rule or by introducing a second pronominal anaphora rule. Some evidence in favor of the former solution was given.

It was then shown that either of these solutions to the ordering paradox eliminated the need for Postal's WH-Constraint, provided that individual speakers are permitted a great deal of leeway in assigning determinateness to WH-words. The absence of an independent criterion for assigning determinateness to WH-words (at least in relatives) detracts to some extent from the force of this argument. It has, however, been shown that much of the evidence purportedly supporting the WH-Constraint has an independent explanation, so the need for the constraint is extremely questionable. Certainly, the burden of proof has been shifted back to its proponents.

NOTES

[1] Postal also claims to show that the constraint cannot be formulated in terms of shallow structure or in terms of any combination of deep structure, surface structure, and shallow structure. However, his arguments for these claims are circular in that they depend on acceptance of his claim about what the relevant generalization is. Since I cannot see any way to account for the facts in terms of one or more of these levels, I will not consider the question of whether there is some argument against doing so in principle.

[2] These terms are used below in a more general sense, viz., to denote any sentence in which an NP is crossed over a pronoun to which it is anaphorically related. In what follows, the context should indicate fairly clearly which sense is intended.

[3] There is a great deal of individual variation in judgements of weakly crossed sentences. However, all speakers recognize that they are incomparably better than strongly crossed sentences. In many cases, I found it necessary to explain to informants that the indicated anaphoric relations in examples (1b) and (2b) were logically possible. On the other hand, judgements about the examples in (7) tend to be unsure, often taking the form of remarks

to the effect that the examples were awkward, but comprehensible. Notice that three of the sentences in (7) were published; in contrast, it is inconceivable that strongly crossed sentences would ever be used.

[4] This proposal might be objected to on the grounds that it in essence formulates "chopping rules" (Ross (1967a), Chapter 6) as copying rules in which the copy is phonetically null. This obscures to a large degree the distinction between these types of rules (see Ross (1967a)). If this distinction is indeed as vital as Ross claims, it might be possible to say that chopping rules are those in which the trace is ultimately deleted. If this proposal is tenable, then the Complex NP Constraint (and perhaps Ross' other constraints) can be restricted to deletion rules alone (cf. Chapter 5, § 2). This might also make it possible to account naturally for dialects in which sentences like (i) are acceptable (cf. Ross (1967a), § 6.2.3).

    (i) *King Kong* is a movie which you'll laugh yourself sick if you see *it*.

[5] It might be argued that (12) involves WH-fronting followed by optional deletion of the WH-word, i.e., that sentences like (i) are derived from sentences like (ii).

    (i) It was John that left.
    (ii) It was John who left.

The judgements in (12) would then be an immediate consequence of such an analysis, given example (2). Under this analysis, however, it would be difficult to account for the fact that (iii) and (v) are so much better than their purported sources, viz., (iv) and (vi).

    (iii) ?It was a doctor that John wanted to become.
    (iv) *It was a doctor ⟨ which ⟩ John wanted to become.
                   ⟨ who ⟩
    (v) It was a blonde that John brought to your party.
    (vi) ??It was a blonde who John brought to your party.

It seems likely that whatever analysis is adopted for (iii) and (v) could also account for (i). If this is so, then the deviance of (12b) does not follow from the deviance of (2b).

[6] (15a) is rather awkward, but this has nothing to do with anaphora, as evidenced by the fact that (i) is equally awkward.

    (i) John, Mary claims said Jane kissed Bill.

On the other hand, the deviance of (15b) definitely has something to do with anaphora, as the grammaticality of (ii) shows.

    (ii) John, Mary claims Bill said Jane kissed.

[7] These examples are not out for all speakers because of the individual variation regarding the definition of "less deeply embedded than"; see Chapter 4, § 2.1.

[8] The examples of (17) are somewhat better than those of (16), but they are considerably less natural than the superficially similar sentences in (i) and (ii).

    (i) *John* is eager for *his* brother to help.
    (ii) *John* writes to *his* brother to be careful.

[9] I hesitate to label this a case of "idiolect" variation. Rather, I tend to believe that determinateness cannot really be clearly defined, so that there is often a good deal of doubt regarding the feasibility of right-to-left anaphora. This view is supported by the fact that it often happens that a given speaker will respond differently on different days to examples of this sort.

[10] If the relative clause is restrictive, there is some reason to think that the head NP is indeterminate, for the restrictiveness of the relative clause indicates that the rest of the context fails to provide sufficient information to assign a referent to the head. If, for example, a complex NP like *the man Mary saw* is used, it is implicit that the use of the NP *the man* in its place would not have sufficed to indicate what man is intended. Thus, it seems intuitively correct to stipulate that the head of a restrictive clause is indeterminate. Since the head of a relative is anaphorically related to (and hence non-distinct from) the relative pronoun, it seems reasonable to suppose that relative pronouns in restrictive relative clauses are indeterminate.

Similar reasoning leads to the conclusion that the heads of non-restrictive relative clauses are determinate. The non-restrictiveness of a relative clause is an indication that the information contained in that relative clause is not needed for the purpose of identifying the referent of the head NP, i.e., that the head is determinate.

In spite of the very informal character of the above discussion, the hypothesis that the restrictive-non-restrictive distinction for relative clauses corresponds to the determinate-indeterminate distinction for the NP's makes certain empirical predictions which can be tested. In particular, it predicts that proper and generic NP's allow only non-restrictive relatives, and that necessarily indeterminate NP's allow only restrictive relatives. Some facts, given in (i)-(x), seem to bear this prediction out, but others, such as (28), contradict it.

   (i) John, who was here yersterday, is now gone.
   (ii) *John who was here yersterday is now gone.
   (iii) I don't trust anyone who votes.
   (iv) *I don't trust anyone, who votes.
   (v) John is a man who keeps his word.
   (vi) *John is a man, who keeps his word.
   (vii) I met someone who knows you yesterday.
   (viii) ??I met someone, who knows you, yesterday.
   (ix) Something that I own is very valuable.
   (x) ??Something, which I own, is very valuable.

[11] This fact is a mystery to me. No existing theory of anaphora can come close to accounting for it.

[12] None of these is bad enough to establish my point very strongly. This is because the pronouns are all objects of prepositions, thus leaving somewhat uncertain the question of whether they are less deeply embedded than their antecedents. Sentences like (i)-(iii) might constitute stronger evidence for my position, but their significance is somewhat dubious because considerations of stress may be sufficient to exclude (ii) and (iii).

   (i) The woman who loved *John* betrayed *him*.
   (ii) *It was *him* that the woman who loved *John* betrayed.
   (iii) *Him*, the woman who loved *John* betrayed.

[13] This argument is not terribly decisive, since it would be quite simple for Postal to modify his proposed second pronominal anaphora rule to account for (33b). Nevertheless, (33) does show clearly that the specific proposal Postal made in the lecture cited above is inadequate.

A third difference between the analyses in question has to do with the ordering of Tough movement and It-replacement. Postal orders these rules before the pronominal anaphora rule, unlike the other NP fronting rules discussed. In contrast, the trace proposal treats these rules just like other NP fronting rules. The crucial examples here are sentences like (17). The trace analysis predicts that they should be just as bad as (16), whereas, according to Postal's analysis, they should be fully grammatical. Unfortunately, it appears that both predictions fail here, for the examples of (17) are too good for my analysis and not good enough for Postal's.

[14] There is a problem regarding the notion "WH-form". Postal (1970a) uses (34) in excluding (i).

   (i) *Whose *friend's father* did *he* criticize?

If the italicized NP in (i) is a WH form, why are sentences like (ii) not similarly excluded?

   (ii) How many of *John's* teachers does *he* call by their first names?

Postal (1970a) recognizes this problem and devotes a lengthy footnote (footnote 14) to it, but instead of providing an answer, he merely assures the reader that it is possible to provide one. It is interesting to note, by the way, that in his discussion of this problem, Postal refers to "WH-marked nominals". If he conceives of WH-marking as a process which precedes WH-fronting, then he has implicitly abandoned his "orphan preposition" argument against cyclic WH-fronting, for, as Jackendoff (1969), p. 51, shows, the orphan preposition argument fails if WH is a feature of entire nominal phrases.

[15] Postal uses the phrase "stipulated coreferents" to mean what I would call "anaphorically related NP's."

16 Since my intuitions on weakly crossed sentences tend to differ from those of most other speakers, I have checked Postal's claims with a number of informants. I have been unable to find a speaker who agress with Postal's judgements.

17 (37a) and similar sentences seem to be fully acceptable to most speakers only if they receive the heavy stress of incredulity. If pronounced as normal echo questions, the reactions are mixed.

18 As noted, Postal makes the opposite claim about (41) and (42), but I have been unable to find other speakers who share his judgements.

BIBLIOGRAPHY

AKMAJIAN, A. (1970), *Aspects of the Grammar of Focus in English*, unpublished MIT dissertation.

AKMAJIAN, A. (1973), "An Interpretive Principle for Certain Anaphoric Expressions", in Anderson and Kiparsky (1973).

AKMAJIAN, A. and R. JACKENDOFF (1970), "Coreferentiality and Stress", *Linguistic Inquiry*, I.1.

AKMAJIAN, A. and T. WASOW (1975), "The Constituent Structure of VP and AUX and the Position of the Verb *Be*," *Linguistic Analysis* I.2.

ANDERSON, S. and P. KIPARSKY (eds.) (1973), *Festschrift for Morris Halle*, MIT Press, Cambridge, Massachusetts.

ARONOFF, M. (1971), "Stress and Anaphoric Objects," paper delivered at the second annual North Eastern Linguistic Society Conference in Montreal.

BACH, E. (1969), "Anti-pronominalization," unpublished University of Texas paper.

BACH, E. (1970), "Problominalization," *Linguistic Inquiry* I.1.

BACH, E. (1971), "Syntax Since *Aspects*," in R.J. O'Brien (ed.), *22nd Annual Round Table Linguistics : Developments of the Sixties — Viewpoints for the Seventies*, Georgetown University Monograph Series on Language and Linguistics, Georgetown University Press, Washington, D.C.

BACH, E., J. BRESNAN, and T. WASOW (1974), "Sloppy Identity : An Unnecessary and Insufficient Criterion for Deletion," *Linguistic Inquiry* V.4.

BAKER, C.L. (1966), "Definiteness and Indefiniteness in English," unpublished University of Illinois Masters Thesis.

BAKER, C.L. and M. BRAME (1971), "Global Rules : a rejoinder," *Language* 47.

BOWERS, J. (1968), "Adjectives and Adverbs in English," unpublished MIT paper.

BOWERS, J. (1969), "Generic Sentences in English," unpublished MIT paper.

BRESNAN, J. (1968), "Adsententials," unpublished MIT paper.

BRESNAN, J. (1970), "An Argument Against Pronominalization," *Linguistic Inquiry* I.1.

BRESNAN, J. (1971a), "Sentence Stress and Syntactic Transformations," *Language* 47.

BRESNAN, J. (1971b), "Contraction and the Transformational Cycle in English," unpublished MIT paper.

BRESNAN, J. (1972a), *The Theory of Complementation in English Syntax,* unpublished MIT dissertation.

BRESNAN, J. (1972b), "A Note on the Notion 'Identity of Sense Anaphora'," *Linguistic Inquiry* II.4.

BRESNAN, J. (1971c), "Stress and Syntax : a Reply," *Language,* 48.

BRESNAN, J. (1973), "The Syntax of Comparative Clause Constructions in English," *Linguistic Inquiry,* IV.3.

BURT, M.K. (1971), *From Deep Structure to Surface Structure,* Harper and Row, New York.

CHOMSKY, N. (1955), *The Logical Structure of Linguistic Theory,* Plenum Press, New York.

CHOMSKY, N. (1957), *Syntactic Structures,* Mouton, The Hague.

CHOMSKY, N. (1964), *Current Issues in Linguistic Theory,* Mouton, The Hague.

CHOMSKY, N. (1965), *Aspects of the Theory of Syntax,* MIT Press, Cambridge, Massachusetts.

CHOMSKY, N. (1968), *Language and Mind,* Harcourt, Brace, and World, New York.

CHOMSKY, N. (1969), "Deep Structure, Surface Structure, and Semantic Representation," in Steinberg and Jakobovits (1971).

CHOMSKY, N. (1970a), "Some Empirical Issues in the Theory of Transformational Grammar," in Peters (1972).

CHOMSKY, N. (1970b), "Remarks on Nominalization," in Jacobs and Rosenbaum (1970).

CHOMSKY, N. (1971), "Conditions on Transformations," in Anderson and Kiparsky (1973).

CHOMSKY, N. (1972), *Studies on Semantics in Generative Grammar,* Mouton, The Hague.

CHOMSKY, N. and M. HALLE (1968), *The Sound Pattern of English,* Harper and Row, New York.

CHOMSKY, N. and G. MILLER (1963), "Introduction to the Formal Analysis of Natural Languages," in *Handbook of Mathematical Psychology,* Vol. II, R. D. Luce, R. Bush, and E. Galanter (eds), Wiley, New York.

CULICOVER, P. (1970), *Syntactic and Semantic Investigations,* unpublished MIT dissertation.

DIK, S.C. (1973), "Crossing Coreference Again," *Foundations of Language,* 9.3.

DONELLAN, K. (1966), "Reference and Definite Descriptions," in Steinberg and Jakobovits (1971).

DOUGHERTY, R. (1969), "An Interpretive Theory of Pronominal Reference," *Foundations of Language,* 5.

DOUGHERTY, R. (1970), "A Grammar of Coordinate Conjoined Structures : I," *Language,* 46.4.

EMONDS, J. (1970), *Root and Structure Preserving Transformations,* unpublished MIT dissertation.

EMONDS, J. (1972), "Evidence that Indirect Object Movement is a Structure Preserving Rule," *Foundations of Language,* 8.4.

FIENGO, R. and H. LASNIK (1973), "The Logical Structure of Reciprocal Sentences in English," *Foundations of Language,* 9.4.

FODOR, J. (1970), *The Linguistic Description of Opaque Contexts,* unpublished MIT dissertation.

FODOR, J. and J. J. KATZ (1964), *The Structure of Language,* Prentice-Hall, Englewood Cliffs, New Jersey.

FRASER, B. (1970), "Some Remarks on the Action Nominalization," in Jacobs and Rosenbaum (1970).

FREIDEN, R. (1970), *Interpretative Semantics and the Syntax of English Complement Constructions,* unpublished University of Indiana dissertation.

GEACH, P. (1967), "Intentional Identity," *Journal of Philosophy,* 6.4.

GRINDER, J. (1970), "Super Equi-NP Deletion," in *Papers from the Sixth Meeting of the Chicago Linguistic Society,* Department of Linguistics, University of Chicago, Chicago, Ill.

GRINDER, J. (1971a), *On Deletion Phenomena,* unpublished University of California at San Diego dissertation.

GRINDER, J. (1971b), "A Reply to 'Super Equi-NP Deletion as Dative Deletion'," in *Papers from the Seventh Meeting of the Chicago Linguistics Society,* Department of Linguistics, University of Chicago, Chicago, Ill.

GRINDER, J. and P. POSTAL (1971), "Missing Antecedents," *Linguistic Inquiry,* II.3.

GROSU, A. (1972), *The Strategic Content of Island Constraints,* Ohio State University Working Papers in Linguistics, Columbus.

GRUBER, J. (1965), *Studies in Lexical Relations,* unpublished MIT dissertation.

HAMMERTON, M. (1970), "Disputed Interpretation of a Pronoun," *Nature*, 227, p. 202.

HANKAMER, J. (1971), *Constraints on Deletion*, unpublished Yale University dissertation.

HARMAN, G. (1972), "Noun Phrases Derived from Variable Binding Operators," in B. Freed, A. Marras, and P. Maynard (eds), *Forms of Representation*, North Holland, Amsterdam.

HELKE, M. (1970), *The Grammar of English Reflexivization*, unpublished MIT dissertation.

JACKENDOFF, R. (1969), *Some Rules of Semantic Interpretation for English*, unpublished MIT dissertation.

JACKENDOFF, R. (1971a), "Gapping and Related Rules," *Linguistics Inquiry*, II.1.

JACKENDOFF, R. (1971b), "Modal Structure in Semantic Representation," *Linguistic Inquiry*, II.4.

JACKENDOFF, R. (1971c), "On Some Questionable Arguments about Quantifiers and Negation," *Language*, 47.

JACKENDOFF, R. (1972), *Semantic Interpretation in Generative Grammar*, MIT Press, Cambridge, Massachusetts.

JACOBS, R. and P. ROSENBAUM (1970), *Readings in English Transformational Grammar*, Ginn and Co., Waltham, Massachusetts.

KARTTUNEN, L. (1969a), "Discourse Referents," paper presented to the 1969 International Conference on Computational Linguistics, Stockholm.

KARTTUNEN, L. (1969b), "What do Referential Indices Refer to?," unpublished University of Texas paper.

KARTTUNEN, L. (1971), "Definite Descriptions with Crossing Coreference," *Foundations of Language*, 7.2.

KATZ, J.J. (1973), "On Defining 'Presupposition'," *Linguistic Inquiry*, IV.2.

KATZ, J.J. and J. FODOR (1963), "The Structure of a Semantic Theory," in Fodor and Katz (1964).

KATZ, J.J. and P. POSTAL (1964), *An Integrated Theory of Linguistic Descriptions*, MIT Press, Cambridge, Massachusetts.

KAYNE, R. (1969a), "On the Inappropriateness of Rule Features," *Quarterly Progress Report of the Research Laboratory of Electronics of MIT*, 95.

KAYNE, R. (1969b), *The Transformational Cycle in French Syntax*, unpublished MIT dissertation.

KAYNE, R. (1971), "A Pronominalization Paradox in French," *Linguistic Inquiry*, II.2.

KIMBALL, J. (1971), "Super Equi-NP Deletion as Dative Deletion," in *Papers from the Seventh Regional Meeting of the Chicago Linguistics Society*, Dept. of Linguistics, U. of Chicago, Chicago, Ill.

KIPARSKY, P. and C. KIPARSKY (1971), "Fact," in Steinberg and Jakobovits (1971).

KLIMA, E. (1964), "Negation in English," in Fodor and Katz (1964).

KRAVIF, D. (1971), "Weak Generative Capacity and Emonds' Constraint," *Linguistic Inquiry*, II.1.

KURODA, S.-Y. (1969), "English Relativization and Certain Related Problems," in Reibel and Schane (1970).

KURODA, S.-Y. (1971), "Two Remarks on Pronominalization," *Foundations of Language*, 7.2.

LAKOFF, G. (1965), *On the Nature of Syntactic Irregularity*, in *Mathematical Linguistics and Automatic Translation*, Report no. NSF-16 to the National Science Foundation, Harvard University Computation Laboratory.

LAKOFF, G. (1968a), "Counterparts, or the Problem of Reference in a Transformational Grammar," unpublished paper.

LAKOFF, G. (1968b), "Pronouns and Reference," unpublished paper.

LAKOFF, G. (1970a), "Global Rules," *Language*, 46.3.

LAKOFF, G. (1970b), *Linguistics and Natural Logic,* Studies in Generative Semantics, No. 1, Phoenitics Laboratory, The University of Michigan, Ann Arbor, Michigan.

LAKOFF, G. (1970c), "On Generative Semantics," in Steinberg and Jakobovits (1971).

LAKOFF, G. (1971), *Irregularity in Syntax,* Holt, Rinehart, and Winston, New York.

LAKOFF, G. (1973), "Deep Language," letter to *The New York Review of Books,* XX.1.

LAKOFF, G. (1973), "Some Thoughts on Transderivational Constraints," in B. Kachru, et. al., (eds.), *Issues in Linguistics,* U. of Illinois Press, Urbana.

LANGACKER, R. (1966), "On Pronominalization and the Chain of Command," in Reibel and Schane (1970).

LASNIK, H. (1971), "A General Constraint : Some Evidence from Negation," in *Quarterly Progress Report of the Research Laboratory of Electronics of the Massachusetts Institute of Technology.*

LASNIK, H. (1972), *Theories of Negation in English,* unpublished MIT dissertation.

LASNIK, H. (1976), "Some Thoughts on Coreference," *Linguistic Analysis,* 2.1.

LASNIK, H. and R. FIENGO (1973), "Complement Object Deletion," *Linguistic Inquiry,* V.3.

LEBEN, W. (1970), "On the Status of VP Deletion," unpublished MIT paper.

LEES, R. B. and E. KLIMA (1963), "Rules for English Pronominalization," *Language,* 39.

MACCOLL, S. (1972), "A Note on Dougherty's Anapornia," *Foundations of Language,* 9.1.

McCAWLEY, J. (1970), "Where Do Noun Phrases Come From?," in Jacobs and Rosenbaum (1970).

PARTEE, B. (1970), "Opacity, Coreference, and Pronouns," *Synthese,* 21.

PARTEE, B. (1973), "Variable Binding and Deletion," unpublished paper.

PERLMUTTER, D. (1968), *Deep and Surface Structure Constraints in Syntax,* MIT dissertation, published (1971) by Holt, Rinehart, and Winston, New York.

PERLMUTTER, D. (1972), "Shadow Pronouns in French," in *The Great Chicago Which Hunt,* Department of Linguistics, University of Chicago, Chicago, Ill.

PETERS, S. (1972), *Goals of Linguistic Theory,* Prentice-Hall, Englewood Cliffs, New Jersey.

PETERS, S. and R.W. RITCHIE (1969), "On the Generative Power of Transformational Grammars," Technical Report CSci 69-2-3, University of Washington, Seattle, Washington.

POSTAL, P. (1966), "On So-Called 'Pronouns' in English," in Reibel and Schane (1970).

POSTAL, P. (1970a), "Global Constraints on Pronominalization," early unpublished version of Postal (1972a).

POSTAL, P. (1970b), "On Coreferential Complement Subject Deletion," *Linguistic Inquiry,* I.4.

POSTAL, P. (1971), *Cross-over Phenomena,* Holt, Rinehart and Winston, New York.

POSTAL, P. (1972a), "A Global Constraint on Pronominalization," *Linguistic Inquiry,* III.1.

POSTAL, P. (1972b), "Some Further Limitations of Interpretive Theories of Anaphora," *Linguistic Inquiry,* III.3.

POSTAL, P. (1972c), "The Best Theory," in Peters (1972).

POSTAL, P. (1972d), "'Pronominal Epithets' and Similar Items," *Foundations of Language,* 9.2.

PREMACK, A. and D. PREMACK (1972), "Teaching Language to an Ape," *Scientific American,* October, 1972.

REIBEL, D.A. and S.A. SCHANE (1970), *Modern Studies in English,* Prentice-Hall, Englewood Cliffs, New Jersey.

REINHART, T. (1974), "On the non-relevance of Precedence and Command to Coreferentiality," unpublished MIT paper.

VAN RIEMSDIJK and F. ZWARTS (1974), "Left Dislocation in Dutch and the Status of Copying Rules," unpublished University of Amsterdam paper.

ROGERS, H. (1967), *Theory of Recursive Functions and Effective Computability*, McGraw-Hill, New York.

ROSS, J.R. (1967a), *Constraints on Variables in Syntax*, unpublished MIT dissertation.

ROSS, J.R. (1967b), "On the Cyclic Nature of English Pronominalization," in Reibel and Schane (1970).

ROSS, J.R. (1969), "Guess Who?," in *Papers from the Fifth Regional Meeting of the Chicago Linguistic Society*, R.I. Binnick, et al, Department of Linguistics, University of Chicago, Chicago, Illinois.

ROSS, J.R. (1970), "Gapping and The Order of Constituents," in M. Bierwisch and K. Heidolph (eds), *Progress in Linguistics*, Mouton, The Hague.

SELKIRK, E. (1970), "On the Determiner Systems of Noun Phrase and Adjective Phrase," unpublished MIT paper.

SELKIRK, E. (1972), *The Phrase Phonology of English and French*, unpublished MIT dissertation.

SIEGEL, M. (1973), "The Anaphoric Adventures of Oscar," unpublished paper, University of Massachusetts, Amherst, Mass.

STALNAKER, R. (1973), "Presupposition," *Journal of Philosophical Logic*, I.

STEINBERG, D. and L.A. JAKOBOVITS (1970), *Semantics*, Cambridge University Press, Cambridge, England.

STRAWSON, P.F. (1950), "On Referring," *Mind*.

TAVAKOLIAN, S. (1973), "Complement Subject Deletion and Dative Deletion," unpublished paper, University of Massachusetts, Amherst, Mass.

WASOW, T. (1970), "Some thoughts about Anaphora," unpublished MIT paper.

WASOW, T. (1973a), "More Migs and Pilots," *Foundations of Language*, 9.3.

WASOW, T. (1973b), "The Innateness Hypothesis and Grammatical Relations," *Synthese*, 26.1.

WASOW, T. (1973c), "The Transitivity Condition," unpublished paper.

WASOW, T. (1975), "Anaphoric Pronouns and Bound Variables," *Language*, 51.

WASOW, T. and T. ROEPER (1972), "On the Subject of Gerunds," in *Foundations of Language*, 7.1.

WILLIAMS, G. (1969), "Two Rules of Pronominalization," unpublished MIT paper.

WILLIAMS, G. (1971), *Networks of Anaphora*, unpublished MIT dissertation.

WITTEN, E. (1970), "Pronominalization: a Handbook for Secret Agents," unpublished Brandeis University paper.

Printed in Belgium by

S.V. Groeninghe Drukkerij, Buda 56, 8500 Kortrijk - Typo-offset